# Tree Leaf Talk

# Tree Leaf Talk

## A Heideggerian Anthropology

### James F. Weiner

*Oxford • New York*

First published in 2001 by
**Berg**
Editorial offices:
150 Cowley Road, Oxford, OX4 1JJ, UK
838 Broadway, Third Floor, New York, NY 10003-4812, USA

Berg is an imprint of Oxford International Publishers Ltd.

**Library of Congress Cataloging-in-Publication Data**
A catalogue record for this book is available from the Library of Congress.

**British Library Cataloguing-in-Publication Data**
A catalogue record for this book is available from the British Library.

ISBN 978-1-85973-721-7

Typeset by JS Typesetting, Wellingborough, Northants.

To the Memory of My Father

David Weiner
1918–1996

# Contents

# Contents

# Acknowledgements

I am indebted to Roy Wagner, Marilyn Strathern, Jadran Mimica, Chris Pinney, Don Gardner, Richard Handler, and Michael Jackson, who all taught me something important about both Heidegger and anthropology. I would also like to thank Kathryn Earle of Berg Press, and to the reviewer of this manuscript, who was later revealed to me to be Eric Hirsch, for his astute and helpful comments. The Department of Social Anthropology, University of Manchester, the Department of Anthropology, University of Adelaide, and the Research School of Pacific and Asian Studies, Australian National University, all deserve my gratitude for the support I received, both collegial and otherwise, while at work on this manuscript.

Portions of this book appeared, either in whole or in part, in the following:

1991    *The Empty Place.* Indiana University Press. Bloomington, Indiana.
1992    'Anthropology *Contra* Heidegger: Part I: Anthropology's Nihilism'. *Critique of Anthropology* 12(1): 75–90.
1993    'Anthropology *Contra* Heidegger: Part II: The Limit of Relationship'. *Critique of Anthropology* 13(3): 285–301.
1993    'To Be At Home with Others in an Empty Place: A Reply to Mimica.' *The Australian Journal of Anthropology* 4(3): 233–244.
1995    'Technology and *Techne* in Trobriand and Yolngu Art'. In *Too Many Meanings: A Critique of the Anthropology of Aesthetics*, ed. J. Weiner. *Social Analysis* 38: 32–46.
1996    'Sherlock Holmes and Martin Heidegger: Comment on Julian Thomas' *Time, Culture and Identity*'. *Archaeological Dialogues* 3(1): 35–9.
1997    'On Televisualist Anthropology: Representation, Aesthetics, Politics'. *Current Anthropology* 38(2): 197–235 (with *CA comment).
1998    'Afterword: Revealing the Grounds of Life in Papua New Guinea'. In S. Bamford (ed.), *Identity, Nature and Culture: Environment and Sociality in Melanesia. Social Analysis* 42(3): 135–42.

I am grateful to all these publications for permission to reprint or paraphrase portions of these works here.

# Preface

'Tree Leaf Talk' is my literal translation of a Foi term, *irisae~medobora*, and refers to metaphorical speech, usually of an allusive or concealing manner, speech that uses imagery at least partially to hide or conceal its meaning. Other ethnographers of Papua New Guinea have come upon similar terms in the languages of their hosts,[1] enough for me to conclude that it is a common adjunct of speech in Papua New Guinea. Since the beginning of my attempts to understand the Foi world of language and meaning, I have thus tried to understand how and why people could give credence and social utility to language and speech behaviours that consciously undermine, restrict and limit speech's communicative functions.

A volume of Martin Heidegger's later essays was first entitled *Holzwege* in German. George Steiner glossed this in English as 'fire breaks', in other words, a path cut in order to prevent the spread of fires. But originally, *holzweg* was a path leading into the woods used mainly by wood-cutters. These paths ended abruptly in the thicket and didn't connect villages with each other. Nowadays in Germany, a *holzweg* is a path used mainly by foresters, or simply a walking trail in the woods. But it is also used colloquially to mean, 'to be on the wrong track, to be mistaken' (*auf dem holzweg sein*).[2] We seem to encounter another of Freud's primal words with antithetical meanings.

What would a literary or an anthropological 'fire break' look like? It might be a mode of ethnographic inquiry, or a manner of ethnographic writing designed so as to *cut-off* rather than extend or produce a flow of cultural and semantic associations. A mode of presentation of this sort might be necessary to shed light on the way in which conventional usages conceal and mislead and restrict the flow of common understandings, rather than join, connect, construct or facilitate them. The woodsman's, or the hunter's or forager's path through the forest is not designed intentionally to connect points, but is a purposeful movement in search of *matériel*, or sustenance. It makes of human time and labour a track across the earth, something that can be seen, followed, imagined, but that only ever reduces to the life-line of a single person. These are paths for which the travelling is done without a destination in mind, and for which such a destination can only be supplied after the journey is over.

In the same way, we can see the task of writing, ethnographic writing, as a way not just to construct a set of connections that we already assume are there, but to demonstrate that a way of getting there, a way of asking questions, is as important as a plan for anticipating answers.

When Foi men and women are in the forest searching for food or game, they sometimes find themselves on the wrong path. One can be in the forest and find oneself on a path that may end abruptly in an impassable thicket. So it may be with the task of writing; we may find that our tropes close off a path for us, and that we must confront the limits of our expositional strategy at the same time as we confront the limits of our cross-cultural and cross-linguistic understanding and comprehension. One of the things I want to do by way of this book is to suggest that this is not a negative experience that we should hope to avoid, but an inevitable consequence of the translative, descriptive endeavour. And I find the inspiration for this view of language and writing most clearly in the philosophy of Martin Heidegger.

This book gathers together a number of themes, both theoretical and ethnographic, that I have written about over the past ten years. They all attempt to characterize what an anthropology informed by Heidegger's project of existential phenomenology would look like. I have focused in particular on Heidegger's meditations on the origin and function of the work of art, and use his ideas on art as a way of commenting on one of contemporary anthropology's pressing issues: to what extent is our subject-matter, our craft and our theorizing affected by the increasing tendency to see more and more of social life in aesthetic terms?

This book is divided into three parts. The first part revisits my earliest attempts to describe Foi poetry, space, and temporality in existential terms. It presents ethnographic evidence from Foi speech usages for their pervasive preoccupation with forces, objects and actions that 'cut off' the flow and movement of life and meaning. Ultimately this preoccupation is at the centre of how the Foi understand language, art and gender.

If art is the ethnographic focus of the first part, the second part of the book hypothesizes that the same preoccupation with cutting off or severing might also apply to Foi social relationality more generally. It brings the key notions of aesthetics as explicated by Marilyn Strathern in her book *The Gender of the Gift* (1988) into juxtaposition with Heidegger's ideas on the revelation of form through art. The last chapter of that section anticipates the final section: I suggest some of the analytical and interpretational problems of a contemporary anthropology that seems to have replaced the social anthropological task of describing human sociality with a preoccupation with its visual and aesthetic imaging.

*Preface*

The theme running through all three sections is the critique of social constructionism, today's dominant anthropological theory and methodology. Constructionism, simply put, avows that the cultural significance people make of the world is the way that the world achieves an effect and reality for them. The emphasis is on the ability and tendency of human beings actively to fashion a world of meaning and relevance for themselves. The prominence of constructionism reflects I think two important contemporary trends: one is the increasing imaging of human life through a variety of media, of which the visual seems poised to eclipse the verbal and textual. The second is the late Marxist focus on consumption-driven production in which the aestheticization of these two twinned economic processes is its most important feature.

Constructionism therefore often poises itself against the previous structuralist and Marxist understandings of the limitations of the human subject's ability to control and exhaust the meaning and effects of the world. Constructionism is commonly invoked in recent descriptions of achieving self-actualization through art, cinema and other contemporary electronic media. These activities become important because they express a certain subjective understanding of the world, and externalize it so that this understanding can be brokered against others. This emphasis on the negotiation of subjectivities obscures, however, many of the sociocentric properties of ritual, art and local relationality that make their global appearance visible. The Heideggerian anthropology I envision here balances the current fascination with the electronic speed of mouse-clicks[3] and the lineal blur of cinematographic frames against the still pervasive human step-by-step depositing of place names and iconic designs over a local landscape, the telling of a myth in a darkened longhouse, and the singing into being of a humanized and historicized territory, which do not have as their avowed intent the imaging of a subject. The utter disparity of the scale of these processes might at first cause us anthropologists to retreat into a variety of relativisms, not all of them wholesome, useful or ethically defensible for the discipline. My intent in this book is to show how the questions that anthropology must pose in both of these human worlds can and should remain the same.

Some may be prone to construe such a position as a conservative one, and perhaps this is a good place to acknowledge the conservatism of Heidegger's phenomenology. Of course this contributed to his now infamous involvement with the National Socialist regime in Hitler's Germany, which has been the subject of much of the secondary literature on Heidegger in recent times. However, this is *not* a book about Heidegger, but about anthropology. There is a place for the recognition of what is conservative about all human behaviour, especially in an era in which we tend to exalt the novel, the mutable, the hybrid, and the avant-garde. But it makes as little sense to focus solely on the limitless plasticity and creativity of culture as it does to insist that it is restricted to a core of unchanging traditions and habits. As did Roy Wagner in *The Invention of Culture* (1981), I see innovation and convention as emergent effects of a single temporally constituted process of human symbolic articulation. In one sense, I use Heidegger to illuminate in a different way how fundamental this dialectic still must be to anthropological analysis.

As I've said, all this is implicit in the conservatism of Heidegger's notion of human Being; but this is a long way from maintaining, as many have, that everything Heidegger wrote was tainted with the ideology of Nazism. Moreover, there is a resilient conservatism in some of anthropology's responses to some pressing current global issues, notably: (1) the role of culture in maintaining biodiversity, which at some level is a programme for maintaining a certain level of *differentiation,* and of the mechanisms of differentiation, both 'natural' and cultural; and (2) the preservation and enhancement of indigenous heritage and culture in the face of global commercial and political pressures. Although 'radical' in their opposition to the encroachment of global capitalism, they are inherently conservative. The anthropological response to both of these issues is congruent in that, in both cases, there is a prior acceptance of what technology, culture and nature are. One of the side-effects of this book I hope will be to create the conditions under which these terms can be subject to some anthropological scrutiny within the framework of late modernity.

The two most important interpreters of Heidegger for me have been Lacoue-Labarthe (1990) and Zimmerman (1990). Both focused, correctly in my view, on Heidegger's critique of technology and his philosophical struggle with modernity. It is the manner in which Heidegger thought and wrote through the issues of technology and modernism – issues that were even more compelling in his time than they are for us now – that has much to offer contemporary anthropology and its future.

# Notes

1. For example, E. Schieffelin (1976) and S. Feld (1982), for the Kaluli: 'turned over words'; A. Strathern (1975), for the Melpa: 'veiled speech'.
2. My gratitude to Ulrike Hanna Meinhof for conversations with her about *holzwege*.
3. As so effectively characterized by Geertz 2001.

# Heidegger and Anthropology's Nihilism

## Bourdieu and Heidegger

'I always tend to transform philosophical problems into practical problems of scientific politics', Pierre Bourdieu said (1989: 33), and in so doing, he maintains the opposition that Marx in the *Communist Manifesto* established 'between French thinkers who always think politically and German thinkers who ask universal, abstract questions "on ways of realizing human nature" . . .' (ibid.). That might have been true when Marx was writing but one would certainly have trouble sticking to it in this century. What Bourdieu's re-imposition of this Cartesian, Romantic schism glosses over is the peculiar debt of origin that most major twentieth-century French thinkers have owed to German ones – specifically Marx and Nietzsche, who did more than any other European thinkers to rid German thought of spiritualism. But let's accept Bourdieu's distinction for now, for certainly no sociologist has done more than Bourdieu to reaffirm the centrality of the most pragmatic aspects of nineteenth-century German thought, in the figures of Marx, Nietzsche and Weber, to current social science.

But criticism is after all engagement of the most positive kind, and in demarcating a no-man's-land between philosophy and social science, Bourdieu only ensures by that much more a continuing commitment to bridge-building. It may have gone unnoticed by anthropologists that, in the late 1980s, numerous French scholars were engaged in a vigorous debate concerning Martin Heidegger's involvement, both personal and intellectual, with Nazism and with conservative political theory in general in the Weimar and Third Reich years in Germany. What interests us as anthropologists is Bourdieu's role in this debate. Why did he feel it necessary to make his statement on the place of Heidegger's philosophy in political and historical context? Does he foresee a danger to the social sciences that Heidegger's theories represent, and does he therefore wish to obviate the possibility that Heidegger's philosophy will be seen to have something to offer European social science? Does he anticipate that others might perceive a convergence of his own ideas and those of Heidegger and wish to forestall such a perception? And more to the point, are there larger issues involved that are of any interest to anthropologists and to social science?

I want to use Bourdieu's critique of Heidegger as an excuse to open up the more general question of what phenomenology, existential philosophy and hermeneutics could offer anthropology. Because it is in Bourdieu's own work that a debt to a variety of phenomenological hermeneutic is most evident in recent times – so much so, apparently, that Hubert Dreyfus, in his commentary on Heidegger's *Being and Time* (1991), commented on the similarities between Heidegger's and Bourdieu's formulations. In this chapter, I want to address the question of why Bourdieu should react so negatively to Heidegger and why others should think to perceive an affinity between them.

If Marx made a scientific study of history possible by the end of the nineteenth century, Heidegger, of course, has provided something altogether different in our own *fin de siècle*: a resurfacing of nihilism in the period of late and post-Marxism, the sense that Western philosophy, science and political economy have exhausted their possibilities. Some may feel that the transition between the nineteenth-century Marx and the twentieth-century Heidegger is part of what the history of European intellectual thought is all about – one has in mind Marcuse, Foucault and Derrida, for example. But in Bourdieu's eyes, this is a conclusion to be avoided at all costs. For while he is no stranger to nihilism, what Bourdieu prefers is Weber's routinized version of it, supported by the enduring constants of social and historical life – power and interest – rather than Heidegger's spiritual nihilism.

Where does this nihilism originate? Heidegger felt that the West had 'forgotten the meaning of being'; it had reposited meaning in machines and science, rather than in poetry and philosophy. With the Enlightenment, Western society became convinced of human supremacy over earth, that reason was the God-given faculty that allowed man dominion over nature. While reason and rationality were also envisioned as the ultimate source of a future utopian social and political world, this view also arrayed all of nature as a store of things awaiting human appropriation and disposition; all things in the world were henceforth judged in terms of their usefulness to human rational purposes. It is this shift in metaphysical groundings, rather than a simple historical development such as the 'rise of the scientific method', that really grounds our twentieth-century attitude towards technology, Heidegger maintained. The reason why Heidegger considered technology as a symptom of European spiritual *malaise* is because he had already apotheosized its antithesis – the primordial Language of Being that was first revealed in the Greek Temple, the home of gods and men, the source and object of the poetic/sacrificial bond of sky and earth.

But we haven't apotheosized technology, Bourdieu would say, any more than we have sanctified language; we have merely naturalized both, as we naturalize all of our socially-derived modes of understanding the world. Foundational contrasts, such as that between technology and poetry, are not something that 'happens' to Western culture, but are our glosses on an (always incompletely understood) series of historical developments in philosophy, science, and art, and especially on the language in which these pursuits are phrased and communicated.

In *Being and Time* [*BT*] (1962), Heidegger explicitly rejected the suggestion that he was doing 'anthropology' (in Kant's sense), that is, a philosophy that starts off with Man as an objective (empirical) being. What he maintained is that before such anthropological issues can be made visible, one must first pose properly *ontological* issues: questions about the conditions under which the study of anthropology, or anything else, is possible. The latter include asking the questions that are left unstated in the course of doing any 'normal' science, such as: What kinds of assumptions about what human beings *are* do anthropologists make before their inquiry even starts? What are the conditions under which the things on which we focus our attention – the everyday objects in our world as well as the intellectual objects of thought like 'human being', 'society', and 'culture' within anthropology – stand forth? Despite our still avowed commitment to describing and analysing cultural difference, every anthropologist makes some assumptions about human nature, assumptions that usually pass themselves off as just the opposite, as empirical generalizations – for example, that our behaviour is rule-ordered; that social relations are unequal; that productive relations determine other kinds of relations – that themselves conceal a host of questions about the nature of 'a rule', 'social relations', and 'production'. Ontology then becomes the excavation of epistemology, a cataloguing of the steps that are taken and the assumptions that are made to get to a particular view of things.

Heidegger considered anthropology to be the study of 'Man' as a thing already delimited, or of the 'body', 'soul' or 'spirit', as 'phenomenal domains which can be detached as themes for definite investigations' (*BT*: 74). But with respect to the manner in which humans question their own being, 'their nature has not yet been determined' (ibid.). The conditions under which they emerge as steps towards the understanding of human being remain to be investigated. This latter question is the domain of *Dasein.*

> ... to work out the question of Being adequately, we must make an entity – the inquirer – transparent in his own Being ... This entity which each of us is himself and which includes inquiring as one of the possibilities of its Being, we shall denote by the term '*Dasein*' (*BT*: 27).

In other words, there are two questions that Heidegger posed, both of which take priority over so-called anthropological questions. The first is, What does it mean for humans *to be* in a particular manner? (see Gelven 1989: 33). This is the *existential analytic* that Heidegger describes in Division I of *Being and Time.* In the most basic terms, it details how, in our everyday, transparent modes of coping in the world, we for the most part do not have subject–object relations with the entities in our world; we merely use them unreflectively. We use them in carrying out tasks the completion of which we *anticipate*: hence, we are *oriented towards the future*, and this anticipation provides the circular ground of our hermeneutic understanding: we understand the past as a confirmation of our possible future, and we project on to that future our understanding of the world as we have interpreted it. Finally, in this hermeneutic orientation that is our temporal mode of being, *Dasein*'s awareness of its own possibilities is revealed (Gelven 1989: 120); it *cares about* itself.

Now obviously both Heidegger and Bourdieu are engaged in a phenomenological project: both are asking, 'How have we already engaged with the objects and people around us before these entities appear to us before our consciousness?' But Bourdieu's 'reflexive sociology' is concerned to elucidate the objective conditions under which the illusions of objectivism are made effective or natural; Heidegger strives for some account of how understanding and self-understanding take shape within the same conditions. Hubert Dreyfus sees the contrast in the following way:

> Heidegger would differ from Bourdieu ... in holding that Dasein's shared ways of behaving are not mere facts to be studied *objectively* by a 'scientific' discipline such as anthropology or sociology (although they are that too). Rather, because they contain an understanding of being they must be studied as an *interpretation* (1991: 19).

Dreyfus wants us to see Heidegger's nihilism as a Nietzschean recognition that there are no facts behind interpretations, there are just the interpretations themselves. But Dreyfus too quickly glosses over the search for fundamental ontology, the core human characteristics, that dominated Heidegger's philosophy.[1] Heidegger thus maintained that after having answered the first question – the subject of the existential analytic – one must then go on and ask the second question: "what does it mean to be *at all?*" This is the subject of Division II of *Being and Time*, where the essential historicity of *Dasein* is explicated, and where Heidegger reveals the fateful associations he makes between temporality, history and the destiny of a community, associations that found and ultimately reveal the instability of anthropological terminology at the current time.

## Heidegger's Social Ontology

*Being and Time* is nothing less than an inquiry into the way humans *are*, the characteristics humans possess that allow awareness and knowledge of the world, including the social world, to emerge. It is, as I've indicated, an ontological exercise, which means it is concerned with stipulating a proper order to the kinds of questions we can ask: we have first to learn about human nature, specifically, how we learn about things around us, before other questions about those things and the world they constitute can be posed. Now, from this point of view, Bourdieu's exercise in *Outline of a Theory of Practice* (1977) might also be called ontological. Bourdieu asks: 'What are the conditions under which the objective properties of social institutions acquire their objectivity?' and 'What do we have to know about the way humans are in their world before we can properly assess the characteristics of any social theory, judgement or classification, including those that the social scientist him/herself makes?'

In this regard, Bourdieu and Heidegger importantly share an opposition to Cartesianism. Both Heidegger and Bourdieu accept that as individuals we are *thrown*: we come into a world not of our making. This world polarizes us, mediates and constrains our understanding of ourselves in it. We *exist* in it, first and foremost, and it is 'existingly' – through our traffic or engagement with the things and with others in the world – that we arrive at this understanding:

> In interpreting, we do not, so to speak, throw a 'signification' over some naked thing which is present-at-hand, we do not stick a value on it; but when something within-the-world is encountered as such, the thing in question already has an involvement which is disclosed in our understanding of the world, and this involvement is one which gets laid out by the interpretation (*BT*: 190–1).

In a proposition that Bourdieu makes one of the linchpins of his analytic, we become adept in our 'existential skills' without becoming aware of the skills as objects of contemplation: 'The essential part of the modus operandi which defines practical mastery is transmitted in practice, in its practical state, without attaining the level of discourse' (Bourdieu 1977: 87). We use words without thinking of their meaning, and utter sentences without attending to a mental lexicon or grammar (which doesn't mean that syntactic rules don't provide an illuminating description of language once we have already agreed to hypostatize it). Similarly, one of the major foundations of Heidegger's existential analytic is the phenomenon of *zuhandenheit*: 'readiness-to-hand' or what Dreyfus calls 'availableness'. Our world is oriented not by an attitude of detached contemplation, but of 'practical circumspection':

> The view in which equipmental contexture stands at first, completely unobtru-sive and unthought, is the view and sight of practical *circumspection*, of our practical everyday orientation. 'Unthought' means that it is not thematically apprehended for deliberate thinking about things; instead, in circumspection, we find our bearings in regard to them (Heidegger 1982b: 163).

But if Bourdieu shares Heidegger's distrust of cognitivism, he wants to avoid putting these patterns of circumspection beyond the reach of causality. Such patterns of circumspection, even though they are unthought, nevertheless exert an *objective* effect and can conflict with our conscious, objective theories of such patterns, and, in Marxian style, what this conflict leads to in terms of influences on people's motivation is what makes our existence historical. Bourdieu as sociologist borrows from just those philosophers – Wittgenstein and Quine for example – who have always tried to *naturalize* epistemological and ontological questions, to make them just other questions about the contingency of fact and discourse about fact that history is all about (which is why Bourdieu's *habitus* contains a proper recognition of the behaviourist component of human action and conception).

The critical chapter of *Being and Time*, at least as it concerns Bourdieu – and anthropology – is Chapter 4 of Division I, entitled 'Being-in-the-World as Being-With and Being-One's-Self. The "They"'. According to Dreyfus, Heidegger is saying here that we are already 'socialized' (Dreyfus's term, not Heidegger's) before we arrive at an understanding of our 'own' world.[2] Heidegger explains that 'being-with (others)', *mitsein*, is an 'existential condition of Being-in-the-world' (*BT*: 163) and maintains that before we can grasp the notion of our own self, we have already to have encountered others:

Not only is Being towards Others an autonomous, irreducible relationship of Being: this relationship, as Being-with, is one which, with Dasein's Being, already is (*BT*: 162).

But for the most part, the way we experience this Being-with is *distantly*:

. . . this distantiality which belongs to Being-with, is such that Dasein, as everyday Being-with-one-another, stands in *subjection* to Others. It itself *is* not; its Being has been *taken away by the Others* . . . The 'who' is not this one, not that one, not oneself, not some people, and not the sum of them all. The 'who' is the neuter, *the 'they' [das Man]* (*BT*: 164, last emphasis added).

In one's everyday, average attitude, when one is not deliberately focusing one's attention on one's state of being, one gets along unreflectively: we use words, implements, clothing, and other pieces of equipment, we engage in casual social encounters without consciously posing the problem of our *relationship to* such entities (for properly speaking, there is no 'relationship', only an unmediated response of habitual familiarity). One automatically conforms to conventions, one does not follow rules.[3]

We can lose ourselves in this familiarity, though, says Heidegger. To mistake the interpretative, questioning responsibility of the self for the average mode of comportment is 'to be' inauthentically.

This Being-with-one-another dissolves one's own Dasein completely into the kind of Being of 'the Others', in such a way, indeed, that the Others, as distinguishable and explicit, vanish more and more. In this inconspicuousness and unascertainability, the real dictatorship of the 'they' is unfolded (*BT*: 164).

Now Bourdieu himself doesn't deny the 'levelling down' effect of such socialization. Within a social class, or, particularly in societies without institutional differentiation, '. . . it is a whole group and whole symbolically structured environment, without specialized agents or specific moments, which exerts an *anonymous, pervasive pedagogic action . . .*' (1977: 87, emphasis added). It is not in the characterization of socialization itself, or of the phenomenological method itself, that the difference between the two is to be found. Both write about the modes of concealment that found human subjectivity and the implications of these socially-engendered concealments on the exercise of human freedom and autonomy. What I try to do in this book is to focus on what Heidegger, Marx, Freud and Bourdieu all have in common – the way concealment emerges in the human engagement with the world that *is* the fundamental phenomenological starting-point for all of them. All of these writers wrote deploringly about the effects of concealment on the exercise of human freedom, creativity and autonomy; yet all of them accepted that concealment itself is generated out of the very exercise of human striving towards these goals. In applying Heidegger to certain non-Western cultural articulations, I try to restore the positive aspects of concealment to human creativity and its social configurations.

## Holmes and Heidegger

Let me continue by invoking, as anthropologists seem to do from time to time, the figure of Sherlock Holmes. Holmes, as we know, classified types of persons, livelihoods, mentalities and criminalities by, among other things, the varieties of dirt on their shoes, the characteristic calluses and grooves on their hands, the imprints they made upon different utensils, the kinds of tobacco, food scraps, and bits of clothing they left behind as traces of their presence. Holmes made a living out of deducing the motivational and moral contours of a human personality from such material indices. He knew the physical components of his environment – the different soils and plants of London, which stores purveyed which implements and goods characteristically utilized by criminals – and he catalogued the sartorial and other visible indices that marked inhabitants of different districts and socioeconomic and ethnic categories. We also learned that he was not unfamiliar with the *Who's Who* of London society of his time, not to mention the London constabulary and the organization of various other professions whose activities related to his interest in crime-solving.

Holmes was a brilliant practical ethnographer and physical anthropologist, but his knowledge of human habits was geared toward deduction and not induction. His theories did service to his particular interest in the world, rather than the other way around. Holmes, as Nicholas Meyer so delightfully reminded us in his novel *The Seven Per Cent Solution* (1974), lived in the world of Sigmund Freud, and if these two keen empirical observers had one thing in common, it is that they made no hypotheses in advance of their data.

There was something else that Holmes and Freud had in common, and that demonstrated what they shared with Martin Heidegger. 'You see, but you do not observe . . .', Holmes said to Watson, early on in their association. All three were aware of the power of *nescience*, not-knowing, the ubiquitous manner in which human beings turn away from the world as a result of their ability to reconstitute it and represent it to themselves.

All three figures drew attention to the way in which humans can become *absorbed* in particular manifestations of the world to the exclusion and disregard of others. The more intense the effort to observe, recall, remember and understand, the more powerfully does this not-knowing and turning-away assert itself and bring recall, remembering, and observation to a halt. Holmes, therefore, like a good ethnographer, from time to time felt compelled to retrace the routes and pathways of criminals, and sometimes, disguised as one himself, to linger at the gathering-places of the London underworld. In other words, like the anthropologist who tries to make a methodological success out of participant observation, he came up with strategies for shifting himself to the side of his own conceptual foci, so as to make aspects of the world reveal themselves to him.

Faced with the efficacy of these Holmesian/ethnographic strategies, we might want to conclude, as W. V. Quine once summed it up, that there is nothing in meaning that is not in behaviour. If our apperceptual strategies emerge in response to what the limits of human knowledge make apparent to us, then, despite the limits to human knowing and remembering and observing, this nescience deposits itself and ultimately makes itself visible in behaviour, in our investigative, ordering, classifying and productive strategies.

What we therefore confront in the products of human labour and intention are all the effects that displace it and deflect it from intentionality, and that to the fabricator therefore seem to originate outside the human world. At different times in Western history we have variously labelled these effects God, evolution, history, class struggle, and power (among other things). They have served, in their respective times, as teleological touchstones, because they seem to originate beyond human subjectivity, motivation and knowledge. Heidegger, however, and those who have been influenced by him, including Foucault, reminded us of their human, and hence historical and cultural, origin.

Marc Augé characterizes ethnology in a similar Holmesian way:

> The ethnologist, for his part, is especially responsive to everything written on the soil, in the life of those he observes, which signifies closure, careful control of relations with the outside, the immanence of the divine in the human, or the close connection between the necessity for a sign and its meaning (1995: 56).

A Heideggerian approach to convention and perception of the sort Augé characterizes above thus offers a most trenchant counterweight to what I identify as the vulgar constructionist accounts that seem to be so popular today in social science and Cultural Studies. A conventional definition of social constructionism avows that meaning is engendered through the operation of communication and other relational processes. A vulgar constructionism, however, distances itself from the sociogenic locus of meaning production and focuses on what is subjectively experienced by the individual in the conscious and deliberate act of identity management and self-definition.

By focusing on the unwitting and undetected deposits, leavings and traces left behind by human beings during their actions and movements in the world, I am drawing attention to the fact that Heidegger's view of technology and the material was not constructivist. And neither was that of Sherlock Holmes. Recall that Watson was amazed that Holmes was unable to deduce from the remains of track, fingerprint, and callus the fact that the earth revolved around the sun. While Heidegger's use of the term gathering would seem to support a constructionist or reflectionist interpretation of the artefact, this term was not a description of human or cultural agency. It described instead the phenomenon by which meaning, relationship and temporality seem to move counter to human subjectivity and intention.

It seems inevitable that some social scientists would choose to take the path taken by many social scientists of postmodernism in our current period, which Marc Augé characterizes as supermodernity – a period when the kinds of spaces we formerly associated with cultures and social systems no longer have much purchase on our attention or imagination; when the very thingly quality of things themselves is a matter of the most pervasive dubiety; when the recorded and played-back character of events and public performances makes time constantly loop back on to itself in an evolution- (but not history-) defying non-linearity. The problem once again is that between Hot and Cold societies, as Marc Augé has so effectively reiterated in his recent essay (1995: 28). We late-twentieth-century Westerners experience and perceive that there are 'more' events now than there used to be, and the implication of this is that there must have been an epoch, before History itself began to accumulate events, when, as it were, there were none to speak of. Under such conditions, every action was an instauration, not of Event or Time, but of Structure and Habitus. Heidegger may have felt nostalgic about a way of life so tied to the rhythms of the soil, plant and sun, and may have valued a religious life where the fundamentally divine, and hence non-human, qualities of these temporalities were exalted. This may have been a manifestation of his oft-interpreted alienation from modern, and modernist, thought.

But we need not succumb to either Heideggerian or postmodern nostalgia. As long as sociology and anthropology do not turn away from what Bourdieu describes at the end of *Distinction* (1984) as the 'humble, easy yet fertile activities' of data collection and the methodical but unglamorous task of formulating 'provisional systems of scientific propositions which strive to combine internal coherence and adequacy to the facts' (1984: 512), it will never succumb to the illusion that spirit or thought could come adrift from the world:

> 'thought', if there is such a thing, can never proclaim itself 'disengaged' from metaphysics. And this, moreover, is what always leaves it *'engagé'* in this world, however great its prudence or its disillusionment (Lacoue-Labarthe 1990: 19).

The Heideggerian anthropology I illustrate in the following chapters emerges from both a methodological and a personal engagement in the world – the world of things, of people, and of the embodied relationality of both. Its apparent moments of transcendence – through art and language – do service to the human attempt to be in that world interpretationally, to bring closure and hence meaning to the open-ended traffic of humans with other beings in that world.

## Notes

1. The problem with Dreyfus's and to a lesser extent Rorty's (1989, 1991) pragmatic view of Heidegger is analogous to the inconsistency that Christopher Boorse (1975) identifies in Quine's theorizing. Boorse says that Quine wants to retain the Duhemian holism – that sentences can only be interpreted with respect to a total theory within which they are embedded – alongside his naturalistic theory of reference, which links utterances to agreed-upon stimulus conditions. Similarly, Dreyfus wants to see Heidegger as deferring to a social construction of being while retaining his quest for the essence of language, art and Being (Rorty identifies these two trends with the earlier and later Heidegger respectively). But in all these cases, the conflict only emerges as such because of the insistence on keeping issues of relativism and foundationalism, or holism and stimulus-meaning, as

ontological stances rather than as mutually-implicated stages in the social constitution of practical knowledge and theoretical knowledge out of each other that Bourdieu describes.

2. 'When, for example, we walk along the edge of a field . . . the field shows itself as belonging to such-and-such a person . . .; the book we have used was bought at So-and-so's shop and given by such-and-such a person, and so forth. The boat anchored at the shore is assigned in its Being-in-itself to an acquaintance who undertakes voyages with it . . . The Others who are thus 'encountered' in a ready-to-hand, environmental context of equipment, are not somehow added on in thought to some Thing . . . such 'Things' are encountered from out of the world in which they are ready-to-hand for Others – a world which is always mine too in advance' (*BT*: 153–4).

3. '. . . we sometimes demand definitions [i.e. rules of behaviour] for the sake not of their content, but of their form. Our requirement is an architectural one; the definition a kind of ornamental coping that supports nothing' (L. Wittgenstein, *Philosophical Investigations* §217).

# Part I
# Place, Death and Voice in Foi

# 2

# Space and Naming: The Inscriptive Effects of Foi Life Activity

Bright, Bright, the flowering tree,
That's taken root upon this spot.
The blossoms that it shone with in the morning,
It will have lost before the night has fallen.
Human life is like a sojourning
Yet for melancholy there is time to spare.
Brooding long in silence on these things
My heart is filled with bitterness and grief.

—T'ao Ch'ien (365–427)[1]

I begin with the emergence of place out of activity that does not have the 'production of place' as such as its avowed goal. For people like the Foi, place is made as a by-product of their focus on certain activities such as food-getting, which demand movement and activity over and through a terrain.

Thus, our intentions and concerns structure the world, but they do not yet 'construct' it; they 'polarize' the world's objects and dimensions in terms of their relation to such concerns. Lived space is constituted as the graphic record of such intentional consciousness over time. Through our acts of concernful appropriation of objects that we put to use, we bring existential space into being: the space in which human intention inscribes itself upon the earth, as Eric Dardel puts it.[2] Relph suggests that 'places in existential space can therefore be understood as centres of meaning, or focuses of intention and purpose' (1976: 22). This inscriptive activity of the body is encompassed within a comprehensive 'linguistic' capacity, of which the verbally descriptive function of speech is only one manifestation.

For Merleau-Ponty, lived space is structured by our patterned acts within it, by the meaning and end of our intentions within it. To structure space in this way means:

... to mark out boundaries and directions in the given world, to establish lines of force, to keep perspectives in view, in a word, to organize the given world in accordance with the projects of the present moment, to build into the geographical setting a behavioural one, a system of meanings outwardly expressive of the subject's internal activity (1962: 112).

In this chapter I would like to describe the lineaments of the Foi spatial world and to explicate the role that naming plays in constituting this world as an intersubjective, social one. I maintain that Foi song poetry is poetic because it reveals to the Foi in their maximally intense moments of social engagement the existential foundations of that world. The poem precisely encapsulates a set of 'meanings outwardly expressive of the subject's internal activity', which Ezra Pound suggested was the essence of imagist poetry and which Merleau-Ponty in the passage above described as the essence of humanly inscribed space.

Heidegger maintained that the poet names things: not in the sense of labelling them, for they already are represented to us by such labels. Names, on the other hand, expose things in their being, that is, in terms of their true relation to our life condition. David White has provided one of the most incisive interpretations of Heidegger's writings on this subject:

> ... names bestow what Heidegger calls a measured command over entities. The measure is the extent to which any given name is a locus wherein may be experienced relations between the being of the entity named and being as totality (White 1978: 25).

In other words, a society's place-names schematically image a people's intentional transformation of their habitat from an unobjectified deposition of lived spaces into a pattern of historically experienced and constituted place and time. 'Space is a society of named places, just as people are landmarks within the group', Lévi-Strauss noted (1966: 168). The bestowing of place names constitutes Foi existential space out of a blank environment; it reveals what Merleau-Ponty described as the figure–ground reversal of nearness and remoteness. Let us first examine how this existential contrast emerges for the Foi.

## Paths and Water: The Conduits of Foi Movement

The system of paths in Hegeso, and throughout the riverine Foi region, resembles the human circulatory system – there are main arteries used by everyone, smaller paths branching off from these, and finally, the paths to individual houses and gardens, made and used only by the current occupiers and users of those spots. These small paths tend to be referred to as 'So-and-so's path'. The larger ones serving a more inclusive region are usually referred to, for example, as 'the Gisa Tono path' or the 'Namikiribibi path'.

The word for path is *iga*. It resembles the verb *i~ga-*, from which it differs only by the lack of a nasalized /i/. In its transitive form, *i~ga-* means 'to make, build, create' and in its intransitive sense it also means 'to turn into, to transform into'. Unlike watercourses, which can only be followed, Foi paths are the graphic effect of intentional, creative movement across the earth. They transform the ground, partition the earth and create human space. Additionally, *iga koro* means the door or entrance to a house; a conduit into highly structured space, just as a path itself eventually leads to a house or other human artefact.

Other words for paths and the use of paths partake of the imagery of points, edges and cutting. In the 1960s the Australian colonial administration upgraded the major footpath between and through the Mubi River villages, widening it and building drains on either side. Until the early 1990s, it had been lined with limestone and was accessible to four-wheel drive vehicles (which had to be flown in by aeroplane).[3] The Foi call this main road a *gifuri*. *Gifu* or *gifo* means 'the tip or point of a knife' or 'the tapered end of a bean' or 'a top knot in one's hair'. An *ira gifu* is the top of a tree. The turning off from a main road or a *gifuri* on to a smaller path is called *hudegeraha-* (alternately, *hugeteraha-*), which also means 'to interrupt, to cut off', from the verb *degeraha-* '1. to stop from flowing; 2. not to show up at an appointment'. It is also used to describe the action of a small group of people breaking off from a larger group and going their separate way while travelling. It is important to understand that this 'cutting' terminology refers not to the severing or dividing up of territory by paths, but to the cutting and channelling of people's intentions and movements, for these are the constitutive source of places and their names in Foi.

Journeying through Hegeso territory on foot is never a matter of merely getting from one point to another. People pause to inspect trees for signs of fruiting, or for the spoor of animals. A length of good-quality rattan may be found, cut down, made into a coil, and placed in a string bag. Sometimes men will see high on a tree trunk the leathery nest of the *O. joiceyii* moth, whose larvae are edible and whose nest itself is used as a wrapping material. A dead and fallen tree trunk may be briefly attacked with axes if there is evidence that the longicorn beetle has laid eggs in it. In these and other casual 'productive' acts, Foi men and women truly turn these paths into conduits of inscribed activity. Motion and movement is always exploitative, productive movement in Foi. There is no artificial distinction between 'commuting' and 'work'.

Sometimes off to the side of a path the remains of an old garden or a lone cordyline shrub may be glimpsed ever so faintly. Where once a path led up to that spot, the marks formerly etched on to the earth have faded; a new path, indicative of other men's concerns in other regions, now focuses travellers' attention away from those earlier sites. But, infrequently, a few handfuls of edible greens, the remains of previous planting, may be quickly gathered and slipped into a string bag, a terse requiem to its previous inhabitants.

Hegeso territory and the names that the Hegeso people use to identify different regions within their village area are dominated by the various watercourses. The Mubi River is, of course, the largest and virtually the only navigable river in the entire region. But the numerous smaller creeks that flow into the Mubi provide the orienting and identifying landmarks. More importantly, they constitute the most common boundaries between clan territories. When Kora Midibaru undertook to take me on a tour through all inhabited Hegeso territory, he did so by first dividing the territory into districts centring on major streams. There were thus 24 such areas in Hegeso named for the streams whose courses delimit them (see Map 1) – flowing water is the dominant feature upon which the Foi focus in creating the regions of their lived space. Each district was thus oriented around the mouth (*tage*: 'end') and the source (*ga*) of its identifying stream, and the place also could be named and subdivided accordingly (for example, the creek Asima encompassed two named areas, Asimaga and Asimatage).

This was the way Hegeso men described where they lived: 'My house is at Namanihimu . . .', 'I have a garden at Yebibu . . .', 'My father planted sago for me at Oyane . . .', and so forth. Men usually have more than one house in different parts of the village territory. Both collective clan and individual holdings are quite dispersed and chequer-boarded. This is the result of a long history of continuous swapping of pieces of land between men and clans: men attempt to obtain access to major swamps, gardening areas and riverine frontage along the Mubi so that they are not denied any subsistence activity or resource.

Hence, in some parts of Hegeso land – the banks of the Mubi, the major swamps at Faibu, Oyane and Gigisabu – nearly every clan has a holding. Land that is some distance from the longhouse or does not have significant swamp areas or riverine frontage and is otherwise without any special attributes, on the other hand, tends to remain controlled by the original clan of possession (though the history of how the early arrivals in Hegeso obtained such holdings is no longer known).

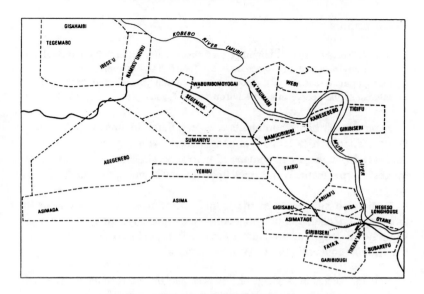

**Map 1.** District names in Hegeso Village territory

As an aside, it seems that this approach to Foi 'land use' leads to a critique of the concept of landownership, so commonly and unreflectively transmitted to our host communities in the tribal world, and so pre-emptive and subversive of the constitutive, ontological role of land and space in tribal consciousness and perception and assessment of the person. For the Foi at least, it is true that entitlement to land is inherited by virtue of one's membership in a clan and as the patrimony received from one's father. But unless this privileged access is 'quickened' and authenticated by actual involvement with and use of the resource, one's proprietary rights over it become harder and harder to assert. Quarrels over land in Hegeso most commonly revolved precisely around this issue, especially in the light of the facts that the Foi population is small relative to their large territory, and that there are often significant inequities in the amount of land controlled by local groups (see Langlas and Weiner 1988).

The names of places a man has occupied, upon which he has built houses, made gardens, caught fish, and so forth – these place-names act as an effective mnemonic for his productive and social history within Hegeso. They encapsulate not only the specific events for which the name was first given, but the lives of the succession of men who have left their mark there. Let us examine these names in more detail.

## Place-names

> It is the vocabulary of a language that most clearly reflects the physical and
> social environment of its speakers . . . [But] it is not merely the fauna or
> topographical features of the country as such that are reflected, but rather the
> interest of the people in such environmental features (Sapir 1912: 228, 229).

Sapir's remarkable comments are very much in line with Merleau-
Ponty's approach to language, and, indeed, with a phenomenological
approach to language and human action in general. And nowhere is human
interest more effectively inscribed upon the environment than in the names
we give to places.

Sapir also suggested in that same article that 'the transparent or
untransparent character of a vocabulary may lead us to infer, if somewhat
vaguely, the length of time that a group of people has been familiar with
a particular concept' (1912: 231). For example:

> Only the student of language history is able to analyze such names as Essex,
> Norfolk, and Sutton into their component elements as East Saxon, North Folk,
> and South Town, while to the lay consciousness these names are etymological
> units as purely as are 'butter' and 'cheese'. The contrast between a country
> inhabited by an historically homogenous group for a long time, full of
> etymologically obscure place names, and a newly settled country with its
> Newtowns, Wildwoods, and Mill Creeks, is apparent (ibid.).

I was able to derive a lexical significance for something over half of
the most important place-names in Hegeso. Like the American Indian
languages that Sapir briefly described in that article, the Foi language
makes use of certain geographically descriptive words in its place-names:
*ibu*, 'creek, river, water' (as in Ibu Segemi); *ibu karua*, 'pond' (as in
Ka'arumaibi Karua); *yeyema*: 'ridge, raised ground' (as in Dau~ga
Yeyema); *tono*: 'island; isolated mountain' (as in Gisa Tono); *merabe*:
'harbour' (as in Saboro Merabe); *fu*: 'swamp' (as in Bubare Fu); *kara*:
'grove' (as in Gagikara); *ka'aga*: 'small hill' (as in Horo Ka'aga); *geno*:
'bend in river' (as in O'oroga Geno); *sabe*: 'ridge, spur' (as in Yagenebo
Sabe); *duma*: 'mountain' (as in Duma Yefua); *ibu komosodi*: 'waterfall'
(as in Ibu Agegenebo Komosodi).

The place-names listed, therefore, do not represent all the different
places in Hegeso territory. They are the names of the regions of the Mubi
Valley of Hegeso. Within each region there are probably many other tiny
spots with their own names, names that they acquired only because
something notable happened there in the past, not necessarily because

the place itself is in some way physically distinct. The designations I listed in the preceding paragraph may inflect a number of names. The different sago swamps (*kuikara*) are named according to the streams near which they are located; there are different canoe mooring-points along the Mubi – Segemi Merabe, Faya'a Merabe and so forth; all groves of bamboo are named according to the stream that lends its name to that district; and so forth. These descriptive adjuncts should not be confused with a place-name itself. For example, the extensive sago swamp near the Faibu Creek (Ibu Faibu) is called Faibu Kuikara, 'Faibu Sago Grove'. But the place Gagikara is itself a name, even though it means 'Thorn Grove'.

Several of the place-names give good evidence that, like the English examples cited by Sapir, their original lexicality decays over time. The small creek Hesa was also referred to as Hesawabo. *Wa-* is the verb 'to come', while *hesa-* is used as an auxiliary verb that modifies more basic verbs of motion. *Hesa-* means 'to follow the contour of a river bank on foot', and is always followed by *wa-* or *u-* ('to go'). In other words, the Foi usually drop the *-wabo* when referring to the place Hesa. Similarly, Kubunuga is a slightly shortened form of Kuibunuga, composed of three words, *kui*, 'sago', *bunu*, 'valley', and *ga*, 'base, source'. The stream Yagikera'abe, composed of the words *yagi*, 'fish', *kera'a*, 'is not', and the particle *be*, was usually shortened in favour of Yikera'abe.

For a few of the names, I was able to obtain a specific explanation linking the place and the name. For example, there is a place near Segemi called Ya, 'hand' (the word *ya* in Foi also means 'bird'). The place is so named because in the past, a Hegeso man was killed and carried away by enemies, who dismembered his body as they fled. When other Hegeso pursued, they came upon the severed hand of the dead man at that spot. Similarly, at Huanobo (*hua*, 'killed'; *nobo*, 'eaten'), a Hegeso man was killed and consumed by raiders from Lake Kutubu.

Yadenabo, or Yadenabibi is a swift-flowing creek near the head of the Sumaniyu Creek, and refers to the birds that are often seen bathing in pools formed by the rocks that litter its bed (*ya*, 'bird'; *dena-* 'to bathe, immerse in water'). Yagenebo Sabe, 'Bird Dancing Ridge', on the other hand, is one of the names of the spur upon which the current Hegeso longhouse is located, and refers to the decorated men who dance within the longhouse at ceremonial occasions.

Particularly notable vegetation commonly lends its names to places, especially if the specimen is unusually large. Most of these names refer to the place in terms of the base of some particular plant, *ga*. For example, Bi'a'aga, 'Black Palm Base'; Dau~ga Yeyema, 'Pandanus Base Hill'.

A lexical breakdown of several place-names consists of a tree name plus *-himu*, 'to chop down', indicating that at one time, the place or creek was notable for such an action's having occurred nearby. Thus, Namanihimu, Digasohimu, and at Ayamo, Gagihimu, 'Thorn Cut'.

Place names incorporating game animal references are not restricted to Ayamo, the hunting area *per se*. In the central Mubi region there are the places Gisa Tono, 'Cassowary Hill'; Gisahaibi, 'Cassowary Lives'; Horo Ka'aga, 'Bush Fowl Hill'; Ya'onobodabikiri, 'Earth Oven Eaten Cave', referring to some incident where meat was cooked and consumed (*ya'o-*: to cook in an earth oven; *nobo*: 'eaten'; *dabi*: 'cave'; *kiri*: 'is').

If places can be morally invigorated, as it were, by naming them after significant human events, then humans can also be named after such places. The Foi make a distinction between the lexical meaning of a name, which, as in the case of place-names, is frequently opaque to them, and the person after whom one is named, one's *ya'o*, which is a socially significant relationship. A name could originally embody a relationship between a birth and the birthplace, but this would be irrelevant to the person upon whom the name is eventually bestowed. However, it is safe to say that most personal names that are also names of trees or other vegetation refer to a birth place where a specimen of that name was located. This speculation is given confirmation by considering the way new names are chosen (for a variety of reasons, a namesake may not be available, and new names sometimes have to be given to infants).[4] Often these refer in some way to the place where the infant was born. Of the 302 Hegeso names I have investigated, 83 unambiguously refer to a place-name or a tree or vegetable name. Some examples are Isaka, 'Isa woman' (*-ka* is a common ending for women's names, just as *-mena*, from the word *amena*, 'man', is a common male name-ending): this woman was named after nearby Mount Isa, after her father perceived the name in a dream shortly after his daughter's birth; Goraka, 'Gora woman', who was named after the Gora Creek where she was born; and the woman Yorame, who was named after the sago variety *yora*, a specimen of which was near the place where she was born (*-ame* is also a common female name ending, like '-ette' or '-ina' in English).

Foi children are also named after significant deaths – these can be called 'memorial names'. The little girl Ibu's namesake was killed by a falling sago palm, and, henceforth, the girl was called Kuiremohui~, 'Sago Killed (Her)'. The infant Sese's namesake committed suicide by hanging himself, and people called the little boy Yogehui~, 'Killed Himself'. These memorial names are passed on to new namesakes along with the original names. I suspect that in the past, when homicide and warfare were far more frequent, as were sudden deaths from sorcery, such memorial names were more common: they survive in names passed on from earlier generations, such as Hoabo, 'Killed'; Humofa'abo, 'Killed and Discarded'; Gebo, 'Weep'.

Along with all the names one's namesake has acquired during his or her life, a young Foi person also acquires the namesake's private or hidden name. (I do not say 'secret' name. These names are not secret; merely not public.) A man's hidden name or names are only revealed in the song poems composed in his memory. I will return to the implications of hidden names shortly.

Keith Basso has effectively demonstrated the usefulness of pheno-menological and existential approaches to language and placedness in his analysis of place-names among the Western Apache (1984, 1988). The Western Apache 'speak with names' during times of difficulty, confusion or emotional stress. These names allegorically anchor a person's worries in the soothing 'good thinking' that attends dwelling upon distant events in different places.

> . . . placenames are arguably among the most highly charged and richly evocative of all linguistic symbols. Because of their inseparable connection to specific localities, placenames may be used to summon forth an enormous range of mental and emotional associations – associations of time and space, of history and events, of persons and social activities, of oneself and stages in one's life (1988: 103).

and:

> Poets and songwriters have long understood that economy of expression may enhance the quality and force of aesthetic discourse, and that placenames stand ready to be exploited for this purpose (ibid.).

Basso, examining such Western Apache names as Tse ligai dah sidil, 'white rocks lie above in a compact cluster', and Tse bika tu yahilii, 'water flows down on top of a regular succession of flat rocks', in words that could not be more appropriate here noted that:

> Sapir's description of Algonkian words as 'tiny imagist poems' applies nicely to Western Apache placenames, and there is little doubt that the practice of 'speaking with names' exhibits poetic qualities (1988: 126 fn.).

Foi place names are not inert, lexical labels for places; place names have their origin in discourse, and it is within discourse – in the encompassing sense that I am using the term– that places are named. As is the case with the Apache, Foi place-names act as mnemonics for the historical actions of humans that make places singular and significant. The Foi examples above indicate that it is not easy to draw a line between where 'names' end and 'descriptive phrases' begin, and this seems to be even more the case with Apache place-names. If place-names have poetic qualities, then they have displacing – ek-static – effects on conventional meaning: as with any construction that exerts a 'trope-ic' effect on publicly attributed significance, names can hide as well as reveal the consequences of human action, a phenomenon to which I now turn.

## Showing and Lostness: The Poetic Nexus within the Inscribed World

During my time in Hegeso, my friends and I spent much time walking along the paths throughout Hegeso territory. At these times, if we happened to be walking across land that belonged to one of the men, I would sometimes be informed that 'this is the sago my father showed me', or 'my father showed me this bamboo stand when I was just a small boy'. Sometimes we would walk through the territory belonging to different clans, and occasionally it would be remarked, 'my brother-in-law showed me this ground here so I could make a garden'.

'Showed', they said. Not 'gave' or 'loaned', though the Foi language had words for these and other similar transactions. Clearly, 'showed' was the appropriate idiom in this context. The Foi word used is *mitina-*, and it carries the connotation not of something 'demonstrated' (as in 'show me how to do it'), but of something previously hidden now being revealed. One can speculate on the etymological associations of the word: *Mi-* is a general causative prefix; it makes an intransitive verb into a transitive one. *Tina-* means 'to abandon, to leave, relinquish, release', already in transitive form. Hence, *mitina-*: 'to cause to abandon; to make released'. I can think of no other word which so perfectly translates Heidegger's own reading of the Greek *aletheia*: 'to unconceal'.[5]

For in formally 'showing' a piece of ground to another, a Foi man is precisely relinquishing control over it (even if only temporarily). More importantly, in 'showing' someone else the extent of his land and resource holdings, a Foi man is revealing the fundamental lived dimension of his *dasein*, 'Being-there', through the attitudes of care and the actions of concernful appropriation of earthly space, the historical record of the impressions he has made on the land, the inscriptive evidence of his life.

This quality of unconcealing characterized authentic language for Heidegger, as Kockelmans describes it:

> Within the horizon of a certain culture, which mainly in and through its language makes the world emerge from hiddenness and places it in "unconcealedness," man and things as well as man and fellow men are concretely related. . . [L]anguage. . . brings about the original interwovenness of man and things in the world (Kockelmans 1972: 29).

Foi men 'unconceal' the land to each other, furtively, reluctantly, privately. Young men often become impatient with the slowness with which their fathers reveal their territorial property. Men approach each other in private to arrange a transfer of or temporary use of a piece of land, just as the initial stages of betrothal are shrouded in stylized, formal and extremely private negotiations between men. With time, these transactions become known publicly: men begin seeking donations of shell wealth for a bride payment from their kinsmen and neighbours; a new garden or house begins to take shape under the eyes of passers-by.

Peoples' inscriptive, productive activity is hidden, privatized, unsignified – until men choose to reveal resources for others' use. But it is only through language that the earth is revealed in its existential nature. Men reveal hidden places, but it is women who, in their poetry, reveal hidden names and bring these hidden names in relation to hidden places. And this nexus is only made possible through death. Women's poetic creations thus constitute in Heidegger's terms an authentic use of names and naming, because they situate the 'fundamental project'[6] of death as the condition of placedness; men, by keeping productive and inscriptive relations hidden, deny the existential fact that it is through death that places 'move' from person to person through time, just as it is through life that persons move from place to place.

For the Foi, the opposite of *mitina-*, 'unconcealedness', is *berebu-* 'lostness'. Men become lost through death, though places live on. And the song poems characteristically juxtapose these images of unconcealing and lostness. Among the most obvious examples of this imagery are the following:

(Song 5):

The large cassowary who sleeps in the cave
He has gone away.

The black marsupial who sleeps in the cave
He too is lost.

(Song 20):

The man who sleeps by the bank of the rushing water
He is lost now.

Twigs and branches clot in the swiftly flowing water
But he who sleeps there is lost.

In the following song, this lostness is seen from the eye's of the deceased's dog who survives him:

(Song 22):

The dog Awaro cries out
How will he find the way now?

The dog Kimi cries out
How will he go?

Even when the word *berebu-* is not used in the poem, the image appealed to is still one of lostness. Lostness is interpreted as a silence where there once was discourse, and in this respect it invokes Heidegger's distinction between speaking and silence. This contrast is effectively utilized as a poignant device in several Foi songs:

(Song 9):

Your Little Eye myth
You can no longer tell.

(Song 3):

Your weakness-causing spell
You didn't tell me before you left.

(Song 30):

The aeroplane buzzed as it flew away
But to us you said nothing.

As I have been maintaining, the relationship between motion and rest is at the heart of Foi poetic imagery. And it was Heidegger who invoked the relationship between stillness and motion as a way of understanding language's dependence upon silence (1971b: 122). In silence or rest, things can be represented, they can be named and brought into relationship with each other. According to David White, the purpose of silence:

> is to emphasize that the relation between language and being can be scrutinized only if we first bracket concrete speaking as such and then examine (in a state of silence, as it were) how beings are established through the actual process of naming representation (1978: 48).

In concealing the land, in concealing magical words and political metaphors, in keeping their names private, Foi men appropriate the representational power of words. And where words can be hidden, so can the things for which they stand. Men's relations with each other become a never-ending strategy of hiding and revealing, of using names as negotiable tokens of things that are never revealed. Women, on the other hand, through poetry reveal language's ontological status: they reveal the nexus of space and time that is encapsulated in personal and place-names and restore the movement of life activity to language and names.

Heidegger distinguished between these two features of language when he elaborated on the distinction between speaking and saying. Speaking employs the power of language to represent things 'as if' they were factical, 'ontic', 'in-themselves'. It gives us the illusion that we can manipulate the world, an illusion that is, after all, true. Saying, on the other hand, is the domain of poetic language in its most comprehensive sense: it is any discourse that reveals the ontological dimensions of the world, that presents things named in their spatial, temporal and historical relation to human concerns. And in so far as Heidegger identifies all art as poetry, it is the function of poetry to reveal these existential properties of language.

> That into which the work [of art] sets itself and which it causes to come forth in this setting back of itself we called the earth . . . Upon the earth, and in it, historical man grounds his dwelling in the world (1971c: 46).

To appreciate what Heidegger meant by this we have to understand his earlier writings on the spatiality of *Dasein* (Being-there) in *Being and Time*. When implements are exposed to our concern, when we appropriate things in our environment and make of them equipment, we put such things in a spatial relationship to ourselves and hence to each other. What is inscribed by the sum total of human acts through time is a space that sets forth a world of historically constituted human being.

> Dasein's spatiality is a function of its commerce with the implements. Dasein places things. It places them by approximation and by direction (Vycinas 1961: 40).

Relationships of 'distance' and 'nearness' are not primarily geometrical – that is, they are not primarily a matter of measurement of absolute units of distance; they are not ontic, in other words, but ontological – that is, defined with reference to human being. Those things that are ready-to-hand for us are characterized by nearness; they enjoy an intimate role in our being-in-the-world (the example that Vycinas uses is the astronomer looking through his telescope, for whom the distant star he focuses on is ready-to-hand and 'nearer than the glasses on his nose' [1961: 39]).

Now what the work of art does, according to Heidegger, is to open the object of contemplation into its full relationship of nearness, presence and remoteness with respect to our life projects; it situates the object within a world ontologically constituted through the continuing accretion of human concern and attention over time. It brings the object out of the seclusion of its everyday-ness, where its significance as a focus of human intention and attention may have been lost, forgotten or concealed; or where its formative relationship with the earth may have simply atrophied over time as a result of our distancing neglect. Though living people's recent paths have led attention away from the abandoned, empty gardens and houses of the deceased, Foi women, through their memorial poetry, unconceal these hidden traces of former lives.

But it is through this distancing neglect that the things in our world come to have relative statuses of revelation and opacity; and they are relative and mutable because of course our concerns and goals change over time. Things revealed to our scrutiny become so against a background of other things that recede into anonymity; we 'de-circumspect' them by virtue of focusing our attention elsewhere. The work of art, however, uncovers or re-reveals this tacit ground; it allows us to see the things of our concern within the totality of their connection to a world and hence to each other. It appresents figure and ground simultaneously to us; in other words, it obviates the dialectic of the figure–ground bracketing.

Heidegger put it this way: 'The setting up of a world and the setting forth of earth are two essential features in the work-being of the work [of art]' (1971c: 48). Here, Heidegger is positing a figure–ground relationship. Our quotidian experience of things involves this ceaseless tension between what we reveal and what we at the same time hide so that it can provide a background against which the revealed object can stand forth. 'What appears hides what does not and draws attention away from the entire context in which it does appear' (Kaelin 1967: 84). Foi men's historical relationship to the earth is impelled by this tension. This is not to say that Foi men are unaware of the earth as the historical ground of being, nor do they fail to contemplate the poetic dimension of their activity-on-the-earth, which is the world of their being, in Heidegger's terminology. I only mean that what convention assigns to men is the possibility of transacting with land, of subordinating its functions as an arena of their historical life to their transient political manoeuvrings. Foi women, on the other hand, reveal hidden names and the earth as an arena of death. There can be no true historicity, no true world without the inclusion of that finality, and this is what is missing in men's discourse about place (though, of course, it is not lacking in their *authentic* relation to place).

\* \* \*

In Foi, the word *me* means the following:

1. 'place, region, area' as in *me ti*, 'this place [here]'; *Foime kasia*, 'Lower Foi area [south]'; *bu'uni me*, lit. 'deadfall place', i.e. a section of the bush where traps are habitually set, or *guru me*, 'cassowary place', a region cassowaries are known to frequent; *me wasi*, 'a good place'.
2. 'language, speech', also used to describe the 'speech' of animals, primarily birds.
3. 'wild, undomesticated; the bush as opposed to the village', as in *me nami*, 'wild pig'; *me dare*, 'wild pitpit' (uncultivated).
4. 'other, another, different' as in *amena me*, 'another man'; *ma'ame mege me*, 'something else, something different'; *feraga me*, 'again, one more time'.

This semantic unity between 'place', 'speech' and 'wild' constitutes the most vivid Heideggerian synthesis in the Foi lifeworld. It calls to mind how the Daribi explained to Roy Wagner: 'eat our pandanus fruit, smoke our tobacco, and you will know our language' (Wagner 1975: 114). Language and place are a unity. The manner in which human action and purposive appropriation inscribes itself upon the earth is an iconography of human intentions. Its mirror image is speech itself, which, in the act of naming, memorializes these intentions, makes of them a history-in-dialogue. Every time the Foi make reference to a place-name, they, like the Western Apache, invoke this iconographic encapsulation of a human history. For the Foi, speech, *me* – Saying – creates the world, but it also brings forth the earth as a collection of human places, as the grounding of that world. Place-names create the world as a humanized, historicized space; but speech, like any other bodily activity, is conditioned and shaped by the tasks to which human interests direct it. The poetic nature of Foi song begins, not with a woman's attempts to give an aesthetic dimension to her emotion, but with the everyday, unremarked-upon rhythms, melodies and mimeses of quotidian speech itself.

## Notes

1. Translated by William Acker (1952).
2. This is a paraphrase of Relph's translation of the original French passage (Relph 1976: 26).
3. In 1993, the Chevron Niugini Company completed the Poroma–Kutubu access road, which linked this local Foi road to the Highlands highway system. The road was widened and upgraded at this time.
4. A description of Foi naming practices can be found in J. Weiner (1988a).
5. I might add that the Foi word *mowa~ga-*, 'to clarify, to make clear, to explain' partakes of the same spatial metaphor as does our English expression: in Foi *me wa~ga* means 'a clearing, a cleared space in the forest'.
6. This phrase is Sartre's.

# 3

# Being and Striving: Death, Gender and Temporality among the Foi

Anthropologists have always been sensitive to the ways in which people throughout the world try to bring the signifying powers of the material to a halt, to erase the inhuman memory of the object world itself. If it is not a matter of explicitly 'finishing the dead', as they do in the Massim region of eastern Papua New Guinea (see Battaglia 1990), it is still a matter of deferring to the degradability of the material and the artefactual to create a memory out of absence. The Foi of the Southern Highlands Province of Papua New Guinea, who show no interest in graphic or plastic art, do however compose and publicly sing poetic songs that are of great poignancy and performative value in Foi communal life (see J. Weiner 1991). Through the medium of these songs they memorialize the lives of deceased men. While men live, they make marks and work transformations on the land, in the form of, for example, gardens, houses, and fish and animal traps. When these men die, the traps, houses and other built artefactual sites rot and decompose: these *things* return to the vegetable world from which they originated. The songs characteristically sing of deceased men as having occupied a series of places that are now being reclaimed by the anonymity of the forest. They celebrate the temporal span of a man's life in spatial terms, a phenomenon which we now understand to be common throughout the non-Western world, where people are still in relations of immediacy to the land, its topography, landscape and resources. These songs make visible much that is central to the Foi experience of social life – most importantly, memory, production, and movement – and are performed on ceremonial occasions in the communal longhouse. For the Foi, what Heidegger called 'being-towards-death', the self-conscious moment at which humans contemplate their own finitude and undertake the responsibility of finding meaning in these acknowledged limits of human life, is a fundamental human *existentielle*.

The role of Foi women in this process is crucial, for it links the Foi understanding of gender contrast to the existential dimensions of finitude

I have introduced in the last chapter. The general association of women and death and mourning that we encountered in Foi song-making in the previous chapter still remains a building-block of the anthropological portraiture of tribal society. In some versions, women emerge as caretakers of the dead body because they themselves biologically create the live body; in other versions, they are given the care of the polluting, dangerous corpse because they themselves are already polluted by their intimate role in physical reproduction. To turn to another contrast, in some cases they stand as repairers of the social network damaged by death's removal of the social actor; while in other cases they are themselves the source of that disruption, as the exclusive source of witchcraft, for example.

Another image has them representing timeless values of nurturance, regeneration or the reconstitution of various enduring social identities, which again are iterated in mortuary ceremonies and exchanges. And in other instances these social identities are evidence for women's association with temporal, finite social processes.

What these formulations thus have in common is not, however, their linking of femininity and death; they also share a view of death as antithetical to life, as the end of life, as a disrupter of life. Women, either as exemplary sources of life on the one hand, or of pollution and death on the other, are paradoxically, outside of life too, by virtue of their intimate association with death, dying and mourning. Here we have an appeal to the notion that the *source* of something is not a part of the thing it creates – the variety of idealism that suggests that a product is *not* determined by the shape of the mechanism that forms it.

There is, then, this variation in women's ontological association with social process; but it is consistently pegged to an association of women with the beginning and end of life itself. It is not that we disagree about what *value* and *interpretation* societies place on death and finality; but we are unsure about the existential status of death itself, and its relation to life. Death in the anthropological portraiture can be both temporal and non-temporal; global and particular; social and individual. A large part of this ambiguity results from our Western delicacy, our impulse to sanitize death and deny it as a legitimate posture of life itself. After all, most of our fieldwork has been carried out long after the most horrific mourning cults that some non-Western people used to practice had been eliminated – practices that involved holding the dead body, smearing the juices of the dead body on one's skin, drinking the juice. These practices were largely, though not exclusively, associated with women too, at least in Papua New Guinea.[1] Death for people such as the Foi was a part of life in a far more complex way than simply as a source of fear and disruption.

In the teknonyms and grief names they used, in the taboos on the names of dead relatives, in the shrines they erect in their houses in the memory of deceased kinsmen, in their constant attempt to communicate with the spirits of the dead, to harness their power for healing, prescience, wealth acquisition, and so forth, rather than simply to avoid or ignore death – in all these ways people like the Foi made death a project of life.

When this project is exclusively allocated to women by the ethnographer, however, women are removed from a consideration of their total authentic life condition. They are made to inhabit some kind of liminal or atemporal zone, removed from sources of power, except perhaps such as are unintentional and uncontrollable. Such an approach denies women an authentic relation to temporality, which I argue *is* the defining feature of being-in-the-world. Associated with the phenomenological movement in European philosophy in the twentieth century and in particular with Martin Heidegger, the phrase 'being-in-the-world' describes a total human situatedness within an encompassing matrix, a physical and social environment, and an awareness of the way human beings, through their actions and consciousness, polarize a world and are in turn polarized by it in their re-confrontation with it.

In repairing women's existential posture, in other words, one must not deny that posture to men too. Annette Weiner, for example, suggests that Trobriand women control the primary arena of affinal mortuary exchange as well as the critical transactions in matrilineage property and names. They therefore control or have power over reproduction in its temporal and historical, as well as its cosmic, immortal and ahistorical features. Men, on the other hand, because they do not pass on matrilineage (*dala*) property to their own offspring, are only indirectly involved in the regeneration of *dala* identity. 'Men can only control objects and persons which remain totally within a generational perspective of social time and space' (1976: 231).

The problem here is that Weiner confuses political and economic asymmetry in power relations with an asymmetry in the constitution of spatial and temporal lived experience itself. Obviously, the differential power alignments of men and women are made visible in their acquisition of and contrasting uses of time and space. But while one can make a claim that some individuals have more power than others, one cannot claim that one gender is 'more authentically temporal' or 'more fully spatial' than another. The problem is that such characterizations of temporality as Annette Weiner attributes to the Trobrianders are as much an abstraction of their lived experience of duration, interval, causality and so forth as are our own timepiece-dominated modes of measuring time. They bear the same relation to the everyday Trobriand constitutions of temporality as the rationalizations 'lineage' and 'clan' bear to the everyday Trobriand activities of production, the implementation of personal power, and the practical assertion of parental and sibling relationships, all of which first and foremost are constituted as historical processes.[2]

In this chapter, I want to outline an existential approach to the problem of women and death. That is, I want to consider a mode of being-in-the-world that attributes to women a particular perspective on temporality and finality. In looking at the Foi of interior Papua New Guinea, I have been suggesting how some of the ideas in Heidegger's *Being and Time* (1962) give us a different perspective on this dilemma. I want to suggest that men and women in Foi have different ontological relations to death; that is, each is responsible for constituting part of the total social creation of death-in-life; but I do so without claiming that either or men or women do or do not lack certain dimensions of spatiotemporality, that men or women are 'confined' to this or that spatiotemporal range, because I do not wish to speak about space and time as essents, or as an empty resource waiting to be filled by a culture (see Casey 1996). I want instead to suggest that men and women constitute a particular temporal condition through a specific *sexually demarcated discursive habitus* – a mode of speaking, learned as embodied technique and anchored by a total life perspective that is engendered in the historical process of socialization.

So, the framework I am appealing to is largely hermeneutic, and hermeneutic specifically in terms of Heidegger's hermeneutic. Heidegger claimed that it was the understanding of one's own death that allowed us to be truly temporal beings. Faced with one's death, one works towards an eventual resolution of one's life, one seeks to make a meaning out of the sum of one's projects. And it is in this forward projection towards death that Heidegger suggested was the true moment of temporality: anticipation of the future. 'There is . . . a literal sense in which futurity is the most immediate, the most present, of the dimensions of temporality' (Steiner 1978: 106). We don't, in other words, want to commit the Cartesian error of seeing ourselves as passively moving through an objective stream of time, or of seeing time as a succession of objective moments with ourselves as the static observers and victims of it. We make time first through the bodily, spatially situatedness of our goals and postures in life, and it is part of our groundedness to be forward-looking towards the anticipated outcome of these goals.[3]

And from this stance of anticipation of the future, the past and its interpretation is always contingent: '. . . past events are altered, are given meaning by, what happens now and will happen tomorrow. . . Heidegger is reminding us of the mutually generative an re-interpretive circularities of past–present–future', Steiner says (1978: 107).

The role of discourse in this construction of lived temporality is of course critical. When the dead are memorialized through rite, memorial litany, eulogy, teknonymy and penthonymy, they are brought into our present. The vivification of our memories of the dead is just one instance of the way the dead can often be closer to us than the living; in the 'intense recall' of the deceased's prior situatedness are instances of what Heidegger called *care*, which he described as our source of interest in our future:

> . . . the death of an individual is very often a modulation towards resurrection in other men's needs and remembrance. Heidegger's term is 'respectful solicitude' (Steiner 1978: 100).

In this lies the understanding of 'how a living community must constitute a "being-along-side" its dead' (ibid.).

Given that the dead live in the manner in which we memorialize them, I am going to examine two different ways in which the Foi accomplish this, one associated with men and one associated with women. Having described these two contrastive discursive modalities, I will then speculate on a Foi nexus of gender, discourse, death, temporality and agency.

## Death, Ghosts and Dreams

When a Foi person's body dies, his/her soul, *i~ ho~*, leaves the body. Ideally it should depart the area of the living and go to the afterworld, an actual physical region that in traditional times was thought to lie far to the southeast, where all rivers and streams ended. But a person's *i~ ho~* also leaves the body during sleep and wanders around, encountering other such spirits, including those that have become permanently detached from bodies after death. It is these activities of the soul that the Foi perceive in dreams.

For the Foi these dreams are sources of power. They are one of the primary avenues of meaningful communication between ghosts and humans. In this way, these spirits or ghosts can impart information to the living. One who can interpret dreams effectively can gain access to the knowledge of ghosts: knowledge, primarily, of magical formulae. But the Foi maintain that what ghosts do and say can never be taken literally; their motives and purposes are concealed and hidden from the society of the living. One must therefore acquire the ability to interpret appropriately the events symbolically perceived in dreams.

Ghosts are associated with specific parts of the landscape. In order to expose themselves to the possibility of dream contact with ghosts, men (the deliberate seeking after dreams is a male interest for the Foi) visit those places where ghosts seem to be found: certain pools of still water; the whirlpools that form near sharp bends in the river; the bases of certain flowering trees that attract many birds; places where powerful magical spells were once performed. A man prepares for contact with ghosts in the same way he prepares for battle: by fasting and avoiding sexual contact with women. He then sleeps alone near one of these spots until he dreams vividly, at which time he will conclude that he has made contact with a ghost.

To the Foi these places are associated with *stillness*, with the *halting of motion*, with the *holding motionless of some movement or flow* – the whirlpool that stops the one-way flow of water; the nectar-filled tree flowers that attract the passing birds; the spells that bind the wandering spirits to a particular spot. Anything that holds that flow or movement in place has a potential, some pent-up reserve or capacity, a possible source of power or revelation.

Because of their immobility, Foi ghosts lack temporal dimension. Foi ghosts do not represent or call forth the memory of historical persons. The Foi do not know the identity of a ghost, do not know which deceased person's *i~ ho~* a ghost represents. Unlike living persons, ghosts are only in the present, with no future to look forward to, and no history that focuses that forward anticipation. And without this double anchoring in a mirrored past/future, they are not memories, nor can they call forth memories. They are not creative in the same sense that Aboriginal or south-coast New Guinea ancestral beings are continuously creative in the present of humans.

When I say that it is magical formulae that men seek from ghosts in dreams, I really mean that in a more encompassing sense: men seek the revelation of auspicious names. A magic spell for the Foi is, in its bare essentials, but the perception of an alternative and secret *name* of an item one wishes to transform in some way.

Consider the following portion of a spell that is recited when preparing a snare trap for cassowaries:

*tudamere, tudayawage*
tudamere, tudayawage

*sawa hae~ hubu guru-o tuda*
Sawa fruit [a variety of pandanus], cassowary come strike it

*kenebo hae~ hubu guru-o tuda*
Kenebo fruit, cassowary come strike it

*gofe hae~ hubu guru-o tuda*
Gofe fruit [a *Ficus* variety], cassowary. . .

*kawari hae~ hubu guru-o tuda*
Kawari fruit [a *Cyrtostachoid* variety], cassowary. . .

*sore hae~ hubu guru-o tuda*
Sore fruit, cassowary . . .

*igini ga'ayare hubu tuda*
Cassowary with multi-coloured fur, come strike it

*game ga'ayare tuda*
Orange-furred cassowary . . .

*furubu sae~ bosodibio tuda*
Cassowary with red comb ['cassowary with a comb hanging down like a red *furubu* leaf'] . . .

*tai o'oni-o tuda*
Female cassowary with small nipples . . .

*gamu sabudibi-o tuda* . . .
Very old cassowary . . .

*igini ga'ayar-o tuda*
Multi-coloured cassowary . . .

*me me haru guru-o tuda*
At another place, cassowary come strike it.

*me me oro guru-o tuda*
The mountain-top cassowary . . .

*me me fai guru-o tuda*
The mountain-side cassowary . . .

*duma me guru-o tuda*
The hilly-place cassowary . . .

*ibu mano me guru-o tuda*
The small-creek cassowary . . .

*hau me guru-o tuda*
The valley cassowary . . .

*ibu mano me guru-o tuda*
The small-creek cassowary . . .

*tuda*
tuda

*me me guru-o tuda*
At another place, cassowary . . .

*igini ga'ayare tuda*
Multi-coloured cassowary . . .

*game ga'ayare tuda*
Orange-furred cassowary . . .

*sigaru hae~ri hera'ame davi'ame giridia-o*
Sigaru fruit, tomorrow perhaps, the day after perhaps, the cassowary will approach.

*hukageraha ferodoba'ayo'o*
The snare will hold the cassowary in its noose.

*bidiyere humotauyere mowaedibubege*
The cassowary will be hung up like a ripe fruit.

*ma'aweyabo*
Ma'aweyabo [finish].

There is a broad comparison being made here between the varieties of fruit that cassowaries eat and the image of the cassowary itself, hanging in the snare like a fruit on the vine. The names of the fruit become alternative names for the cassowary itself, as do the metonymic descriptions of the cassowary ('red comb', 'small nipples', 'orange', 'multi-coloured').

The Foi perceive the cassowary as a wanderer of the bush, and the spell thus calls upon the cassowary by its different haunts – the mountain top, the mountain side, the distant mountain valley, the side of the small creek. The varieties of fruits, the different physical characteristics of the cassowary, and its various places in the bush all become alternative *names* for the cassowary itself.

What is actually revealed to a man when he learns a spell of this nature is never made entirely clear. Although men spoke literally of learning the spell in a dream, it seems as if what is perceived or intuited is a single, secret name, around which the dreamer can then verbally expand upon the spell with a variety of other, already available metaphoric equivalences and spoken cadences specific to spell recitation within a standard format.[4]

There is another way in which names are 'revealed' to the Foi, however. In the men's longhouse, men perform the *sorohabora* memorial song poems. Typically, these poems link the life-course of a deceased man to the places he inhabited during his lifetime. In the closing lines of every Foi memorial song poem, the name of the deceased man who is the subject of the song, his father's and mother's names and clan names, and the deceased's 'private' or 'hidden' name are recited. In contrast to men's solitary outposts in the bush, where they dream of spells, cassowaries, and marsupials, the setting is the interior of the longhouse, crowded with living people.

1. *ba'a na'a namikiribibi iga*
   boy, your Namikiribibi path

   *iga aodiba'ae*
   path tree-covered.

   *ba'a na'a tigifu iga*
   boy, your Tigifu path

   *iga aodiba'ae*
   path tree-covered.

2. *ba'a bamo waya'arihabo iburo'o*
   boy, this Waya'arihabo creek

*aodibihaba'aye*
let the bush cover it.

*ba'a bamo domege ibu*
boy, this Domege creek

*aodoba'aye*
let bush cover it.

3. *ba'a na'a duma orege duma*
   boy, your mountain, Orege mountain

   *memo aginoba'aye*
   another let steal it.

   *ba'a na'a so~a duma*
   boy, your So~a mountain

   *memo aginoba'aye*
   another let steal it.

4. *kibudobo ka yamo*
   Kibudobo woman Ya

   *kabe sese*
   man Sese

   *banimahu'u kabe irahaimabomo*
   Banimahu'u man Irahaimabo

   *kabe sisu'umena*
   man Sisu'umena.

5. *turu ya bari dobo ba'a irahaimabo*
   sky bird banima clan boy Irahaimabo

   *kabe sese*
   man Sese

   *kibudobo ka yamo*
   Kibudobo woman Ya

*kabe sisu'umena*
man Sisu'umena

6. *yo hua ka mege bamo*
his mother woman only that

*kabe sese-o*
man Sese

*yo hua ka mege bamo*
his mother woman only this

*ibudawabo*
ibudawabo

1. Boy, your Namikiribibi path –
That path is covered over.

Boy, your Tigifu path –
That path is hidden by the forest.

2. This boy's Waya'arihabo Creek
It is obliterated by trees.

This man's Domege Creek
Is covered over by the jungle.

3. Boy, your Orege Mountain
Let another man steal it.

Boy your So~a Mountain
Let another man steal it.

4. The Kibudobo woman Ya
Her son Sese

The Banimahu'u man Irihaimabo
His son Sisu'umena.

5. The clan of the high-flying *banima* bird, Irihaimabo
His son Sese

The Kibudobo woman Ya
Her son Sisu'umena

6. His mother, this woman alone
   Her son Sese

   His mother, this lonely woman
   *Ibu Dawabo*.

This song was composed to the memory of a man named Sese. The places he used to occupy during his life – the path he created and used at the places Namikiribibi, Tigifu, the creeks he fished in, Waya'arihabo, Domege; the mountains in which he used to hunt, Orege, So'a – these places have, in his absence, become covered over with bush as the forest works to reclaim the traces he left on these places. But in verse 3, a sardonic equivalence is also hinted at between the impersonal obliteration of the forest and the deliberate appropriation of a dead man's land by his surviving male relatives. 'Let other men also do their part in obliterating your trace', the song also says.

The final three verses of these songs are called the *dawa*, and these are the verses where the deceased's names are called out, as well as the names of his mother and father and their clans and associated totemic species. Finally, in verses 4 and 5, the deceased's private name – Sisu'umena – is also publicly recited, although these names are never used in public when people are alive. The last phrase, *ibudawabo*, for which the Foi gave no literal translation, but which could mean 'water cutting', is the way such songs end: with an appeal to some act of cutting, severing or ending of a flow or movement, like the *kireji*, the 'cutting words' that punctuate Japanese haiku.

These songs, as I have said, are performed by men, and constitute the most compelling performative techniques the Foi possess. But the songs themselves are composed by women. While at work at the long, tedious job of making sago flour, women dwell on their deceased male kinsmen and feel compelled to compose these songs in their memory. It is they who are revealing the hidden names of people, and it is they who are recounting the social, productive history of men. Their husbands might find on occasion that they pass nearby their wives' sago camps and hear them singing. If he hears a song that strikes his fancy, the man may ask his wife to teach it to him later on.

Like ghosts, then, women also reveal hidden names to men in the bush. Men take these verses and names and make of them the songs that are the medium of their flamboyant ceremonial performances, just as they take the names they perceive in dreams and turn them into the magical spells that are the adjuncts of their assertive male productivity.

## The Metaphor of Magic and the Image of Poetry

If I were to sum up the way Foi men attain to power, it would be this: the more a man can become like a ghost, the more power he exerts in life; the more associated he becomes with the souls of the dead, the more decisively he lives among the living. In the often opaque images of dream, men seek the revelation of some metaphoric link that will allow them to exert the ghost's power in their own world. When ghosts reveal cassowaries as fruit, or pearl shells as birds-of-paradise, or pigs as cockatoos, men assume that these equations in themselves constitute a key to exerting a leverage on the world. The Foi man then knows that by invoking the fruit, or the bird-of-paradise or the cockatoo in a spell he will gain access to shells and pigs. He does not have to understand the link between the two domains, though it may be readily apparent to him and the anthropologist alike (in these cases, it is the red colour of birds-of-paradise and pearl shells and their common use as male decorations; or the white colour of cockatoos and pigs and the similarity of their raucous squealing and shouts).

In their oratorical encounters, men also mimic ghosts, so to speak. Foi men of high status have access to a range of metaphoric usages called *irisae~medobora*, 'tree leaf talk', which consists of cryptic or allusive replacements for ordinary semantic items: a '*waru* tree' (a *Ficus* species) is a head man; a 'marsupial' is a woman; a 'mushroom' refers in a derogatory way to a meat prestation; 'paint' can mean sorcery powder. Most men know a stock of such common metaphorical usages; but head men have a large repertoire of them that only they know how to decode. Men of high status thus become ghost-like to the extent that their speech, particularly their oratory, is opaque and needs to be interpreted, just as dreams need to be interpreted.

It can be said that what women's songs reveal is also a metaphoric link: most commonly they depict the life of the deceased in terms of the series of places he inhabited, so that a temporal and a spatial interval are equated. But the link in this case is not an arcane or arbitrary or adventitious one imputed by a ghostly agent. In the case of the poem it is the revelation of the fundamental lived experience of life and death as spatially and temporally constituted states of being.

But this recreation of dead men's life-history takes place against the background practices from which the Foi's everyday understanding of temporality acquires its significance. One's life is envisioned as the serial inhabitation of a set of places upon which one has effected some productive or appropriative transformation – the making of a garden, the erecting of a house, the setting of semi-permanent animal trap lines and fish dams, the paths they habitually created and used, and so forth. Foi women reveal these precise links in their songs. By serially listing place-names, a temporal span is automatically invoked, a sense of life as productive movement is appealed to.

This contrasts quite radically with the static, timeless, conceptual equations of men's metaphoric usages. The intent of magic spells is to turn a movement into stillness: in the example above, men want to *halt* the movement of cassowaries, to make them as still as the tree fruit upon which they feed. The places they invoke to depict the wandering habits of this terrestrial bird are not named. Woman's song, on the other hand, turns the final stillness of death into what was its original historically constituted life movement. Women are the true source of the central *moving* images in Foi society: their menstrual flow, which is so akin to the flowing water that orients the Foi in their cosmos; and the 'flow' of place-names and personal names they initiate in the memorial songs.

It might be argued that men's magical spells depend upon rhythmic repetition, just as women's song does; that they detotalize a field, by serially listing a set of alternative labels, just as a woman's song does. But this would be to exalt the *formal* similarities between the two modes of speech at the expense of their contextualized, perlocutionary properties – their historical properties – which are precisely what is at issue here. Moreover, it would involve a glossing over of the contrastive spatio-temporal frameworks that ground these modes of speech, and their rather different modes of embodiment. Whatever moving properties the imagery of magic has for the Foi, it is a movement that doesn't go anywhere, like the whirlpool, or ghostly activity in *Haisureri*; whereas a woman's song depends upon the listener's calling up the image of people moving through space in a historically significant way. Women's songs are ultimately danced by men, performed before the entire community and literally embodied by men; magic spells are whispered and are not communicative in intent at all.

More importantly, this contrast calls forth the key contribution that Heidegger makes to anthropology in *Being and Time* concerning the historicity of human being. Whatever the memorial song evokes in terms of its commentary on a total life, it requires that the audience accept that the song itself is iconic of human history: that it serially unfolds a set of places that were inhabited and appropriated by the named individual. The song, its performance and what it evokes in an audience are all part of one of the Foi community's important forms of hermeneutic constitution of past, present and future as a coherent field of human temporality. Magical speech, on the other hand, may be temporal, as of course all speech is, but is not constitutive of history for Foi and gives only limited scope to hermeneutical evaluation.

With respect to procreative, productive and discursive flow, men assert themselves as both *initiators* and *interrupters* of these flows: their semen blocks the flow of blood and allows it to coagulate and form a fetus. They also take names and render static their moving characteristics. Magic for the Foi involves the ability to *fix* ghostly power, and to that extent – to the degree, that is, that they bring continuity to a halt – men become more 'ghost-like' in their social impact than women, who, through possessing a ghost-like 'lethal influence' – contact with their menstrual secretions is debilitating to men – nevertheless are the true sources of life-sustaining motion.

Let me enlarge on this: as I have described elsewhere (J. Weiner 1986, 1987), Foi men traditionally participated in several healing cults, before they were persuaded by the Christian missionaries to abandon the practices sometime in the 1960s. The most important of these cults was called *Usi Nobora*, 'Usi Eating'. While all the healing cults centred around pieces of antique stone – pestles, mortars, club heads, and so forth – that were thought to be the incarnation or residing place of certain ghosts, only the Usi cult involved the actual ingestion by men of subsidiary 'stones' (in the form of human molars). Initiation into the Usi cult involved eating the stones and the bitter-tasting Usi mixture. This was thought to make the initiates lose their senses and make them receptive to possession by a ghost 'familiar'. The initiates ate the Usi mixture a number of times, until traces of the 'stones' could no longer be found in their faeces. At this point, the initiates were considered to have incorporated a ghost, and its powers of life and death, within them.

To the extent that they thus became as lethal as ghosts – or as women, for that matter – men as much as women caricatured some version of 'death in life'. The point is that the Usi power was deployed as a power to heal illness, even though it could also be used to sorcerize; just as women's power to create new life, centred in their menstrual blood, is also harmful to men. The difference is that men's power is the result of *holding something motionless*, in this case, the peripatetic ghosts, while women's power is a function of *the moving flow of life* within her.

However, I caution against a too literal Platonic extension of this central Foi aesthetic – I suggest that its role in the constitution of social and sexual categorizations is not essential, determinate or structural, but rather interpretative, or analogical, encompassing simultaneously both a 'model of' and 'model for' the roles that the Foi see as constituting their social universe. Like any trope, the contrasts between metaphor and image, distance and nearness, stillness and motion, demand an interpretative realization as well as an idealization in terms of structural homologies. Neither does an asymmetry in interpretative *habitus* necessarily depend upon a real sociopolitical asymmetry.

I want to suggest that at the core of the dynamic of Foi tropic and poetic discourse lies the realization and confirmation of contrastive male and female discursive modalities – *provided* we realize right from the start that the Foi demarcation of this contrast is as much a *comment upon* or *interpretation of* as it is a *normative summation of* behavioural tendencies.

## Death, Temporality and Historicity

Let us return to Annette Weiner's Trobriand Islanders. The Platonic dialectic she appeals to may be summed up as *the [female] atemporality of human being* and the *[male] temporality of human striving.* For her, Trobriand women have the prerogative of iterating the immortal properties of social identity: the social essence of a person, the *baloma* or matrilineage spirit. Men, on the other hand, without access to the immortal and ahistorical mode of reproducing matrilineage identity, are confined to historical, finite cycles surrounding the transfer, use and ultimate return of matrilineage land. They are productive, but this productivity always runs up against matrilineal, female continuity, which continuously short-circuits the efforts of men.

But a Foi perspective of human being inverts this dialectic. It is precisely the temporal nature of being that is its core feature, while the illusion that one has attained goals (in the Trobriand case, the reaffirmation of the matrilineage), what I am calling *striving*, brings continuity to an end; it signals a falling away from the anticipatory atttitude that marks our interest in the world. Obviously, we all strive, in that we work to seek a resolution to our life's story. This is the way we create temporality, as a function of our concernful activities in this forward-looking posture. But in the Foi world of space and time, it is men who strive to bring this link between the acting, sensuous person and temporal continuity to a halt. They seek after the atemporal and ultimately lethal power of ghosts and channel it for their own purposes. In Heidegger's terms, Foi men's cutting of spatial and temporal flows embodies a turning away from what he called being-towards-death: the authentic, concernful being that encompasses its own finality as an integral part of its temporality.

But as much as men are concerned with bringing continuity to a halt, it is women who, in their reveries while making sago, concern themselves with the most central aspect of finality, the death of humans. While women are engaged in the monotonous, rhythmic work of making sago, they dwell on the death of their husbands and male kinsmen. Men are only concerned with ghosts, which is the volitional residue or precipitate of power that remains after men die, which retains no sense of temporality, and which can be tricked, conjured, cajoled or threatened into acting on behalf of living men. Women, on the other hand, immortalize men themselves as they lived. They sing of men in terms of their historical being, rather than in terms of their atemporal spiritual striving and influence.

Through dreams men gain access to metaphor; women, in their reverie over dead kinsmen, create poetic images. Metaphor confines the striving of men in a static, atemporal formula; poetic image embodies the historical nexus of human attachment and loss. Metaphor is anonymous, secret, hoarded, transactable. Poetic image is performative, evocative, intrinsic to women's authorship, publicly displayed and celebrated, valuable only in so far as it cannot be cashed in for the negotiable finalities that valuate the currencies of men's power. Men's dreaming is a silent world of elusive contact with detemporalized spirits; women's poetry is a sung message of love, loss and grief, proclaiming the temporal ascendancy of human relationship.

*concealed vs. revealed*

Am I then merely inverting Annette Weiner's gender contrast by attributing temporality to Foi women and atemporality to Foi men? Of course not, and the whole point of this exercise is precisely to avoid phrasing the dialectic in just those Platonic terms. The poetry that women compose depends upon the innovation of tropic juxtaposition; just as the contextual effectiveness of men's oratory (and dream interpretation generally – see J. Weiner [1986]) depends upon their accurately and insightfully depicting real-life people and events in allegorical terms that enhance their meaningful historicity. Speech is incomplete without both temporal trope and historic image, and men and women can no more do without one of them than they can do without discourse itself. I do not want to depict Foi metaphysics as some version of Bergson's antinomy between lived experience and scientific law (in this case, between poetic and semantic modes of verbalization). Instead, as Dilthey did in his critique of Bergson, I want to show that both the 'experiential' and the 'conceptual' are necessary and reciprocal existential components of a total life condition. What I *am* suggesting is that Foi men and women use the contrast as a way of evaluating their relationship to a world of discursive being. It is not only that image and metaphor have different semiotic or tropic foundations; more importantly, *they embody the contrast in the way discourse is situated with respect to the other temporal processes of the lifeworld, and it is this contrast that is given a gender marking in Foi conceptualization.*

## Conclusion

The contrast centres on what kinds of historicity the Foi recognize and how they apportion and to whom they attribute them. As I have said elsewhere (J. Weiner 1988a), men are by and large the *initiators* of productive activities, especially those that involve the inscription of agency on the land – the building of houses, the planting of gardens, trees, sago stands, bamboo, and so forth. The tasks that are characteristically associated with women are those that *maintain* and preserve these initial efforts. But poetically and metaphorically, it is women who are credited with creativity – they compose songs, whereas men merely take women's songs and perform them on their own social occasions. Similarly, men have to maintain contact with ghosts so that they can obtain the magical metaphors upon which their own productive efficacy depends.

One could be tempted to say that it is in men's activities that the spatial historicity of the Foi community takes shape, as they determine the patterns of habitation and movement of people over the land through time; and that women are then relegated to the 'interpretive work' of making an affective, aesthetic, linguistic 'image' of this spatiotemporal product.[5] But that would be to repeat Annette Weiner's Bergsonism, Trobriand-style: it would buy into a dichotomy between speech and bodily action, and between 'productive' and 'linguistic' action (and ultimately, between history and culture) wholly alien to the Foi. For the pattern of men's inscriptive activity on the earth is thoroughly 'linguistic', while women's poetic creations emerge from their most exemplary rhythmic work, sago processing, and further are intimately tied to their role in mourning, and hence first and foremost *embodied*.

More than that, it is in the nature of men's discursive habitus to *conceal* the conventional effects of their inscriptivity and, by so doing, to conceal from themselves the historical implications of their productive acts. They consider metaphor itself as opaque and elusive; whereas women call attention to and elaborate upon the way discourse itself frames and creates historically significant life acts. The magic spell appeals to Platonic forms and in so doing, removes the act and its discursive manipulation from the world of the contingent, the social and the temporal. Women's song, on the other hand, outlines the moral dimensions of a spatial and temporal life sequence, the manner in which production and discourse fashion the clearings of human historicity.

# Notes

1. Jadran Mimica, in a series of seminars on the experience of death among the Iqwaye given at Australian National University in 1987, brought these themes out vividly.
2. Lest it appear as if I am unfairly singling out Annette Weiner for this particular criticism, it should be pointed out that much pre-Bourdieu writing on time and space was Kantian and hence structural-functionalist in nature (see Pandya 1990), including portions of my early analysis of Foi culture (but see J. Weiner 1985).
3. Aletta Biersack, writing of the Paiela of Papua New Guinea, refers to a 'horizon of agency' as 'the spatial, temporal, and personnel limits of projects and their products' (1990: 63–4).
4. See J. Weiner (1986) for details on the structure of Foi magic spells.
5. 'The authentic "struggle", so the later Heidegger concluded, was not the violent action of the man but rather the receptive attitude of the woman staying by the hearth – remembering what needed to be remembered' (Zimmerman 1990: 121).

# −4−

# To Be At Home with Others in
# an Empty Place

## I

I have tried to bring Heidegger's ideas into the service of ethnography because in my opinion Heidegger's existential analytic belongs squarely and integrally to a crucial strand of twentieth-century social theorizing, which others such as Marx, Freud, Bourdieu, Lacan and Foucault have helped shape and bring into the service of social science. What Heidegger and these figures all have in common is how they have placed the *work of concealment* at the centre of their theories of human action, knowledge and relationship: the recognition of the importance of nescience as a positive component of temporality, progress, knowledge and social transformation. Indeed, one way to characterize our present twenty-first-century social science is to say that we have ceased to force such nescience to function as an ordering, rationalizing force, that is, as a component of the productionist rationale we have attributed to social life and intersubjectivity over the past 150 years. Instead, it has recently emerged as both the starting-point and the end rationale of social action and knowledge, something that frames and delimits such action and knowledge but that stands outside it and cannot be measured in its terms. This is what I described earlier as anthropology's new-found, or newly-uncovered, 'nihilism'.

Nescience is what such Heideggerian concepts as fallenness, averageness, and inauthenticity are all about. Bourdieu (1991), and, I would suspect, many anthropologists, no doubt rightly, see these terms as sinister euphemisms for Heidegger's attitudes concerning the sterility of democracy, capitalism, and modern urban bourgeois existence. But other more pragmatically inclined interpreters of Heidegger such as Hubert Dreyfus (1991; see also Dreyfus and Hall 1992a) see them as pertaining to the everyday processes of *méconnaissance*, 'misrecognition', which social scientists such as Bourdieu accept as components of the human existential.

"lack of awareness"

The terms that Heidegger used may seem less neutral than 'mystification,' 'enchantment', 'alienation', and the others with which Marx thought of the very same processes of ideological concealment in his meditations on the modern European condition. Or their sinister nature may lie in the opposite suggestion that they are *too* neutral, too abstract, too studied in their removal from the workings of power and domination. But it may be precisely because these terms address the same condition of life that Bourdieu was so insistent that Heidegger's and Marx's versions be differentiated from each other. But Marx and Heidegger (as well as Durkheim and Weber) were observing and commenting on the same world, and their concerns grew out of an engagement with that world. Heidegger, no less than Freud, speaks to the overtly social concerns of Marx, Durkheim and Weber, albeit not in terms immediately recognizable as those of social constructionism.

Within anthropology, I see the world of concealment most decisively and advantageously articulated within the writings of Roy Wagner and Marilyn Strathern.[1] To put this work at the centre of our analysis is to recognize that whatever it is that has power over social life and social relations must stand outside that life and those relations themselves (see M. Strathern 1988; Wagner 1986b). The issue of empowering social formations is not then solely a sociological matter, but must include some way of making visible the grounding human conditions upon which such social relations depend. What Heidegger, and anthropologists such as Wagner, Strathern, Crapanzano, Marcus, and others, conclude from these premises is that we must take an interpretative approach to social action. Simply put, this interpretative approach is invoked any time we seek to establish a perspective on some entity from the outside. What a genuine hermeneutic anthropology must realize is that this is as integral a process to the formation of a social world as it is to the ethnographic task of translating any such world into the terms of another. In other words, the interpretative work of anthropology and ethnography must model the very constitutive conditions of the social life we seek to describe. To accept this as our starting-point means that we have already accepted Heidegger's most important characterization of *Dasein* – the basic human existential condition of 'being-there' – and the conditions under which it acquires its particular shape.

## II

What I feel makes anthropology unique is that, like psychoanalysis, it takes as its subject-matter the very ontology-concealing capacity of people and communities. The harder we try to assert the radical *difference* between the Foi world and our own, the more problematic becomes the identification of the common ground automatically created between them through the narrowing of focus that such contrast calls for. To exemplify the subjective, social effects of this work of concealment, I wish to introduce a pair of German terms that fascinated both Heidegger and Freud: the 'at-home' and the 'not-at-home' – somewhat awkward glosses for the German words *heimlich* and *unheimlich*.

*Heimlich*: 'belonging to the house, not strange, familiar, tame, intimate, friendly' (Freud 1919: 222); but also, in the sense that it is something kept within the closed-off domain of the house or hearth, it is 'withdrawn from knowledge, unconscious' (1919: 226); hence, 'concealed, kept from sight, so that others do not get to know of or about it' (1919: 223). From Grimm's dictionary, quoted by Freud: *From the idea of 'homelike', 'belonging to the house', the further idea is developed of something withdrawn from the eyes of strangers, something concealed, secret . . .'* (1919: 225).

*Unheimlich*: strange, forbidding, uncanny, weird, arousing gruesome fear (1919: 224). *'The notion of something hidden and dangerous, . . . is still further developed, so that "heimlich" comes to have the meaning usually ascribed to "unheimlich"'* (1919: 226).

The uncanny, the sudden appearance of strangeness and unknownness, of being not-at-home that the German word *unheimlich* so properly expresses, within a situation one has hitherto taken as familiar – this is what I am trying to bring forth for our consideration.

Why should strangeness only make itself apparent to us within the framework of familiarity? We have to know about something or someone in order to know what it is we do not know. We have to create the feeling of familiarity first, because otherwise the impact of the unknown or unexpected cannot make itself felt. What is at issue is the way we construct a proportionality of social knowledge, because we judge the impact of a significant experience of strangeness only against what we perceive to be a background of things known. The greater and more intimate we feel such knowledge to be, the more forceful will be the impact of even a small unexpected piece of the unknown.

All this is turned awry when we envision anthropological fieldwork. We feel that we start from a totally alien position and then go on to achieve familiarity. By the end of our one year or two years, we know more about our hosts than we did when we first arrived. We feel more at home, we feel more *attuned*, in the words of Steven Feld, to our hosts' life. We have entered, after all, into real and concrete relationships of practical social life with them. The work entailed in such relationships results in more and increasingly successful experiences of anticipation and predictability.

As a result of this posture, do we not eliminate the space of the uncanny during our fieldwork? By labelling it culture shock, by deferring its most structural effects to our anticipated disorientation when we *return home*, do we not suppress an important existential dimension of our relationships with our hosts? Is it not true that our not-knowing, our *unheimlichkeit*, also grows in proportion to our newly-found intimacy?

And what home do we return to anyway? Within what precincts of familiarity do we stabilize our perceptions and expectations of life? As an American who lived in England for four and a half years, I experienced far more alienation, bafflement, and not-at-homeness in England than I ever did in Hegeso village in two and a half years. The illusion that Britons and Americans speak the same language seduces one into a superficial feeling of communicative and social competence. And because the illusion is so much more complete than any I could contrive for myself in Hegeso, one learns to not pay attention, to let fade the forms of social life. Under such conditions, the shock of even small failures in social perception achieve a more piquant and anxiety-provoking power. It is precisely because nearly all of what that social and linguistic competence consists of lies in the world that language invokes without necessarily referring to, that such an initial feeling of mastery is ultimately revealed as little beyond the mimicry of forms. Paradoxically, it is conventionality itself that enables this not-knowing. The more conventional and stylized a behaviour pattern or a linguistic usage becomes, the less it is able to convey anything apart from its own conventionality.

Once when I was sitting in silence with a Foi man whom I had already known for over a year, he turned to me and said in New Guinea Tok Pisin '*aiting yumi bagarap nau*': 'I think you and I are buggered up now!' I have always meditated on how extraordinarily ambiguous that remark was, the more so as I did not demand of my host that he explain what he meant at the time; I merely accepted its seemingly unelicited spontaneity in startled silence. I accepted it because it seemed true in so many ways for me then. My relationship with this Foi man had reached the end of the level of superficial delightful curiosity with our cultural differences and had reached the first barrier, defined by the realization of our inability to communicate. At that moment in Hegeso what I represented as the presence of the European presaged the end of Foi village life as they knew it (less than ten years later, the Chevron Niugini Oil Company's petroleum extraction project would be in full swing). Jadran Mimica

(1993) rightly identified in that statement the Foi moment of abandonment, of nihilism, of the recognition of joyful futility in the face of the appearance of these barriers to knowledge and language, barriers that the Foi were well aware of and that their whole world of knowledge and action was oriented towards revealing. But for me, it was quite simply waking up to the fact that the strangeness of my hosts and of myself would only be magnified and made more profound the more we learned to share and communicate.

In Foi they say 'it is over; we are finished' instead of the more graphic pidgin expression, 'bugger up'. For a person to be finished means that he or she is dead. For two people to be finished means that they have reached the point where the uncanny that always grounded their encounter has been revealed. The uncanny finishes the relationship by resolving its limits. And what is the death to which the Foi are alluding? It cannot be the death of the corporeal body only. It must be an end made possible by the revelation of the spaces of silence and death within language itself. It is speech of the other that provides that body with its most visible punctuations and limitations.

## III

In his sensitive and compelling critique of *The Empty Place*, Jadran Mimica (1993) offered his own strikingly poised notion of 'being-towards-the-beginning', which could well serve as a title for Mimica's own Daseinanalysis of the Papua New Guinea lifeworld, against the 'being-towards-death' that is an integral component of Heidegger's *Being and Time*. It is indisputable that in Papua New Guinea, particularly in the Eastern Highlands where the Yagwoia live, the attachment between male children and their mothers is of a profundity that almost defies description in our own terms. Gillison's (1993) account of the Gimi, who live not far from the Yagwoia, gives us a glimpse of an attachment in which the boundaries between mother's and child's bodies are obliterated, where bodily emissions flow freely between them, where no part of the child's body is spared the bonding, eroticizing caress of the mother's single-minded attention. We have no trouble understanding that it would be the life destiny of Eastern Highlands men to seek to return to this earlier state of non-differentiation from the mother's world-body.

Freud called this drive to restore such a primordial state the *todestriebe*, the death drive. The many accounts of the centrality of mortuary and funerary rituals and exchanges in Melanesia leave no doubt that far from being a negation of or a force opposed to life, it is the pulsion and source of life activity and passion themselves. For Freud, in his insistence that each organism seeks its own appropriate death, death was not an accident that happened to organisms, some adventitious calamity, but was the ownmost internal condition for the bodying forth of life itself. Instead of life then, we might want to speak of lifedeath, both life in death and death in life, as Roy Wagner (1986a) and David Krell (1993) have commented, each in their own way. And what is this but a hermeneutic of life drives, the drives that have the terms of their own limits written into them, so that our other varieties of hermeneutic model this more profound bodily interpretational stance?

But what is needed to resolve these limits of social power and efficacy? I can only repeat that to make these limits appear, some external perspective is necessary. It could be said that we need to place a framing skin around anything we care to isolate and give form to, and that this more broadly conceived 'embodying' grounds and makes possible the particular form of corporeal bodying that Mimica wishes to privilege.

It is thus indisputable that, as Mimica maintains, Heidegger does not address himself to what Merleau-Ponty terms the phenomenal body, the body in its sensuous, corporeal existence. And he comments that my use of Merleau-Ponty along with Heidegger 'never questions its implicit dissonance with Heidegger's poetical ontology in which the libidinal body is glaringly absent'. But where is the dissonance? It is true that Heidegger ignores the libidinal body. But does this mean that he paid no attention to *bodying*, or *embodying*? No – in fact, in his *Nietzsche* lectures he notes:

> In feeling oneself to be, the body is already contained in advance in that self, in such a way that the body in its bodily states permeates the self . . . We do not 'have' a body; rather we 'are' bodily (Heidegger 1986: 98–9).

Heidegger stipulates that the contours of that body are not given solely within the confines of biology:

> Feeling, as feeling oneself to be, belongs to the essence of such Being. Feeling achieves from the outset the inherent internalizing tendency of the body in our Dasein. But because feeling, as feeling oneself to be, always just as essentially has a feeling for beings as a whole, every bodily state involves some way in which the things around us and the people with us lay a claim on us or do not do so (1986: 99).

What we come to identify as the body, its limits, its surfaces, its capacities, and its extensions, is always the learned body in its total historical and cultural constitution; the way we come to have a body *for others* and *through others* at the same time that we come to have one for ourselves. Because our perception of the body is neither more natural nor more cultural than any other perception, the body's physiological functions are subject to the limits of this perceptual faculty as historically and socially constituted, and the time of the body is the hermeneutic of perception itself. Heidegger brings out this notion of the *limits* of bodying as form-producing force much better than does Merleau-Ponty; and when I wrote *The Empty Place* I was fully aware that each account of the body was incomplete as such without the other. As for Mimica's insistence that we pay attention to the solidity of the body's products, fluids, excretions and tissue loss, accidental or otherwise, it could well be that these effusions, taking place for the most part on the body's margins, are more about the perceived *image* of the body and its form and less about corporeality *per se*. They are as much refractions and distortions of the body's outline and capacities as speech, adornments, clothing and vision itself, which also outline the body in a transformative, perspectival manner.

## IV

But ultimately, it is language that outlines the body most effectively, and it is because Merleau-Ponty fails to consider *language*, as opposed to the phenomenon of speech, that I ultimately find Heidegger's phenomenology of more use to anthropology. Because if it is true that we reveal the body through speech, so it is just as true that we reveal language through the body, that language speaks through us as much as we speak through language and with it. And without this interpretative stance to which language gives us access, there is no temporality and hence no human relationality. Moreover, without the concealing, euphemizing properties of language there is no concealment or misrecognition as a core existential condition of human life. And without this nescience, there is no deferred knowledge, there are no retroactive understandings, and hence no perspective on how the present illuminates the past as well as anticipates a future, no understanding of the temporality of social knowledge.

But this is precisely where I locate the historicity of Foi speech as well as the historicity of the Foi body itself. Mimica's most pressing criticism of the Heideggerian terminology I used in *The Empty Place*, one echoed by Alfred Gell (1995), is directed at the self-poeticizing of the Foi and their world: the sacralization of what Heidegger called the 'fourfold' as the existential dimensions of poetic language, and the Romantic and idealist connotations of such characterizations. I would like to respond to this by comparing Heidegger's poetic account of the fourfold with Roy Wagner's notions of the expansion of point metaphor into frame metaphor, and what Wagner terms 'third order trope': 'The trope of . . . embodiment [which] . . . folds figure–ground reversal around itself to constitute bodily microcosm and macrocosm respectively as bounding parameters of the human condition' (1986a: 127).

What Wagner means by 'expansion' refers to the *mode of elicitation* of any particular metaphoric equation. The mode of elicitation, the path along which its associational world is laid out, is as much a part of any specific metaphor as the point equation itself. This is why the unfolding of an obviation sequence opens up further possibilities of incorporation at the same time that it narrows our focus onto a particular associational path. It does not so much provide an interpretation as make visible the alternative images opened up by interpretational procedure itself.

It is important to understand, however, that the scale, or complexity, of these metaphoric equations is not altered by such expansions – what is shown in an obviation sequence is the tacit and unarticulated associational paths that tether them within a particular contextual matrix. An obviation sequence simultaneously opens up such paths and in the act of achieving closure restricts itself, and this is evidence that, in this case, expansion and restriction refer to types of symbolic contrast and not to quantitatively assessed units of meaning.

The connections opened up are not the residuum or trace of the conscious, associational thinking that people do, the structures and orders they concoct as a *post factum* gloss on a social symbolic effect. Rather, they are a testimony to what Heidegger calls our vigilance:

> When and in what way do things appear as things? They do not appear *by means of* human making. But neither do they appear without the vigilance of mortals. The first step toward such vigilance is the step back from the thinking that merely represents – that is, explains – to the thinking that responds and recalls (1971c: 181).

Heidegger thought that activities he glossed under the Aristotelian term *techne*, such as poetry, architecture and skilled crafting, call forth the parameters of a total life world, and that these parameters can be spoken of as delimiting a space or region. This space is bounded by earth and sky, the mortal and the divine. The jug that holds sacramental wine, for example, captures the essence of the fruit of the earth, nourished by the sun and rain, which are the sky's bounty. In unmistakably Maussian terms, he saw the sacrificial function of wine as effecting a bond or exchange between human and deity as paramount.

These same dimensions, and hence the same 'sized' space, are also found in the dimensions of the Greek temple. The points that delineate this space are not multiplied or made more complex in the bigger artefact of the temple. At most we can say that the temple reaches out to encompass more of the everyday words and things of the world, it exposes their place in this region.

I find significant parallels between the expansion of the Heideggerian fourfold through such non-representational acts as poetry and architecture, and the expansion of metaphor through obviation I have just described. Both Heidegger and Wagner have a sense of the *topology* of meaning, of how language is anchored by the three-dimensional kinaesthetic imagination of our productive capacity and desire.

The most vivid exemplification of the shape this Heideggerian/ Wagnerian vigilance takes for the Foi can be found in their pearl shell (Figure 1), the image with which I end *The Empty Place*. In Foi, the word for pearl shell is *ma'ame*, which means 'thing, something, anything'. Not the pearl shell as it is found in the sea, for the Foi never knew of it traditionally in that form, but only in the crescent shape and red colouring that is the form in which they are obtained from their trading partners to the north. What is *the* pearl shell? It is the medium of exchange, says one answer, used to obtain brides when given as bridewealth; for pork when given at a ceremony; for a variety of compensatory payments surrounding injury, insult and death. So many of us are content to reduce pearl shell's significance to its undeniably functional role. With several exceptions (A. Strathern, M. Strathern, Jeffrey Clarke, Paul Sillitoe, Douglas Dalton) few people are very interested in the fact that the pearl shell is also an adornment, worn around the necks of most men, women and children. These pearl shells do not circulate and have no exchange value strictly speaking. They are worn, as adjuncts of the body's presentation of self in the everyday communal world. How much more visible and ubiquitous they are than the formally-exchanged pearl shells which spend most of their time wrapped up in cardboard and pandanus leaves, are locked away in cartons, suitcases and metal boxes, are brought out intermittently, are briefly displayed and transferred, and are then hidden once again.

Since these shells are after all carved by the hand of men, how many of us have bothered to comment on the shape of the pearl shell, its half-crescent with up-turned ends, suggestive of a crescent moon (as the Daribi say) or a woman's string bag (as the Chimbu say). When worn around the neck, the pearl shell frames the face and head of its wearer, the head that is the metonymic person in so much of New Guinea, as indeed everywhere. The pearl shell borders the face of each person, frames the person with a social headline, focuses the gaze on the publicly captioned and capitated identity. The upturned ends are also suggestive of birds' wings, the brightly coloured red wings of the parrots and birds-of-paradise that the Foi and other New Guinea people so intimately identify with pearl shells. A captured bird in flight worn by every person, a pair of still wings to remind them of pearl shell's restless, ceaseless motion, the difficulty in capturing it without killing it, without stopping its life-giving flow.

But birds are also the most common manifestation of the spirits of the dead. Ghosts of deceased people take the form of different species of birds, depending on the manner of the person's death. And more than that, Foi men characteristically require the aid of ghosts in obtaining pearl shells and pearl shell magic. That is, under certain circumstances ghosts reveal to men magical formulae by which they can become successful in gathering pearl shells to themselves. Finally, especially large specimens of pearl shells that resist men's attempts to valuate in standard terms are called *denane ma'ame*, 'ghost pearl shells', and are not used in transactions. They stay in the houses of their owners, immobile, and hence beyond the realm of value.

Man–pearl shell–bird–spirit: alone, each item can only be taken at face value, and thus can only be equated with our bare semantic rendering (and notice how little is lost [or gained, in terms of semantic value] if one pairs each with any other). To extract from this complex the 'pearl shell as such' and then to reduce it to its transactional or economic features is to describe only a part of a complex that is simultaneously thought and lived. Man/pearl shell/bird/spirit is a space, a region wherein the Foi situate the human world between the earth and the sky and between the world of the living and the world of the dead. Pearl shell is above all else a spatial image, and the four points it tethers delimit a *topos* or perhaps a chronotope, in Bahktin's words, within which everyday Foi subjectivity and discursivity unfold. This is not a semantic structure, nor is it exhausted in linguistic terms, though language – particularly Foi magic and poetry – brings it out in the open. It's enabled by language, but not reducible to it.

The pearl shell is the space of the appropriated, human world. But it is not the only thing that defines the lineaments of this world. In *The Empty Place*, I describe how during the construction of the Foi longhouse, certain magic spells must be recited at various phases of its building. In summary, these spells detotalize the body of several mythical hunters, drawing an identity between the parts of the body and the analogous parts of the house: the house posts become the toes of the mythical hunter; the battens of the roof, its ribs; the central walkway floorboards, its chest;

**Figure 1.** The Pearl Shell (Photo by the author)

and so forth. In the final spell, the entirety of the house is retotalized when the magician recites: 'Yibumena [one of the mythical hunters] is sleeping with his arms and legs spread out'. The detotalizing of Yibumena establishes the longhouse as a community of male hunters, but also fixes the immortal cultural heroes corporeally into the very architecture of the house.

At the same time that the magicians accomplish this, each pair of Foi men sharing a fireplace place in the clay of the new firepit the feathers of those birds associated with pearl shell magic. The feathers and the spell recited over them will 'pull' wealth to the longhouse and ensure the future renown of its inhabitants. You could say that the performing of this magic is essential to the integrity and (male) vitality of the house; but it would be just as accurate to see the erecting of the house as Foi men's excuse to do pearl shell magic. Without the house, men would be like bush fowls, laying their pearl shells in hidden nests in the bush.

The Foi longhouse is not, then, just the embodiment of the mythical hunters, but is also the space created by the intercourse between the living Foi and the primordial hunters/creators. The *techne* of its magical procedures turns it into the poetic clearing of human language. The road between sky and earth, the path of shells and meat, is fixed into the fireplaces by individual men; but the most compelling of life's journeys – the search for meat – is also corporeally detotalized in the form of Yibumena's body parts. This Foi existential clearing, the pearl shell enhoused, and the house itself, built of detotalized shells and meat items, is presented, or perhaps 'made present' would be more accurate, in these poetic magical utterances, and is built as the house is built. The house/pearl shell becomes one of Foi men's edifices, as is their language itself.

The human head is also tethered by these horizons, as are the 'head' pearl shells, which are what the Foi term the ten or twelve large shells that form the body of a bridewealth payment. For the Foi, the mouth is opposed to the coronal suture, as earth to sky and more importantly as mortality is to the ghosts; the mouth, the source of speech and hence of earthly, historical sociality, versus the coronal suture, from which the soul escapes in its atemporal life apart from the corporeal body. In other words, the existential dimensions of pearl shell are corporeal ones through and through, even though we are forced to conclude that this body acquires its temporal and spatial shape against the atemporal immortality of ghosts and the historical body of the earth.

## V

The space of the Foi pearl shell is turned into a moral landscape through its expansion in several crucial myths (see J. Weiner 1988a). There we find traced out the critical comparison between the eggs of birds and the 'immortal' eggs of humans: the pearl shells that hatch themselves and, in so self-destructing, bring forth reproductive life, and the pearl shells that never hatch and so never die, but keep circulating amongst humans in a deathless movement of social life itself (see also Wagner 1986a).

Human sexuality in its erotogenic, libidinal constitution seems very much retracted in this version of Foi originary sociality, though, as was clear in *The Heart of the Pearl Shell*, it figured centrally in other Foi mythic images of the foundation of their sociality. Perhaps we should see the effacement of the sexual and the corporeal and the moral as part of the oblivion that each culture and language makes possible for itself. While the Foi seem to make room for their encounter with this oblivion in the form of myth and poetry, it was Heidegger's view that it is precisely this oblivion that has slipped away from the modern Western person's control.

Mimica's oblivion takes the form of accepting the Cartesian schism, which itself covers over the corporeal, reproductive foundation of Western Christianity. He retains the phenomenal body but jettisons the projective

space – a space largely of language and the liturgical form that is its
enhoused body, and of the graphic images of which medieval artists saw
themselves as containers, rather than creators – within which that body
acquires a historical and moral outline.

In *The Sexuality of Christ in Renaissance Art and in Modern Oblivion*,
Leo Steinberg (1983) shows how commonly the sexual attributes of Jesus
were depicted in European Christian iconography of the fifteenth and
sixteenth centuries – the maternal erotic caresses between the Christ child
and the Madonna, the inspection and fondling of the Christ child's
genitals, the unmistakable evidence of erection both in the infant Jesus
and in the ithyphallic depictions of the Christ in the rigor of death and
crucifixion. The painting of the *Pietà* by Jean Malouel (*c.* 1400), or the
*Retable of Saint Denis* by Henri Bellechose in 1416 (Figure 2) established
a visual connection between the blood of Christ's spear wound and the
imagined first blood he shed upon his circumcision as a Jewish male.
Most remarkably, in paintings such as the *Throne of Grace*, attributed to
Roger van der Weyden in 1443, God the Father holds his dying Son and
places his left hand protectively over Jesus' loins. Steinberg, remarking
on the gulf of sexual shame that severs father and son in Western culture,
suggests that in van der Weyden's depiction:

> . . . precisely this shame caves in now before our eyes. Natural distance
> collapses in this coalition of Persons wherein the divine Father's only-begotten
> is (as theology has it) a virgin, virginally-conceived; enfleshed, sexed,
> circumcized, sacrificed, and so restored to the Throne of Grace; there
> symbolizing not only the aboriginal unity of the godhead, but in its more
> dramatic, more urgent message, a conciliation which stands for the atonement,
> the being-at-one, of man and God (1983: 108).

Nearly three hundred and fifty years later, we would witness another,
though diametrically opposed, version of the unity of man and the
godhead. In *The Magic Flute*, Sarastro and his followers would think
that the exercise of reason, wisdom and a correct understanding of nature
would allow men to be as gods, and that if men acted with virtue and
justice, heaven would exist on earth. The price of this heaven would be
the off-loading of the corporeal, the fleshly, the sexual and the libidinal
constitution of such virtue, reason and knowledge on to the likes of
Papageno the Bird Catcher, whom thenceforth we would seek in his Foi,
Yagwoia and Kayapo guises among the fantastic landscapes and scary
monsters of the equatorial world. By that time, we had learned to not-see
the carnal, corporeal, sexual Christ, and it is this incomprehension that is

**Figure 2.** Henri Bellechose: The Retable of Saint Denis (Courtesy The Louvre)

the oblivion of modern Western culture, as Steinberg terms it. This stunning insight of Steinberg stands as a summating image of my response to Mimica: that our phenomenology of the body historically nests itself within the death, resurrection and transfiguration of the body of God, just as the Foi and Yagwoia phenomenology of the spirit world manifests itself through the afflictions and transfigurations of the body. A Heideggerian anthropology of the body must, by my reading, thus contend simultaneously with the issues of the divine, the human body in its sexual configuration, and the poeticizing and self-poeticizing of the world (by which I mean all artistic, including ethnographic, imaging), a world that must include both what is human and what measures or interprets the limits of such humanness.

I would like to end by returning to the uncanny, *das unheimlich*. If we see our task as anthropologists as only to describe and codify the conventional, we work against the task of interpretation, for conventionality by itself short-circuits meaning. What resists convention, what surfaces as perceptions of the uncanniness and strangeness of social life, is as much a part of that life and its constitution, even though their effects seem to originate beyond it.

In my concern to investigate how it is that an image of humanness is articulated in different cultures, I urge us to consider that every social form, and by implication every social science, has inscribed within it the possibility of its own negation, its own effacement, and that such a possibility is not made visible by conventional social processes. What Steinberg's image points to is the same social science that Omalyce of the Yagwoia, Souw of the Daribi, and the Foi woman memorial song composer all call for: an anthropology that can theorize the obliteration of man, the oblivion at the heart of culture that anthropology, and every social science, must ultimately admit as inevitable and necessary.

## Notes

1. I will not address the implied corollary of this observation, namely, the failure of Marxist and Freudian anthropology to place negation at the centre of their social appropriation of Marx and Freud. Both Marxist and neo-Freudian psychoanalytic anthropology have mainly ignored the effects of nescience within the mechanisms of the ideological support of production and of ego-formation respectively.

# Part II
# The Limits of Human Relationship

# 5

# The Limit of Relationship

## I: Anthropology's Mode of Questioning

In *The Heart of the Pearl Shell* (1988a: 243–7), I analysed a Foi myth that I entitled 'The Sky Village'. The plot of the myth is as follows: A young man, in the course of setting marsupial traps, manages one day to trap a young maiden rather than a marsupial. She takes him to her village in the sky, and she warns him not to accept food or tobacco from anyone except her. They live as man and wife and she bears him a male child. One day his sky wife's father shows him, through a hole in the ground, the surface world he left behind. There he sees his former relatives preparing mourning ceremonies for his elder brother who has just died. His father-in-law permits him to return to the surface world with his wife and child to present a pig to his brother's maternal relatives as a mortuary payment, but warns him not to cry for his brother, lest he put the child in danger. The sky realm 'is not a place of sorrow', he tells his daughter's husband. However, the young man is unable to prevent himself from doing precisely that when he confronts his brother's body. His wife 'cries in fear' upon witnessing him do so.

The woman begins to mistreat their son and, shortly afterwards, disappears altogether. The young man goes in search of her, only to discover that she has returned to the sky realm. He then goes back to the house of his relatives and tells them the story of his sojourn in the Sky Village. 'Because I mourned and disobeyed my father-in-law, my wife has returned to the sky land' he tells them finally. He then dies himself and his ghost returns to the Sky Village, while his son remains in the human world.

Another time, he and his wife's father once again look down to the surface and see the boy wandering around aimlessly by himself, uncared for. When the man cries, his wife's father says to him, 'Do not cry. You abandoned that boy and came here.' After another interval they look down one final time and see that the boy has grown to adulthood and is in the middle of a battle: he has become a war leader.

Despite the fact that she originally was caught in a marsupial trap, the young woman tricks the young man into thinking he is in a human world in the sky village by becoming the sole provider of the man's food and other consumable items (hence he has no chance to learn that, as ghosts, the other inhabitants do not subsist on real food). He is prevented from learning that he is in a place where there is no human relationship, and does not understand when his wife's father tells him that 'this is not a place of sorrow'. He goes back as a ghost (unknowingly) to the surface world, as did the woman originally, and cannot resist trying to make a human relationship while there – he shows grief at the sight of his dead brother. But how can one who is already dead show grief? The maternal payment of the pig he makes on the surface world does not, as intended, sever the affinal relations of his brother, but causes the man unwittingly to lose his son, with whom, as a dead man, he cannot possibly have a relationship either.

The appearance of the Sky Village fooled the young man into thinking he was in a human, social world; but the exchanges he subsequently enters into on the surface finally make known to him his incapacity for human relationship – they reveal that he is in fact a ghost, who, like Eurydice, is twice lost from the human world.[1]

'We have now reached the point', Marilyn Strathern concluded in 1989 in her initial argument in favour of the motion, *The Concept of Society is Theoretically Obsolete*, 'of having to tell ourselves *over again* that if we are to produce adequate theories of social reality, then the first step is to apprehend persons as simultaneously containing the potential for relationships and always embedded in a matrix of relations with others' (1990a: 10, emphasis added). The 'over again' refers to the preceding sentence, in which she reminded her audience that social theorists such as Leach, Durkheim and Marx in their own ways and at different times all arrived at the same point, only to see it degenerate into the same Anglo-Saxon antinomy of society versus the individual that seems to have been a defining feature of British anthropology for most of the 20th century.

Strathern's perception that our anthropological theories of society 'have exhausted themselves' (1990a: 7) is thus coupled with a simultaneous admission that this point of epistemological collapse had already been noted in the last century by Marx. This double perception of a unique moment in history that is only unique because it has already happened seems uncannily parallel to the famous assertion of Martin Heidegger: that Western philosophy in the twentieth century had arrived at the end of metaphysics, and that Nietzsche had already proclaimed that end in

FAILED INTERLOCUTION!

the preceding century when he announced the death of God, a gloss on his self-styled 'inverted Platonism'.

But what if the end of metaphysics, or of social science, is something that is there at the origin of philosophy or of anthropology?[2] In discarding such an anthropology, we would be losing a science that already had caused-to-disappear the source of human relationality. In ridding ourselves of this science, we would then be losing human relationship twice over. We would in such a case want to reclaim a theory of society that had its own limitations, its own cancellation or point of collapse already pre-figured, already defined. We could, in other words, after confronting Strathern's announcement of the (double) demise of social anthropology's founding assumption, ask ourselves the following question: Once we have agreed that anthropology's starting and ending points are the elucidation of social relationships, what then is our task? What kinds of problems are given to us to solve against this grounding proposition?

When I ask, in effect, 'What is there left for us to say?', I am posing the following question: Against what epistemological limits will such a mode of questioning eventually run up? Such a question can only arise within the prior understanding that although such limits are part of the subject-matter, they are not directly addressed through its explanatory apparatus alone. A theory – that is, a mode of explanation – is a world, and a world can not provide its own grounding.[3]

Heidegger felt that philosophy, by which he meant the 'task of thinking', provided the means by which a science's fundamental orientation could be illuminated. 'The *grounds* of science must rather be what philosophy alone sets in relief and founds, namely, the cognizable *truth of beings* as such' (Heidegger 1984: 112, emphasis added). How would we render this in specifically anthropological terms? By suggesting that anthropology must address itself not only to identifying and analysing the various forms and processes of human sociality but also to specifying the kinds of beings for whom the question of society and its analysis are issues of life – which is what people like the Foi address in the form of myths such as 'The Sky Village'. In other words, *we want to specify the conditions under which the world is perceived to be relationally based (by ourselves as well as our hosts) prior to our analysis of it*. Let us examine what the terms of such a task might be.

(1) I begin with the notion of 'grounds'. Heidegger here speaks not of Leibnizian grounds, as the 'reason' behind certain states of affairs, but something more like Kant's conditions of possibility: the conditions under which the reasoning and its resulting state of affairs together emerge as a mode of questioning, of making a world visible. 'Hence, to say that a

science is philosophical means that it . . . *sets itself in motion* within the fundamental positions we take towards beings, and allows these positions to have an impact on scientific work' (ibid.). No mode of scientific inquiry is insulated from the form of life and style of understanding of the scientist. It is often said that because anthropology as a human science studies human interpretation as well as embodying interpretation as its own methodology, it can not help but constantly confront the reflexive, relativizing exposure of its grounds. But precisely because its thinking is constrained by academic lifeworld practices of codification, abstraction and transmission, it commonly appears as a 'science' – and thus it frequently seeks to hide that ground of reflexivity as a step toward naturalizing its own view of the world. It presses this basic interpretational mode into the service of making, constructing and asserting. But when interpretation and the awareness of reflexivity are themselves harnessed in such a manner to the task of providing models of cohesiveness and integration, their relativizing effects are cancelled, circumvented, obviated. They cease to be sources of perspective and become recipes for the domestication of data and, through data, the world (cf. Rorty 1979; Bourdieu 1977).[4]

(2) Let us turn now to the 'truth of beings'. Questions of this sort concerning the very grounds and terms of any inquiry are ontological questions. It might at first be thought that anthropologists might be able to ignore such questions without much suffering, because we 'know very well' that we are 'thrown' into a social world. That is, we start out with an acceptance of the cultural, social and historical specificity of any set of foundational or orienting terms and propositions. This was what I have referred to as anthropology's nihilism, the recognition that the most foundational, *a priori* conditions and values of human life ultimately devalue themselves when their historical and political contingency is recognized.[5]

But Gilles Deleuze, writing about Nietzsche's *The Genealogy of Morals*, made the following observation: 'Every historical law is arbitrary, but what is not arbitrary, what is prehistoric and generic, is the law of obeying laws' (1983: 133). Anthropology has shifted its attention many times this century from one focal, foundational source of sociality to another – from kinship, to politics, to reciprocity, to the body, and so forth – without calling into question the search for sociality itself (see J. Weiner 1988b).

'Truth' was Heidegger's own etymological rendering of the Greek *aletheia*, a 'being uncovered' or 'revealed'; an 'unconcealing' (see Okrent 1992: 146). What is revealed in such an encounter is the full scope of a being's (an entity's) attachment to or involvement in a world of human concerns: the simultaneous disclosure of the entity, its form of disclosure, and the mode of being of the discloser. The recognition of the implicatedness of these disclosures with respect to each other is what characterizes a hermeneutic stance in social science.

But for something to be capable of being unconcealed in such a fashion, it necessarily must already have first been concealed. How then does the scope of the involvement of entities in our world and the nature of that world become concealed in the first place? Heidegger responds: Through the everyday or practical attitude with which human beings use and manipulate entities without being aware of them, without attending to their entityness; that is, as a result of the same process of 'misrecognition' through which the *habitus*, as Bourdieu defines it (1977, 1984), is generated (see also Dreyfus 1991). Or, in somewhat different terms, according to Roy Wagner, the way the human origin of external fact and incident is 'masked' through the Western allocation to humankind of the responsibility for action (1981).

For Heidegger, then, human being arises in the tension between the way our non-reflective involvement in the world conceals our relationship to entities, and the procedures at our disposal for revealing these taken-for-granted relationships. Any procedure that calls forth the frames that make visible a particular entity is an unconcealing – a truth of that being.

The manner in which humans are confronted with the unintended products of their habitual activity is at the heart of Bourdieu's theory of practice. But it is perhaps more importantly brought out in Roy Wagner's notion of obviation (1981, 1986a) and Marilyn Strathern's analysis of sociality (1988, 1991), which builds upon the Wagnerian terminology of obviation. I want to argue that because social relations are the prefigured end-product of anthropological analysis, they model both our subject-matter *and* our procedures for making them visible. Not only are we often unaware of the steps we take epistemologically to make social relations appear; we systematically exclude from such epistemology a consideration of the non-relational in human life. Like the protagonist of the Sky Village, despite the evidence before us, we continue to model our own procedures and theories on the assumption of relationship and reciprocity. We confuse a mode of eliciting with the thing elicited (see J. Weiner 1992b).

## Strathern's Melanesian Social Science

The young man who was taken to the Sky Village by the maiden failed to consider that a woman obtained through the activities of hunting, trapping and killing was likely to come from a world where death and not exchange was the founding condition of human life. He is like the social scientist who starts off in any given case by asking, 'What is the form of social relations?' rather than something like, 'What are the practices and conditions that cause social relations to be revealed as an issue of life?'

For Marilyn Strathern, as well as summarizing the difference between a non-reflexive and a reflexive Western social science, these two alternative questions can also stand for the respective contrast between a Western and a Melanesian approach to sociality *tout court*, the contrast between a tradition that takes responsibility for the conscious construction or faithful modelling of the world and its components – the Aristotelean *techne* of thinking – and another that seeks to provide an interpretational strategy with which to elicit or make visible such a world.[6]

In a recent exchange with three critics of *The Gender of the Gift* (Brown *et al.* 1992), Strathern writes in effect that her book was not meant as a contribution to sociological analysis. Rather, it sought to make visible the mode of disclosure of the anthropological observer by contriving an analogous and hypothetical concern for the 'truth of beings' on the part of Melanesians themselves. What Strathern compares is not Melanesian and Western social relations as such but the contrastive ways of eliciting them or making them visible in each case – in other words, she is comparing something very close to what we could call in Heideggerian terms Melanesian and Western *being*. In Melanesia, certain ceremonial wealth objects – the pigs and pearl shells of the interior Papua New Guinea mainland, the ceremonial axes and shell ensembles of the islands off the eastern coast of Papua New Guinea – embody the relational capacity of persons. They are part of the person, but their value, power and significance lie in the fact that they are detachable – they can go proxy for persons, they can be made to move between people and hence quite literally be parts of persons that serve as material tokens of social connection.

But these connections are not always visible. When they are not in use, pearl shells are commonly kept wrapped up and hidden in the recesses of men's houses. When men bring them out, they do not just unwrap them – they display them in a particular way. Depending on the mode of display, different relational capacities of the shell and of the persons of whom they are icons are made to appear or 'unconcealed'. A pearl shell crescent cemented into a resin board in Mount Hagen elicits an altogether different figure for its Melpa owners than a pearl shell placed in a small version of a woman's string bag hanging from the head of a Foi man (a ceremonial display of pearl shells by Foi men who seek publicly to solicit

*kula ring*

an exchange partner) – or, they could be said to be eliciting the same image (that of an unborn child or fetus in a womb) in different ways. In what sense are the pearl shells displayed in these two cases the 'same thing'? We would have to say that the only way we could compare the Foi and Melpa pearl shells *by themselves* would be as a consequence of a prior excising of the shells from their resin board and net bag so that what was distinctive about the shell *to us* was above all preserved and confirmed. A view of the pearl shell that accepted its thingness and its own boundedness as self-evident in such a manner, that isolated the characteristics of the shell that make it resemble Western tokens of power, credit and solidarity, might be inclined to elide these contrastive framing contexts of the shell among the Melpa and the Foi, to relegate these contexts to a subordinate symbolic function that left the (Western-defined) tokenness and thingness of the shell untouched. Under such terms, we confront the shell as standing outside the dominion of the subject. Strathern's argument is that the particular modes of display mentioned above reveal the fact that the shells already have relationship and subjectivity in their very constitution, are in fact material markers for the parts of persons that engage with and make connections with others.

But let me return to the image of the Foi man with a woman's string bag hanging down his back with a pearl shell inside it. My Foi male acquaintances called this practice *dasigo~ hagibu*, which though I cannot translate it well, literally means 'a filled-up string bag carried from the head'.[7] The Foi man who solicits a response from a potential exchange partner by putting a shell in a string bag and hanging it from his head is using the imagery of feminine productivity, nurturance and child care as a lure to trap an exchange partner, just as the young man in the Sky Village myth used wild fruit in an animal trap to lure a marsupial who was a woman. The images that emerge from these modes of display are not simply those of particular kinds of social relations, but of the life conditions, the *mode of being*, that make such relations necessary and inevitable. In such a way, people like the Melpa and the Foi affirm to themselves relationship as the ground upon which human action proceeds – it is a fact of life that is always precipitated or led to by human action. Wagner thus concludes:

> Pigs, pearl shells, axes, bark cloaks are already relational and implicated in the congruence that underlies the remaking of human form, feeling and relationship . . . Minus the sense of their essential unity with body and life-process (in their subjective as well as objective enhancement), items exchanged become . . . mere 'wealth objects' . . . – a 'representation' of human values through utility . . . (1991: 165).

Here Wagner articulates something very close to Heidegger's reading of Nietzsche's *will to power* as life- or form-enhancing force (Heidegger 1979: Chapter 14). The young man in the Sky Village is *compelled* to marry, beget, acquire affines and enter into exchanges through the irresistible appeal of hunting and trapping (which is largely but not exclusively a masculine appeal), and the idioms of hunting and the presentation of gifts of meat pervade all those other activities.

## II: The Limits of Relationship

In a world such as that of the Foi or the Melpa that is relationally based, the task confronting humans is not to sustain human relationship. The very bodily compulsions of life – appetite, sexuality, anger, conflict – do that of themselves. What people must do is place a limit on relationship, on this 'form-enhancing force'; they must restrict its extension. The protocols surrounding the giving and receiving of pearl shells do not have as their rationale the making of affinal alliance. Rather, they control the flow of relationship between wife-giving and wife-taking groups that a marriage sets into motion through procreation and childbirth (see Wagner 1967, 1977; J. Weiner 1988a).

The problem that we now confront is the one the hero of the Sky Village myth faced: How can a human being 'have a relationship' with a woman who herself (as a marsupial, that is, an item of exchange) is the medium through which such relationships are made visible? How can relationship be at one and the same time the mode of elicitation and the thing elicited? Given Heidegger's assertion of what the ground of any thinking, including Melanesian, must include, how is the whole mode of being we term 'relationality' itself thrown into relief?

According to Strathern's reading of this Wagnerian observation, in Melanesia, mediated relationships are those that are composed and sustained through the transaction of recognized ceremonial valuables. The valuables, as I've mentioned, 'stand for' parts of persons. Thus, people exert social leverage on each other chiefly through the *medium* of these objects. In unmediated relations, on the other hand, such social effects are 'experienced directly' (1988: 178). A man and woman who are married, for example, have merely to carry out characteristic male and female productive activity – their complementary work in gardening, food-sharing, copulating and so forth – and the 'relationship between husband and wife' appears as a result. Whereas in so-called gift exchange the relationship itself is the focus of attention, in unmediated relationships 'the fact of relatedness may be taken for granted' (1988: 180).

But what then do we make of the objects that a husband and wife constantly pass back and forth between them – food, sexual fluids, the Bourdieuian 'small, uncommented-upon gifts' of conjugal and domestic intimacy and cooperation; how then do we characterize an exchange relationship, particularly one between trade partners, that subsists only on the hope or the idea of a transaction rather than the transfer of tangible wealth items? In such a case, all that lies between such partners is the anticipation of common interest that brought them together in the first place, but whose public confirmation must forever elude them.

Wherever relationship surfaces in these Melanesian societies according to this model, in other words, it calls forth mediation as the form of its own relationality, whether it is consciously articulated or not. Husband and wife are still as categorically separated, and hence in a potential relationship, as are exchange partners.[8] Thus, Strathern's opposition articulates a sense of unmediation; but this opposition itself does not 'come free' or cancel the effects of the relational. There may be relationships 'conceived of' as unmediated; but they are mediated just the same. Thus, there is no limit to relationship in such a society. For Strathern, and for many of us writing on Melanesian sociality, relationality may well have the status of a Kantian *a priori* category of intuition. *[handwritten: gifts + commodities]*

But if this is the case, then nothing can make it appear. Relationality would already be a part of any device that Melanesians possess to make social relations visible, as Roy Wagner's quotation above seems to indicate. A statement such as the following by Marilyn Strathern on Gawan canoe decorating would thus be tautologous: '. . . the very process of making something visible is a social act that orients the entity (person, vessel) outwards towards those in whose eyes it appears' (1992: 57). Relationality is protected from an imposition of limits because of the assertion that it prevenes its own disclosure. The hero of the Sky Village was led into his dilemma because he focused his attention on the *form* of sociality and not on the mode of being that founds such forms. He thought that the death payment he made only concerned his brother's life, when it was his life that was in question all along. And perhaps he made the same mistake that the anthropologist does. *[handwritten: → discovery = scientific discourse]*

I am proposing a search for a form of sociality that is not mediated, that is not directly articulated, that is only made visible when one's attention is directed elsewhere. If we fail to make this form appear in some way, the ones that are recognized would have no form themselves, no limit, no temporality. *[handwritten: →no existence/no reference]*

Perhaps we can now ask the following question more directly: How do social relations acquire their outline? What acts stipulate a boundary beyond which they cease? Against what is a social relationship poised such that this something shows the limit of relationship itself? Relationship would, in such a case, have to be foregrounded against something that is not relationship. The isolated atomic individual perhaps? No, we know that is wrong, because the definition of the individual presupposes the social milieu, within which are distributed certain agencies, identities, powers and so forth that make the individual discrete – hence, the negation as such of social relationship can not itself be conceived of within a social world.

Let us continue by proposing that our conscious, rational, symbolizing mind does not do all the work of human being. Subject–object relationships do not exhaust our ways of being-in-the-world. The mediated relationships that reach the conscious, theoretical mind presuppose an unmediated – what Bourdieu calls a practical – engagement with a world. The ways in which these unmediated modes of engagement are brought forth, made visible to us, Heidegger described in various ways, as I've indicated – an unconcealing, a disclosedness, a bringing-forth, a releasement, for example. It's not that these unmediated forms of engagement are not also learned – they are learned, and hence are social. It's just that not all of them serve as a means of projecting a human scheme or theory on to a posited external world of fact or incident, and not all of them serve to establish relations between people in that world.

Heidegger explains that when a human being uses a tool or implement with which one is skilled, the tool 'disappears' or becomes transparent. It is a part of one, there is no boundary between the tool and one's body. We can call the relationship between tool and human one of unmediated difference, as does Fell (1979: 217). Heidegger calls such a characteristic of the tool 'readiness-to-hand' (Dreyfus [1991] glosses it as 'availability'). But can we properly speak of a 'relationship' between the tool and the person in this case? I think not.

The notion of such unmediated connections between people and tools poses no real conceptual problems for us. Marilyn Strathern expresses it succinctly with the Melpa idiom of having wealth and decorations 'on the skin'. But in what manner are other people 'ready-to-hand'? In what ways do we confront or engage with others that would allow us to identify unmediated differences between people? Would we want to characterize these by such terms as non-relationship, indifference, apathy? No – these are terms of detachment and uninvolvement, when what I am discussing is just the opposite: an absorption with the world and with others that is so complete and total that it loses sight of itself and its modes of engagement and possibility.

Foi ghosts such as the hapless inhabitants of the Sky Village are involved intimately with people's lives – but are not part of them. Ghosts feel no sorrow – and no pity – and hence their ghostly anger only makes children and animals sick. Their effects are constantly felt, but these effects are not social, for they have no origin, source or explanation. What *is* social is the gloss that living Foi put on the hypothetical reason for the ghosts' actions, the *interpretation of speech and action* that is missing from ghostly life. 'Beings are those for whom being is an issue,' Heidegger said (1962), by which he meant that the interpretational stance was integral to human being and its temporal constitution – and it is precisely the point that for ghosts, being is not an issue because they have departed the spatial and temporal world, outside which interpretation is impossible.

I return now to a topic I discussed in Chapter 1, Heidegger's discussion of *das Man*. Maquarrie and Robinson first glossed this as 'the "They"' and Dreyfus subsequently rendered it 'the One'. What Bourdieu calls the *habitus* is the result of socialization from a very young age in a social world where the presence of others and the general 'form of life' is taken-for-granted, where the boundary between one's perception of oneself and all others is unarticulated. In Melanesian Pidgin, as Wagner reminds us (1981), speakers use the term *ol*, 'All', the transcendent human pronoun when describing just how things are done (as in *oli save wokim olsem*, 'It's done in such-and-such a manner'). 'The One' is always external, distant, yet one's being and motivation and point-of-view are wholly absorbed in it. Wagner calls it the world of 'immanent humanity' (1981) and reminds us that it takes its most concrete form in the Melanesian theories of the 'soul':

> ... the soul sums up the ways in which its possessor is similar to others, over and above the ways in which he differs from them. It comes into being as an inadvertent result of the actor's efforts to differentiate himself, as a felt, motivating 'resistance' to those efforts (1981: 94).

We experience the One distantly, says Heidegger, yet the One presses down into the very core of each of us all the time (1962: 167):

> *Proximally*, it is not 'I', in the sense of my own self, that 'am', but rather the Others, whose way is that of the 'they'. In terms of the 'they'. and as the 'they', I am 'given' proximally to 'myself' ...

The 'All' exerts a levelling force of averageness on each agent; it is only felt as such when the agent resists it (1962: 167–8). And this is not just a particularly Melanesian way of constituting the person: we Westerners are every bit as relationally constituted, just as much thrown into a world of immanent humanity. What we do in contrast to Melanesians is make that relational constitution of the self visible in a different manner (as natural or God-given Law). Which is why, as Strathern notes, the problem of human effectiveness in the world in *all* societies revolves around making the form of this 'All' appear.

> For a body or mind to be in a position of eliciting an effect from another, to evince power or capability, it must manifest itself in a particular concrete way, which then becomes the elicitory trigger. This can only be done through the appropriate aesthetic (1988: 181).

In other words, a certain form of life or sociality is hidden in the day-to-day Melanesian world, as indeed it is in our own, and it requires 'an aesthetic' in order to reveal its contours. With these words, Strathern simultaneously recognizes the Kantian foundation of anthropology (as philosophy – an inquiry into how human beings *are*) but stops short of endorsing a Heideggerian (and Bourdieuian) attempt to overturn the Kantian metaphysic (the phenomenological critique of these forms of intuition).

Heidegger, unlike Strathern, in the end opts for a hermeneutic definition of the manner of human being's disclosedness (cf. Haugeland 1992). What is disclosed is not just the extent of the relationship, but also the framing definition of the *kind* of human being that calls forth relationship as one of its existential conditions. A relationship is itself a style, has in it a particular understanding of what it means *to be* in such-and-such a way. For anthropologists, this is likely to be phrased in terms of culture or morality (see Wagner 1987), but it is the very core of what Heidegger concerned himself with in his existential analytic (cf. Gelven 1989). Hence, in much the same way as Strathern responded recently to her three critics of *The Gender of the Gift*, Heidegger responded to critics of *Being and Time*:

> What is said in *Being and Time* . . . sections 27 and 35, about the 'they' in no way means to furnish an incidental contribution to sociology. Just as little do the 'they' mean merely the opposite, understood in an ethical-existentiell way, of the selfhood of persons (1977a).

He claimed that such references should contain a disclosure to the fundamental possibilities of existence. 'This relation', however, 'remains concealed beneath the dominance of subjectivity that presents itself as the public realm' (1977a: 197–8). The subjectivity he refers to here could well be a gloss on the anthropological assumption of relationality. Under the terms of that assumption, humans unconceal or make visible such subjectivity through their relations with others who are also subjects. What was concealed was always right before our eyes, as the medium through which the revelation was achieved. But in this final revelation anthropology reaffirms the triumph of the subject, the triumph of the viewpoint that would make of the Foi myth 'The Sky Village' a disquisition on exchange, rather than the illusion of subjectivity upon which the fiction of exchange is based.

## Conclusion

The victim of the double death in the Sky Village is trapped by his own animal trap. His own death is secured by the mortuary payment he made to his brother's matrilateral relatives. Finally, he looks down upon the earth and sees the point of life: His own son, having grown up without social relations, is in the middle of a battle, in the middle of death, unconcerned with grief, pity or exchange, like the ghosts themselves, from whose vantage point he can only view but not make contact. He looks down and sees, as if from a distance, the real human world, the limits of which he himself discovered in their most piquant form.

One thing I am saying, therefore, is that we cannot characterize both poles of a dialectic of social life in relational terms. In order for something to stand forth for us, it must have a clearing around it; if it were only contiguous with other things that were identical to it, it could not be distinguished. These are the problems that exercised Heidegger, and that guided his thinking about being-in-the-world and his theory of the role that art and community (*polis*) played in that being. But because Heidegger was not driven by anthropological interests, he did not prioritize the social. He saw it as one component of being within the total human posture in the world. Within that posture were a range of attitudes – of concern, of fallenness, of solicitude, authenticity and inauthenticity, and so forth – that encompassed the social instead of being overarched by it. What fascinates me about Heidegger's account of human being is that although he considers all the things we as social anthropologists view as central to our interests – the community, historicity, the effect of art and language, the sacred, the person, the self and the other – the manner in which he disposes these things in relation to one another is very far removed from conventional social science concerns, and attempts to render this Heideggerian topology in social terms seem to me to be beside the point:

Heidegger intended this topology not to buttress or underpin a mechanism of normative integration, but rather to reveal a mode of 'interrogating being'. To the extent that we are serious about the attempt to critique the whole idea of social relations as our starting and ending point, an inspection of Heidegger's notion of being-in-the-world may provide an image of one kind of social anthropology that might result from such a critique.

## Notes

1. This Orphic imagery recurs in Foi mythology (see the myth 'Return from the Dead' in J. Weiner 1988a).
2. Without a doubt, Heidegger's statement on post-Socratic philosophy applies equally as a summation of the task of twentieth-century social science: 'Plato and Aristotle . . . take thinking to be a *techne*, a process of reflection in service of doing and making' (Heidegger, *Letter on Humanism* ([1977a: 194]; see also Rorty's discussion in his article 'Heidegger, Contingency and Pragmatism' [1991]).
3. Heidegger spent much of his second and third lecture courses on Nietzsche exploring the implications of this understanding of the limits of theory: 'The fact that every science as such, being the specific science it is, gains no access to its fundamental concepts and to what those concepts grasp, goes hand in hand with the fact that no science can assert something about itself with the help of its own scientific resources' [Heidegger, *Nietzsche* II (1984): 112]).
4. 'The researcher always operates on the foundation of what has already been decided: the fact that there are such things as nature, history, art, and that such things can be made the subject of consideration' (Heidegger 1987: 6).
5. See Foucault 'Nietzsche, Genealogy, History' (in Rabinow 1980).
6. A social science of the latter form might not be very distinguishable from other critical and interpretative disciplines. These conclusions encourage us to think that *all* ethnography is a critique of Western culture and by implication Western philosophy, as numerous anthropologists have pointed out recently (for example, Clifford 1988; Marcus and Fischer 1986).
7. *Go~* means 'string bag', and *hagibu* is a participial form of the verb *hagi-*, 'to carry from the head', as women normally carry large, heavy

string bags filled with food or with an infant inside. *Dasi* could be related to the verb *dase(dase)di-*, to fill up a bamboo tube (by banging it down on the ground so that the pieces of food stuffed in slide down to the bottom); or the noun *dasi*, which is the tip of a new seedling. None of these associations were ventured by Foi men, who however may have considered felicitous the idea that a shell can peek out of the holes in a string bag like a chick breaking through an eggshell, or a seedling breaking through the ground; or that a string bag filled with shells could make a satisfying thumping noise as it was plopped heavily on the ground; or that its contents might settle to the bottom of such a bag as a result of the stylized bobbing movements of the man who displays them in such a fashion.

8. The two types of relationships are, for Strathern, articulated in the same manner. They are both conceptual separations (1988: 179: '. . . both mediated and unmediated modes . . . are created within the frame of a single conceptual system'), and they both do functional work on the same level in a social system, that is, they both exert an effect that is evaluated socially.

# 6

# Technology and *Techne* in Trobriand and Yolngu Art[1]

In a comment on Trobriand garden magic, Alfred Gell asserted that 'magical technology is the reverse side of productive technology, and . . . this magical technology consists of *representing* the technical domain in magical form' (1992a: 59, emphasis added). He further suggested that this is a model for what happens in artwork. If, Gell said, we accept that:

> what really characterizes art objects is the way in which they tend to transcend the technical schemas of the spectator, his normal sense of self-possession, then we can see that there is a convergence between the characteristics of objects produced through the enchanted technology of art and objects produced through the enchanted technology of magic, and that, in fact, these categories tend to coincide (ibid.)

It might now occur to the reader to inquire as to the status of the acts of production implicated in each type of technology. In the same article, Gell defined social relations themselves as:

> generated by the technical processes of which society at large can be said to consist, that is, broadly, the technical processes of the production of subsistence and other goods, and the production (reproduction) of human beings by domesticating them and breeding them (1992a: 57).

As his comments in a debate on the status of aesthetics as a cross-cultural category confirm (Ingold 1996), Gell's stance with respect to Trobriand magic, art and enchantment could very well do as a position piece for those who wish to deny a distinctiveness to aesthetic judgements, acts or effects in the constitution of a social world – and in fact, I see it as very close to the views of Pierre Bourdieu, who has been one of the most eloquent advocates of such an anti-aesthetic (1984, 1989).

But the question of aesthetics has not been erased but merely, through the elimination of one term of its dialectic, been subjected to something opposite to sublation, *aufheben* – perhaps we can call it *verdrucken*, 'pressed down or pushed away' or *zuruckziehen* – withdrawn. For if social relations are themselves outcomes of a technology, and if that technology has enchanted forms, we must conclude that there are enchanted forms of the relations through which such technology is manifested. And yet we would surely deny that such is possible – the *relational constitution* of magic and art – the instructing, the learning, the speaking, the reciting, the painting, the carving, the displaying, and so forth – must surely always be, at some level, practical, intraworldly and non-transcendent. We are left with the very problem that we encountered in the preceding chapter, the same problem that Gell began with, and that Bourdieu also has not disposed of: we have located the distinction between intraworldly and transcendent modes of perception within the same concrete world of human relationality, and hence are no closer to drawing any real contrast between them.

For Gell, the normative and the conventional are equivalent to the domains of production and of the technical, and the figurativeness of other representational forms is measured by the degree to which they distance themselves from such domains. What if, however, it was magic and art that were foundational, as indeed our Papua New Guinea hosts constantly tell us, and techniques and products and things made are only revealed in their thingly quality through magic, myth, art and poetry? We might then want to consider art and magic not as an enchanted form of technology, but *our* technology as a concealed or repressed form of *their* art.

Because magic, art and technology are all socially constituted in this practical sense, our search for a contrast between the worldliness of technology and the transcendence of art must focus on the interpretational stance we take towards the *effects* or *outcome* of such acts of perception rather than the forms of sociality through which they are manifested. One of Marilyn Strathern's main points in *The Gender of the Gift* (1988) builds upon the observation that in Melanesia, these forms of sociality are *not* given conventional articulation. They can only be hinted at, or exposed, or alluded to in the acts, or pattern of acts, through which persons strive to *elicit* relationality between themselves. These acts are only judged appropriate, or conventional, if they are seen to bring forth social relations in a proper form:

> ... there is a very small number of (conventional) forms that will do as evidence that relations have been thus activated. They must display certain attributes. Establishing attributes, the nature of things, is not the explicit focus

of these symbolic operations, but it is present as an implicit technique of
operation. From our point of view, the operation thus conceals its conventional
base (1988: 180).

As I pointed out in the last chapter, with this realization, Strathern
understands that anthropology is no longer restricted to the realm of
conventional sociological analysis, but also includes something that might
even be called comparative aesthetics. And it is important to realize that
by the term 'aesthetic' she does not appeal to the subjective or the sensual
or the beautiful, but invokes the Kantian transcendental aesthetic: the
specification of the forms of perception by which phenomena are made
to appear.

The reasoning that Strathern employs is very similar to that which
Martin Heidegger uses in his essay 'The Question Concerning Technology' (1977c). He pointed out that the word technology comes from
the Greek *techne*. *Techne*, he claimed, was a label not just for the 'activities
and skills of the craftsmen, but also for the arts of the mind and the fine
arts' (1977c: 13). *Techne* is a form of *poiesis*, something that brings-forth.

Such a bringing-forth is a revealing in the same sense as Strathern's
Melanesians reveal sociality through patterned acts of elicitation. Heidegger
concludes that 'what is decisive in *techne* does not lie at all in making or
manipulating nor in the using of means, but rather in the forementioned
revealing. It is as revealing, and not as manufacturing, that *techne* is a
bringing-forth' (ibid.).

Strathern speaks in the same way about Western 'making and manipulating' – 'establishing attributes', as she puts it in the above quote. But
for her, Melanesians provide the same critique of such Western modes of
doing as the Greeks did for Heidegger:

> . . . Westerners apprehend as symbolic a relationship between an item and
> what it expresses, as we imagine a shell valuable depicting a child, for the
> relationship is between 'things' each with their own form. Where Melanesians
> personify relations – endow valuables with human attributes and human
> capabilities – they must instead *make the form appear* (1988: 181).

If Strathern's conclusions are correct, they are made possible by
anthropology's special attribute as a mode of inquiry into the social: that
the subject-matter of our discipline – social relations and the forms they
take – is also the medium through which we study them and make them
visible ourselves. We cannot, in other words, study social relations without
employing and implicating our own. If we thus conclude that social

relations, or culture, are only made visible through an appropriate aesthetic form, then our own inquiry is similarly aesthetic, and our investigative procedures must eventually model their subject-matter.

If this is the case, then we can make two further observations. One is positive: We understand now that such an aesthetic is not merely an attitude of detached contemplation, but is an integral part of our life-constituting activities, including the activities of representing and interpreting as well as producing and making. Through our engagement in such activities, we discover the lineaments and forms of the world and remake them in the very act of encountering them. Our work of interpretation models that of our hosts, in that it too conceals its tacit assumptions.

However, what we and Melanesians are likely to identify as the activity of interpretation is likely to take on very different appearances. From this point of view, what we wish to compare between Melanesian and Western lifeworlds is how the *work of concealment* itself operates. The second observation I wish to make leads on from this point and is more cautionary: Because the language and aesthetic of our own Western mode of engagement in the world is so heavily centred on the activities of producing, making, ordering and controlling, and the conscious, intentional postures that underlie them, the work and effects of elicitation come to occupy a subordinate position with respect to such activities. What is elicited for us is usually an unintended by-product of conscious, deliberate intention. But what if it were the other way around, especially in the case of the non-Western societies that anthropologists commonly focus on? What if the world of production and making, of consumption and controlling, was only elicited, what if it were the reflexive by-product of something else, like magic and art?

What needs to be examined, in other words, is the question of whether a culture or world is a 'product' of the relational processes I have been describing. I want to draw upon Martin Heidegger's critique of Western metaphysics to aid me in this, specifically, on Heidegger's characterization of the Western productionist bias. I argue that productionist metaphysics is at the heart of our social theories, including our theories of art. I identify in Roy Wagner's *The Invention of Culture* (1981) a critique of such social productionism that parallels Heidegger's in important respects. I then go on to suggest that, in certain non-Western societies, art is not a condensed version of technology, but something very much opposed to it, for it serves to expose the mode of being upon which the whole normative regime of ordering, producing and making is founded. I then attempt to retrieve an anthropology of art through an appeal to the work of concealment and restriction of meaning, rather than its opposite.

\* \* \*

Although his argument is phrased in linguistic terms, Roy Wagner's theory of symbolic and cultural articulation in *The Invention of Culture* focuses on how general perceptions of identity and difference are established within any given symbolic world. He begins by saying that for any such world, there are two opposed processes of symbolic articulation: one is restriction, whereby some limit is placed on referential accretion or proliferation; and the other is its opposite, expansion, whereby the analogic properties of coding are allowed to multiply. Every speech community must at some point act as if units of speech have fixed designations or *references*. But by the same token, every effort to achieve this only multiplies the possibilities of *analogical* relations between such fixed units. Western theories of language have for the most part tended to see lexical, semantic reference as conventional, and metaphoric or analogic expansion as a perturbation or accretion of language and reference, an adventitious by-product or effect of language use. We tend to view the first as the coding of the world, and the other as figurative image. But neither achieves its force or impact except in relation to the other, and both are involved in any total world of communicated meaning. One might say that code and image are each other's figure and ground.

Wagner then goes on to make a crucial suggestion, one that I feel is consummately Heideggerian: he says that in any given tradition, a distinction always emerges between what human action and thought is seen to do, and what such thought and action exert themselves upon. Societies differ as to which symbolic modality – analogical expansion or semantic coding – is identified as the conventional focus of human action, and which one, by contrast, emerges as the ground of human action and its external limit, so to speak – the external world of fact, nature or incident against which the efforts of humans are poised and against which they seek to effect some transformation.

In the West, we see the world as inherently differentiated into entities. Our task (as Foucault has also characterized it) is to make some order of this differentiation, to turn it into taxonomy, classification, sequence, evolution; to discover the laws that pattern such differentiation. The finding of such laws is always a referential or semantic exercise for us, for it reveals a relationship between entities that we insist is distinct from and independent of the logic of our ordering processes themselves, including the language in which they are phrased. The effects of analogic expansion, however, impinge upon such semantic orders (for example, when the genetic composition of an organism is seen to be like a code;

when the irregularities of a coastline are said to be analogous to the irregularities in wave patterns). Alternatively, analogic expansion has a temporal dimension: the unfolding of transformations in conventional meanings through time, as history or evolution (as when act-final ensembles in Mozartian opera displaced in dramatic centrality the recursive Baroque *da capo* aria of Handelian *opera seria* towards the end of the eighteenth century).

Analogic expansion always works to expose the indissolubility of the world and its mode of representation. But the resulting alterations in convention that such expansion produces are, in the West, perceived as things that affect semantic convention from the *outside*. Their source is seen as something external to the realm of human control and artifice. In the West, such exogenous forces take the form of innate talent or genius, or artistic vision; or, in temporal form, the mechanisms of evolution and historical transformation.[2]

For non-Western people like the Foi, or the Trobrianders, or the Manambu of the Sepik River, or the Umeda, however, the world of analogic expansion is given to them: names are part of the things they label, and the similarities between labels, the resemblances between the sounds of words, are also part of these names; language is laid out in the world as a property of it and not as a result of an artificial imposition of semantic value on to such a world. But because this world has many properties that are hidden from people, there are many names and words that are concealed from people's knowledge – and along with them is concealed the extent of the equivalences between words and the things they label. What the Foi call *kusadobora*, which I have translated as 'spell-talk' or magic, is the revelation of such hidden names, and the way they connect qualities and objects in the world. Commonly, such magical words are revealed to people in dreams with the aid of ghostly intervention.

Actors in such a world allocate to themselves the task of putting a brake on such innate expansion, on introducing the kinds of fastening or tying-down of meaning that these dream revelations represent. Through secrecy, through the ritual use of masking and masked figures, Melanesians contrive to narrow down or control analogic expansion to make it serve socially useful purposes. Characteristically, it is through the focusing of vision, through, say the putting on of a mask, that the world, *as a whole thing* in all its analogic potentiality, is made visible. Thus, the Umeda say that when they put on the Cassowary Mask at the end of the Ida fertility ceremony, 'you can really see everything', which Gell, the ethnographer, interpreted as referring to some panoptic, synthetic vision (1992b: 139) – and it is the paradoxical idea that one's vision is *expanded*

*[margin note: Similar to the copy]*

through the narrowing down of perspective that I find so quintessential to a consideration of the artwork as such.

In other parts of Papua New Guinea, the same process can also be dangerous or deleterious; for the Manambu of the East Sepik:

> To 'see things as they really are' is an experience the [Avatip] villagers fear, because they assume it signifies one's death . . .' (Harrison 1990: 46).

These comments by the Umeda and the Manambu suggest that there are modes of apperception that must not intrude into the conventional realm – and in fact, they bear out the assertion of Roy Wagner that invention and convention cannot normally be simultaneously articulated – one must always be concealed or repressed at the expense of the other. The effect of such a simultaneous revelation would be the compromising of the intention of the actor, who in any case strives to produce a specific effect from her actions. For the Westerner, to have the arbitrary nature of the 'natural' order exposed is to compromise the efficacy of objective knowledge; for the Umeda, the Manambu and Yolngu of north-east Arnhem Land, Australia, as we shall see, there is the threat that restricted knowledge will be released to flow freely and perhaps be exposed as undifferentiated from ordinary knowledge.

But in any case, *what is concealed is the role of concealment itself*, the fact that any mode of symbolic articulation rests on the simultaneous covering over of its opposed mode. And hence, what may be potentially revealed is not necessarily an entity or a word or a formula or an item of knowledge, but the gap or scission between revelation and concealment that makes human intention and striving possible.

The recognition of this concealment of concealment was integral to Heidegger's theorizing of the history of Western thought and the epochal transformations that attended European modernity. He glossed this elsewhere as the 'oblivion of being' (1969; see also Krell 1986) and used it to characterize the mood of anxiety of twentieth-century Europeans. In more sociopolitical terms, Pierre Bourdieu has also made the concealment of concealment a fundamental characteristic of his theory of practice (1977).

Concealment and revelation were also central to Heidegger's conception of the role of the artwork. On the one hand, Heidegger maintained that the artwork served as a node, a point of gathering, a meeting place, a *topos* wherein converge a central constellation of images and values of a community (1971c). His topographical way of speaking of this encouraged him to use sculptural and architectural examples, as we saw in

Chapter 4: in the peasant jug or Greek temple, wherein met earth, sky, humans and deities. The language of spaces and interiors allowed Heidegger to speak of what was 'illuminated' in the interior of such an edifice or artefact, how the play of form created the spaces that impinged on the human perception of boundary and limit – and it is this appeal to the imagery of the space within the artefact, both empty and otherwise, that I have found so helpful in describing the poetic language of the Foi (J. Weiner 1991).

On the other hand, Heidegger did not relinquish his commitment to the Nietzschean view of art as a shattering, a re-enframing (1979), something that was always poised against the everyday structures of the lifeworld. In what way could these two views of art come to the aid of anthropology?

Anthropology has grown out of the Kantian assertion that humans do not encounter the objective world, but a world in which the patterns and possibilities of its accessibility are provided by a total experiential, apperceptual matrix, what Kant called a schematism, which we have conventionally labelled 'culture'. What Bourdieu has pointed out to us, however, is how readily humans accept this environed world *as* the objective one. In taking this objectivist stance, as Bourdieu calls it, humans *conceal* the cultural specificity of that objectivism. Heidegger would say that we fall away from knowledge of that experiential apperceptual apparatus through the attitude of everydayness (1962: 86; cf. Dreyfus 1991: 68). But since every distinct experiential framework hides or conceals the world in some way, what our fallenness amounts to is a double concealment. Or perhaps what could be said is that it is not any real world that is hidden from us, but the fact of concealment itself, which amounts to a recognition of how our very representational strategies have inscribed within them their own resistance and withdrawal.

Heidegger labelled this fundamental tension that arises out of the concealment of a particular historical and cultural mode of perception as the conflict between earth and world. Because each provides the out-of-awareness background against which the other emerges as a distinct form, it is clear that they are not entities as such – earth and world are in fact figure and ground to each other, and one characteristic of a figure–ground is that its form emerges through the articulation of a boundary and not as a concatenation of already-identified entities.

This is a very different mode of bringing-forth than is involved in the technological mode that has dominated Western form-producing, apperceptual strategies. There, the attributes of entities are measured in terms of human usefulness, and the earth as such as a collection of resources-in-potential, which Heidegger labelled 'standing reserve' (1977c: 17). Here, nature (Heidegger's earth) is humanized or anthropomorphized in the image of culture or the human world itself. There is no tension or rift between earth and world. They are only different stages in human mastery over the earth and the resistance that impedes that mastery.

When Gell thus speaks of the technology of art and magic, he uses two idioms fundamentally at odds with each other, in that each brings-forth the world in opposed ways for us. Technology reveals the world as human resource potential, and in so doing conceals its own objectifying effect. Art, on the other hand, reveals the gap or rift, as Heidegger called it, between earth and world that technology serves both to establish and to conceal.[3]

In the gathering together and making visible of the hidden grounds of a human world, the artwork situates itself within the rift or gap between what Heidegger called *earth*, the perceived non-human, external environment, and *world*, the domain of human action, intention and destiny  (Heidegger 1971a). It forces us to confront our most taken-for-granted, concealed everyday procedures, the procedures with which we naturalize the world and our place in it, the procedures that fade into impassivity because of the non-cognitive way we learn to cope in the everyday world (cf. Bourdieu 1977). What must be concealed is the nature of the earth as itself worlded; the nature of signified entities as themselves already given over to us prior to our linguistifying them. What art does is to make visible or give form not to the power of the artist's subjectivity, but to the capacity of the unsymbolized and unspoken world to resist its own representation. The work of art sets itself against the everyday world as something that makes visible its boundaries.[4]

This Heideggerian notion of rift, I believe, corresponds to Roy Wagner's stipulation in *The Invention of Culture* that the two complementary aspects of a trope cannot be simultaneously involved in the articulation of any symbolic construction: an actor is obliged to focus on the collectivizing or the differentiating function of a symbol, but not on both at once, lest the framing intent of the actor be compromised (i.e. lest the construction itself be relativized out of effectiveness).[5]

Heidegger, Wagner and Strathern start with similar goals in mind – they want to question the dominance of productionist models in human social life and social analysis, the kind of models that make the task of 'establishing attributes' the focus of conscious attention. And in their appeal to the alternative social-existential tasks of evocation, elicitation and gathering, they have made the calling forth of a human world of action, relation and production a matter of the elicitation of forms and

paper!

their proper grounding conditions – what we would conventionally label an aesthetic process.

But if we have now totally aestheticized the social world and our means of making it visible, is this tantamount to saying that society and relationality have been turned into a work of art? Must such a comparative aesthetics inexorably lead us to some form of a Richard Wagnerian national aestheticism? Regardless of how unsavoury we might find Richard Wagner's musicological politics, we might yet admire the attempt to achieve some synthetic vision of a total social world through imagistic means. Wyzewa's description of the Wagnerian *gesamtkunstwerk*, cited by James Boon, is useful here, because it aligns such a task with that of the Maussian total social fact with which we are familiar: 'With [Wagner], Art is no longer in painting, nor in literature, nor in music, but in the strict union of these genres and *in the total life which is born thereof*' (Boon 1972: 171, emphasis added).

But at the moment when the total work of art emerges, we might have to abandon the aesthetic as such. For we have a paradox: How can a whole thing, that is, the total work of art, or total social fact, emerge as part of something, or a diminutive or miniaturized version of something? How can the total work of art be at one and the same time the whole thing and less than the whole thing? How can social relationships themselves be made reducible or representable in such a way, when, as I have suggested, they themselves are the media through which such representations are created, when they must, by this token, retain their scale?

These questions appear as paradoxical only if we accept the self-evidence of a particular proportionality of human life and action, a proportionality whereby an artefact, or linguistic usage, or theory is always a compact, less complex, abbreviated form of the whole of which it is part. Science would act by chaining together such artefacts, linguistic usages and theories into a whole that would, point by point, exactly match, in scale and explanatory complexity, the total world it seeks to explain and control.

To see something as a whole is also to remove it from the constraints of scale and proportion, of measurement, contrast and relation, for a thing that is whole, be it the world, the body, society, the longhouse, can be of any size and any scale; it can be both the microcosm and the macrocosm at the same time.

But from the point of view of the bodying of life through form itself, we have something altogether opposite. It could be that such artefacts are useful because they *are* miniaturizable in a way that the social relations they comment on can never be. Aesthetic synthesizers such as Richard Wagner, Baudelaire, Mallarmé and Proust – and such representative anthropologists as Lévi-Strauss, Roy Wagner, Paul Friedrich, David Guss and James Fernandez – all have promoted a conception of artistic creation 'in terms of a view best clarified by Bergson, by which "an ideal perception would thus contain in a single present object the totality of the sensible universe . . . Ordinary perception is a *dimunition* of this ideal perception"' (Boon 1982: 148). And the comments of the Umeda mask-wearer seems to confirm that this is an intuition not restricted to our own Western theory of art. Here, the smaller thing would be actually more complex than the whole that it purportedly represents, because it would obtain the capacity to be subsumed by everything else.

If in this view painting, gardening and exchange all have aesthetic properties, does this mean that the distinctiveness of the artwork vanishes? Must we see the Trobriand garden as much a 'collective work of art', as Gell terms it (1992a), as the Trobriand woman's banana-leaf skirt, or a Trobriand canoe prow? Or must we now attempt to establish the grounds by which we can separate the aesthetic from the artistic? And if not, what then remains of and for an anthropology of art? We have yet to free the work of art from the tasks of social and cultural productionism, which is still its most distinguishing goal for most of us. I am maintaining, however, that the function of the art is not to represent society or any of its components, including relationality itself. We cannot appeal to what the work reveals without understanding that such a revelation involves a suspension, cancellation, or concealment of conventional processes of social elicitation.

Nor, on the other hand, can we appeal to the work of concealment or *méconnaissance* in a society without a simultaneous consideration of the procedures a society has for revelation. We must, that is, continue to think dialectically, and this means that the negation or collapse of the form of sociality is implicated in the same procedures that account for its positive instauration. Because art, unlike technology, focuses on the rift between the world and the limitations of our modes of appresenting it, it exposes the arbitrary differentiation that convention makes between them. It embodies the dialectic between the innate and external, and the human and the artificial, rather than fixing it in some antinomy of the objective, such as nature vs. culture, material vs. ideal, society vs. the individual, or inside vs. outside.

Let us now examine how the play of concealment operates in the artistic practices and language of non-Western people. My first example comes from the Trobriand Islands, from an article written by the Trobriand aesthete, John Kasaipwalova. In this article (1975), he advocates the setting up of a new Art School on Kiriwina, the Sopi Arts Centre, a school in which modern Kiriwina artists could be trained in traditional techniques.

There are two terms that Trobrianders use to describe 'the appreciation of art works' as Kasaipwalova puts it. First, there is *kwegivayelu*, literally, 'the voice that follows'. It is the power of reproduction *as mimesis*, as direct similarity, for the *kwegivayelu* artist has only to listen to the sea or wind and be able to reproduce that sound with his voice. The power to reproduce is not limited to aural skill, but can take the form of carving or painting as well. The second term, *Sopi*, on the other hand, is the power to enframe that reproduction, it involves learning a *theory* of art: one has to learn *Sopi* magic at childhood, which 'involves the intimate transmission of magic, history etc. from the adult relative with that knowledge' (1975: 5). In other words, *Sopi* is the appreciation of art framed by a world of historically derived meanings; while *kwegivayelu* is a more primordial reflection of the elements in the person of the artist. Kasaipwalova's grandfather told him: '. . . the biggest qualitative difference between *kwegivayelu* and *sopi* is that the artists of the former magic will go to either the sea or the caves for inspiration while the latter will go to both and return to the midst of the village surroundings to create' (ibid.).

Kasaipwalova says: 'The school for the *sopi* artists is the seas, the caves and the village, the sea representing the outside world, the caves representing the subjective human potential and the village representing the complex of human inter-relatedness.' What Kasaipwalova seems to be saying is that it is not enough to recognize that the art of the Trobrianders is iconic of nature (*kwegivayelu*); some interpretational ambience (*sopi*) must also stipulate the essential *arbitrariness* of that resemblance and hence the contingency of nature *vis-à-vis* the social and vice versa. Some ground must disclose the essential historicity of the perception of this iconism, must set limits to the expansion of 'natural' mimesis.

A parallel case is found in Howard Morphy's recent description of the art of the Yolngu of north-east Arnhem Land, Australia. He first distinguishes between two broad systems of representation that the Yolngu employ in painting. The first he calls *figurative representation*, 'iconically motivated representations of objects of the human and natural environments' (1991: 152). They are 'intended to "look like" the object represented and to be interpreted as such by those familiar with the iconographic code' (ibid.). But the extent and criteria of figurative representation are determined not by the accuracy of the resemblance, but by the acceptance of the representational relation 'to all interpreters' (ibid.). 'The [figurative] representation . . . is intended to be interpreted as such by all who see it, and indeed its interpretation as (for example) a shark is a prerequisite for any other meanings' (ibid.).

The other system of representation Morphy calls the *geometric*. Each geometric element:

> can represent a range of different meanings, for example, a circle can represent a water hole, a campsite, a mat, a campfire, eggs, holes left by maggots, nuts, and so on (1991: 167).

Now Morphy states that in the context of a specific design, the figurative elements are never seen as having multiple significations. For geometric elements, on the other hand, 'multivalency is an essential part of their meaning' (1991: 168). A 'key' is needed in order to interpret geometric designs; this key is some knowledge or prior experience of the element.

In talking about their iconographic designs, Yolngu painters make use of the word *likan*. In 'non-ritual' contexts:

> *likan* means 'elbow,' 'fork between the branches of a tree and its trunk,' and 'bay between two promontories.' All these meanings have something in common: they refer to objects which are discrete yet at the same time link other objects in relation to which they are defined (Morphy 1991: 187–8).

In ritual contexts, *likan* refers to the connection between the designs or any other ritual object, and the actions, powers or physical make-up of the creator beings, the *wangarr* beings. '*Likan* is a metaphor of connection or connectivity. It focuses on the way paintings are linked with ancestral action' (1991: 189).

This connectivity for the most part is specifically between what the Yolngu refer to as 'inside' and 'outside' things. 'Inside' things refer to the primordial, creative acts of the ancestral *wangarr*; to the true significance, hidden motives, or underlying import of actions. 'Outside' things are the way things appear or are made to appear, the face that things take in their public exposure and superficial, indiscriminate assessment.

But as Morphy notes, 'what is inside shifts according to the perspective adopted' (1991.: 83), and in fact:

> . . . secrecy is a mask, not the means by which knowledge is controlled. The mask of secrecy is an illusion and a tease; knowledge slips out from behind its locked door into the public arena and back again . . . in most respects the body of public knowledge is broadly equivalent to and overlaps with the body of secret knowledge, covering the same ground and conveying similar understandings about the world (Morphy 1991: 96).

These two examples show that there is always a counter-invented world that emerges along with the intended objects of our conscious efforts, but that remains concealed or unknown. This world is created as an unintended by-product of the focusedness of people's perception, and makes itself felt as a resistance to those efforts. It is not brought out directly, but only indirectly – hence, our conventional terminology of production, construction, and ordering do not accurately characterize its origins. And because it is a reflexive effect, as it were, of intentionality – a parodying of our forward-looking, ecstatic temporality as resistance and reversibility – it requires specific techniques, which are themselves non-productionist, non-relational, non-constructionist, and non-representational, to make them visible.

## Conclusion

Heidegger particularly addresses the possibility of anthropology in his article 'The Age of the World Picture' (1977b). One of the characteristics of the productionist metaphysic is the interdependency of subjectivity and representation that are constitutive of it. To be a subject means that 'Man becomes the being upon which all that is, is grounded as regards the manner of its Being, and its truth. Man becomes the *relational center* of that which is as such' (1977b: 128, emphasis added). To occupy such a position gives the possibility of putting everything before oneself as object of representation; to see oneself *in relation to a world*, and to a *totality of entities* in that world. It also involves viewing these entities in terms of their utility, as resources in the service of production and consumption, and once utility in production becomes the dominant essence of things, then the issue of the function of the artwork, and of art, becomes the irresolvable and futile language of Western aesthetic analysis.

Once the subject is put at the centre of the world, then the art work becomes a species of the aesthetic, and the aesthetic eclipses the art work because of its concern with the internal experience of the subject.

> Instead of changing the way things are open and available to us, art now manipulates our feelings. The whole phenomenon of art is absorbed into a way of thinking and living centered on the subject–object division. Besides the art business, this produces the endless debates in modern aesthetic theory about the nature of the inner experiences involves in art, whether they are cognitive or emotive, how they link with sensible stimuli, and so on (Kolb 1986: 122).

But I think no strong case can be made that either Trobriand or Yolngu art has as its function the imaging of the subjectivity of the artist. If we believed otherwise, we would be making the sociality elicited by such art works contingent on such subjectivity. But it is probably more nearly the other way around – subjectivity only arises within a specific field of social perception, and art draws attention to the way such a field and its media limit and shape the kinds of subjectivity possible within it.[6]

One of the most important critiques of this subjectivity is found within Heidegger's phenomenological ontology. Heidegger's reading of Kant's first critique is decisive here, for he locates the fundamental ambiguity in Kant's relation between the objectivity of the object, human subjectivity and its relation to the human schematism, the cognitive faculty:

> The thing does not relate to a cognitive faculty interior to the subject; instead, the cognitive faculty itself and with it this subject are structured intentionally in their ontological constitution. *The cognitive faculty is not the terminal member of the relation between an external thing and the internal subject; rather, its essence is the relating itself*, and indeed in such a way that the intentional Dasein which thus relates itself as an existent is always already immediately dwelling among things. For the Dasein there is no outside, for which reason it is also absurd to talk about an inside (Heidegger 1982b: 66, emphasis added).

The inside and outside of Yolngu knowledge refers not to the way such social and political conditions differentiate types of knowledge – rather, the facts of social and political differentiation are themselves contingent upon how such knowledge is brought forth in particular ways, through the displaying of painting or the reciting of myths, for example. Inside and outside are descriptions of the contrasting limits within the Yolngu's form-producing procedures, and what such limits make it possible to create as socially enacted perceptual contrasts. The iconicity of Yolngu designs is not the true shape of their world, but a visual rendering of the kinds of forces that make connectivity a vital constituting force of that world.

## Notes

1. A shorter version of this chapter was first presented to the Department of Anthropology, University College London in 1991. I would like to thank Georgina Born and Bruce Kapferer for their valuable comments at that time. I am also indebted to the late Alfred Gell for his inspiration.

2. The difference in the *form* this articulation took between the medieval period and the modern period that replaced it is profound. In the medieval period, it was not science but religion that provided the shape of analogic expansion. Language and representation were seen as a restricted power of the Divine God, and hence the world at large was a Divine product. Analogic expansion in the form of art took religious imagery as its sole legitimate subject, and man, through the mechanism of religious vision, was the mediator of such analogic expansion, but not its source.

3. Michael Zimmerman puts it in these words:

   'The conflict between the disclosing which wants to measure and the self-arising which contains its own law involves an essential conflict, a rift (*Riss*) which makes the "innerness" of the event of being, the event of truth. The art work can never *represent* the primal rift, the struggle between earth and world, but it does somehow *embody* it. *Gestalt* or figure names the way in which this rift is "set in place" in the work of art. As the particular embodiment of this enduring rift, the work of art constitutes the primordial sketch or outline which measures and gives meaning to entities: "Figure is the structure in whose shape the rift composes and submits itself . . ." (1990: 64).

4· Paul Klee (1970) said 'Art does not reproduce what is visible, instead, it makes visible.'

5. Habermas, in contrasting psychoanalysis and conventional hermeneutics, reaches the same conclusion:

   '. . . the acting subject belies himself only for others who interact with him and observe his deviation from the grammatical rules of the language game. The acting subject himself cannot observe the discrepancy; or, if he observes it, he cannot understand it, because he both expresses and misunderstands himself in this discrepancy. His self-understanding must keep to what is consciously intended, to linguistic expression – or at least to what can be verbalized. *Nonetheless, the intention content that comes into view in discrepant actions and expressions is as much a part of the subject's life-historical structure as are subjectively intended meanings.*

The subject must deceive itself about these non-verbal expressions that are not coordinated with linguistic expression. And since it objectivates itself in them, it also deceives itself about itself' (1987: 218, emphasis added).

6. I am very grateful to Henrietta Moore for the valuable comments she made in her ASA Decennial paper, 'What is Social Knowledge For?'.

# Part III
# The Aestheticization of
# Social Relations

# 7

# The Community as a Work of Art

One essential way in which truth establishes itself in the entities that it has opened up is truth setting itself into [the] work [of art]. Another way in which truth comes to presence is the deed that founds a political state — Heidegger (1971a), 'The Origin of the Work of Art'.

In the last chapter, I brought Heidegger's notion of unconcealment to bear on two anthropological issues: the making visible of social relations, and the function of the work of art. I also drew attention to Marilyn Strathern's suggestion in *The Gender of the Gift* (1988) that social relations in Melanesia were elicited by a certain form-inducing process, and that this gloss on human relationality served to broaden what we meant by the 'aesthetic'. I then observed that Wagner, Strathern and Heidegger all share a concern with the role of these aesthetic, form-inducing processes in human social and cultural life in general and not just with respect to the artwork narrowly conceived.

In this chapter, I want to push the notion of the aesthetic further, to its own limit, in order later to critique the current anthropological fascination with the spectacle, the performance, the cinematographic, the display, and the representational in general. My concern is to demonstrate the limits of these ostensive representational strategies, which are more assumed than demonstrated in much contemporary anthropological writing. This critique rests on the anti-constructionist argument I have been making with respect to the task of social analysis.

In the last chapter, I characterized two ways in which social relations can and have been aestheticized in recent anthropological analysis. The first preserves the transcendent effect of the art work, as a technique for exposing the limits of human relationality. It is here that I locate one point of similarity in the Western and non-Western artwork. As I demonstrated in the last section, forms such as Yolngu painting and Foi poetry poise themselves deliberately against the conventions of 'normative' sociality and achieve their interpretational effects through this external positioning.

The second approach takes the opposite tack – it collapses the artwork into conventional relationality. It seeks to 'demystify' the artwork by focusing on its constitutive productive relations and its social and political contexts of creation. This second approach has also been used by some anthropologists of art as a way of equating the function of the artwork in Western and non-Western worlds.

In an obvious sense, these approaches are in conflict with each other, although they both embody a truth about the function of art, as I intimated in Chapter 6. In the remaining chapters, however, I will continue to criticize the latter, Bourdieuian approach. I maintain that not only does this approach elide what we intuitively feel to be the distinction and non-conventionality of the artwork, but that it also, perhaps unwittingly, supports the aestheticization of social and political life through the unintended reflexive effect of art's transcendent properties. To put it another way, it avows the reflexive effects of objectification while disavowing the work of interpretation that this reflexivity also makes necessary. This, I will argue, is most visible in the way some anthropologists have analysed the role of cinematographic media in non-Western societies.

Let me return first to the notion of the uncanny I introduced in Chapter 4. What seems to characterize the lifeworlds of all the non-Western people to which I have referred is the place of the unknown, the unseen, or the uncanny as an articulated limit to knowledge, vision and perception. Social relations, including the ones we are most likely to isolate as productive, reproductive, ritual/religious, and artistic, all have some capacity to draw forth some perspective on what we can call, for lack of a better term, this *unworld*. What we isolate as *artistic* procedures as such are perhaps the most perspicuous and forceful versions of such a drawing-forth.

In this sense, what founds sociality for people like the Foi, the Manambu, the Trobrianders, the Yolngu, is not something that is self-evident and visible to them. It is not enshrined in law or constitution or a sacred tablet or document attesting to the Divine rights and nature of Man. It is, in fact, unknown, and perhaps ultimately unknowable. In the form in which we encounter it – the uncanny – nescience thus founds social life.[1]

What people like the Foi have are various devices for bringing this unworld into view, making it visible. How can we see this process of elicitation account for a society or polity, as opposed to an art style, be it verbal or graphic? Let me now return to the analysis of Manambu sociality provided by Simon Harrison.

The Manambu of the Sepik River lowlands are a people closely related to and neighbours of the Iatmul, who were described in Gregory Bateson's famous monograph *Naven* (1968). Harrison first identifies his theoretical interest in the following way: traditional analyses of small-scale social organization tend to accept the atomic individual as the innate unit of social analysis, out of which groups are constructed from the culturally-specified rules of social engagement. Harrison oppositely argues, in much the same vein as have Roy Wagner and Marilyn Strathern, that onto-logically, people such as the Manambu of the Sepik River area in Papua New Guinea accept interrelationship as innate, prior and taken-for-granted. What *is* problematic for them is *restricting* the range of social relationality. Thus, for the Manambu, Harrison argues that: 'an inde-pendent polity is an entity needing constantly to be achieved by *counter-acting* its external ties and dependencies' (1993: 14, emphasis added).

For the Manambu of Avatip Village, warfare is one of the ways that such political entities can come into existence; other ways include ceremonial exchange or marriage. Harrison thus concludes that 'violent and peaceful sociability are often aspects of the *same relationship*' (1993: 18). The violent leader, the war leader in Papua New Guinea society, is socially valued precisely because he successfully exemplifies the mascu-line ethos of self-assertion and aggressive will to power. In order to prepare for warfare, men impersonated the totemic spirits. These spirits are themselves hostile to each other and spur men on to fight as their proxies or avatars. The totemic spirits' sociality is viewed as fundamentally negative and hostile.

The ties that link people are thus not problematic, for the clan system is global. That is, the totemic system of clans is assumed to be the same for all peoples of the region, perhaps for all humankind as they conceive it. What people focus their efforts on is 'how to create and preserve distinct polities *for these ties to exist between*' (1993: 46). For the Manambu, it is sociality, in the form of inescapable obligations of reciprocity between people, that is prior and foundational, not individuality. Violence is one kind of social relationship, one form of sociality played off against others (like domesticity or exchange). It is creative and positive, and cannot be dismissed as mere absence of social relationships or a breakdown in normative communal functioning.

Harrison goes on to suggest (1993: 89) that in cooperating in murder and cannibalism, Manambu men achieved a sense of solidarity with each other, 'not a sense of Durkheimian moral solidarity but a shared experience of transgressing norms'. What men have to accomplish in order to be successful warriors, assassins and murderers is not to release some repressed natural violent impulse, but on the contrary, to stifle the inner core of sociability and affect that is the source of Manambu 'being-with-others', to take on a mask of autonomy and cruelty, to become something like the Nietzschean 'Overman', beyond all values. 'To Avatip men aggression implies . . . an impassiveness, a dispassionate withdrawal or non-reciprocity of emotion' (1993: 111).

Echoing what Wagner concludes for the Usen Barok, Harrison says, 'Polity is perhaps most real at the climax of articulatory rituals, and it is a hard-won, rare and momentary achievement' (Harrison 1990: 193–4). The image of the mask figures prominently in these ritual devices: 'The villages call living human beings *kwamakanduta'akw*: people with revealed, or visible faces. The totemic ancestral spirits, they say, are men and women too, but their faces (*mak*) are hidden because these beings do not show themselves to living people in their true form' (1990: 46).

In the totemic names they acquired access to, in the magic spells they learned and that gave them power, in the decorations men used that were tantamount to assuming the *persona* or mask of the totemic spirit, Harrison sees violence as an aesthetic complex. One Nietzschean reading of this could be that, through violence, Manambu men achieve a sort of transcendence, a power to shatter the normal conventions of life. But as was the case with Gell, Harrison does not consider this transcendental violence itself to be non-social, or outside the social. But in these terms, the idea that Mananmbu men can share the experience of transgressing norms becomes paradoxical, for in the moment when a shared way of transgressing norms emerges as a consensual image among men, it becomes as thoroughly normative and conventional as that which it purportedly transgresses. My point is that there is a dilemma in Harrison's analysis: although he defines the realm of the aesthetic in social terms, one is unable to conclude from it that it achieves its effects wholly within that realm. For is it not the case that Harrison is trying to theorize what Gell is preoccupied with, that is, how society can give form to *enchanted social relations*?

In the last sentence of his book, Harrison concludes that Manambu men '. . . fostered war in their cult, not because they lacked the normative ties beyond the village but, quite the opposite, *precisely because they had such ties* and could only define themselves as a polity by acting collectively to overcome and transcend them' (1993: 150). It is significant that Harrison ends by articulating the Manambu political ethos in terms of what we have classically identified with the 'Nuer paradox' – in this case, it would go something like, 'the Manambu are so solidary and collective that fighting, murder and warfare themselves served socially integrative purposes'. But the Nuer paradox has always been, without our necessarily having been aware of the fact, a function of our effort to make commensurate two different, incommensurable articulations of polity, community and sociality: the normative and the aesthetic.

What is valuable about Harrison's analysis is the manner in which it confirms one of Marilyn Strathern's characterizations of Melanesian social articulation: 'In lieu . . . of a theory of symbolic construction as we would reckon it, we find a . . . theory of social action' (M. Strathern 1988: 174). As Harrison observes, persons, and their capacities, have to be made distinct from each other; some disparity or difference must be established, in order to create the space in which a social effect can be made visible, can be seen to be making a connection.[2]

Harrison concludes that 'the basic preoccupation of the [Avatip] men's cult is with *representing the identity of the community as an enduring political entity* . . .' (1993: 147, emphasis added). But they do so primarily in a negative sense, by prescribing hostile relations of violence and homicide with outsiders, and by modelling their form-producing behaviour after the non-social totemic spirits. Thus, if this is a representation, then it is a representation that can only work by depicting something in terms of its opposite or negation. Is it not then the case that the whole Durkheimian problematic of the ritual/aesthetic representation of society is called into question by the Manambu case? That it is more fair to say that the community cannot be represented but only contained or elicited through such acts?

We are now in a position to consider again the steps that we must take to see social relations as themselves enchanted, as I did in the last chapter. To do so, we would have to begin by seeing the Manambu warrior turning his will to power into a work of art, a Papua New Guinea version of Ernst Jünger's modern German worker, 'accustomed to endure the fearsome and to do the fearsome'. Ernst Jünger was one of the most important forerunners of National Socialist philosophy in Germany before the Second World War. Jünger felt, largely as a result of his own first-hand combat experience during the First World War, that warfare 'was a manifestation of elemental, mythical, irrational forces that transcended "bourgeois" economic concepts and political ideologies' (Zimmerman 1990: 50). And as we know, men like Jünger contributed to the mythologizing of military technology and its bizarre fusion with a pagan organicism of blood and soil that was one of the defining features of National Socialist ideology.

In his book *The Worker*, Jünger described his concept of the *Gestalt* of the worker. It was what arose in opposition to civilization and was intended to overcome and triumph over it. The Gestalt of the worker fused man and technology within the ambit of a transcendental Will, which represented the very 'being [*Sein*]' of the worker (Zimmerman 1990: 58). In his surrender to the Gestalt, the worker is stripped of his bourgeois individuality and becomes a *Typus* or type. Jünger would go on to describe this *Typus* as a mask, '. . . the gas mask of a soldier, the mask of the industrial welder, the face mask of the hockey player, or even the make-up of the modern woman' (Zimmerman 1990: 59).

The mask, however, was not a human mask; the mask was the incarnate form of something altogether without qualities, namely Will to Power itself – something that could not be explained in human terms but which nevertheless moulded human character, society and destiny.

Jünger and Harrison reach the same conclusions about warfare – that it is made possible by a *suppression* of mundane sociality; that it is a transcendent, category-destroying act; that it stands outside or beyond the social, and yet is supremely creative, perhaps the most intensely creative act that the communities in question are capable of.

They both significantly make use of the imagery of the mask, the *personae*, and this is very important, because it signals to us that what is at issue, as is the case with any modernist excursion into the realm of the aesthetic, is the question of the identity of the perceiving subject, and in fact, the broader issue of the subject as the point of reference for all social science.[3]

How would we analyse Jünger's social theory in anthropological terms? As do Heidegger, Marx and Bourdieu, Wagner accepts that the process of masking or concealment is fundamental to human conceptualization. All living things evince a movement, without which change and development would not be possible, and, as Marx noted (see H. Lefebvre, *The Sociology of Marx* (1968)), it is impossible to consider growth apart from change in form. It is this Platonic form which is hidden, because it is (Western) human nature to focus on the entities themselves and ignore the originating conditions that give entities their shape and form.

The term itself 'masking' deserves to be taken literally here. A mask does not just cover up a person's face; it sets up the possibility, in fact the necessity, that the mask will be taken off and the person underneath revealed. The possibility of putting on an ostensive mask covers up the other day-to-day masking we engage in all the time, which has to go unnoticed in order for social convention to reveal itself in the 'normal' way.

If, as I suggested, the Manambu warrior achieves his convention-preserving effect by an act that is explicitly opposed to that convention, then in the terms I have advocated it so far, his actions and strategies and effects are 'artistic'. If art is everywhere poised against the conventional, then it does not have a function (in the social anthropological sense): it does not integrate, nor does it relate. Its effects are *social*, but not conventional. If the work of art does not articulate a relationship, then Western society conceived of as a work of art cannot be relationally based either. This is why Jünger's aesthetic is anti-modernist, because he mythologized technology and derived a socio-political logic from it that was deliberately intended to obliterate conventional sociality. But for the Manambu, because the relational is taken for granted, because its production and representation are not the realm of convention, then their acts of aesthetic, mythopoietic rupture through warfare, as Harrison suggests, will always serve to make the social visible.

By inspecting the Manambu and juxtaposing them to the anti-modernist credo of men like Ernst Jünger, we have illuminated a paradox in the social evaluation of the artwork. But though Ernst Jünger, like Nietzsche, also felt that life could only be "justified" as an aesthetic phenomenon' (Zimmerman 1990: 54), we have no cause to see the Manambu as 'anti-modern', or even 'pre-modern', because it is not in modernist terms that the Manambu are 'opposing' relationality. Few anthropologists would identify their pursuit with this 'modernist credo' of 'the triumph of spirit and will over reason and the subsequent fusion of this will to an aesthetic mode' (Herf 1984: 12). The problem with aestheticizing the culture of non-Western people like the Manambu in this way is that it poses the danger of a blurring of our theory of their social life and their own, because we accept that representation is the final goal of all cultural articulation. Because it was modern thinkers such as Kant who originated our concept of aesthetics, it has always been constituted through 'metaphysical subjectivism and representationalism' (Zimmerman 1990: 107). This became so conventionalized by Lévi-Strauss's structuralism that it has attained the status of methodological *habitus* within anthropology. Within such a definition, the social acts through which aesthetic events materialize likewise first and foremost serve the interests of representation and communication. It then becomes easy to model social relations themselves on the semantic relations of words and images, to make them a form of representation.

Both Harrison and Jünger characterize the subjectivity of the Manambu and the German worker in the same Western terms, the terms that Heidegger identified as the language of production and making, the Aristotelian *techne*, and that Zimmerman has so aptly described as productionist metaphysics. It is productionist metaphysics that still dominates anthropology, in the form of social constructionism, the notions that society, social relations and a moral world in general are artefacts in some important sense; and that the personhood of persons can be measured in terms of production and its obverse, consumption. Is it not the case that both Harrison's Manambu and Jünger's German worker strive for some form of *enchanted social relations*?

In a roundabout way, I have returned to the topic of social drama, a concept that has been at the heart of what anthropology has attempted to find in different societies since Spencer and Gillen first described the Aranda *intichiuma* ceremonies, which Durkheim would go on to formulate in his now-classic terms as a total venue of societal self-representation. This legacy has been passed on virtually unchanged through most of this century, and has reached its modern form in another now-classic work, that of Clifford Geertz, 'Deep Play: Notes on the Balinese Cockfight'. There Geertz suggested that:

> . . . art forms generate and regenerate the very subjectivity they pretend only to display. Quartets, still-lifes, and cockfights are not merely reflections of a preexisting sensibility analogically represented; they are positive agents in the creation and maintenance of such a sensibility (1973: 28).

It seems that anthropology has had only two ways of dealing with the 'problem' of art: either it serves to represent what is already there, or it 'constructs' the form in the very process of representing it. What is thus written into what I am calling this productionist approach is the antinomy created between the act of production and the act of contemplating art. Each one is made to have its own very different metaphysics. From a Durkheimian, Tönniesian perspective, we might think that art or artistic activity is the medium through which a society *creates* its social mode of engagement. If, on the other hand, we were in the mindset of a Boasian aesthetics of culture, we might conclude differently that what art (and here we can say 'ritual' to preserve a more specifically anthropological dimension to this question) does is to *reveal* a certain pattern to our life, our social life, that we don't normally think of as an object of contemplation.

Is there a big difference between saying that art *creates* something that is not there, and saying that art *reveals* something that *is* there all the time, but that for one reason or another we are not or cannot be aware of? Is there any practical way of distinguishing creation from the imposition of a frame or procedure within which some thing can be isolated that has not been isolated before? For how can we tell on the face of things whether we are perceiving a new entity or an old entity in a new context?

According to Charles Spinosa (1992), however, Heidegger circumvents making an artificial choice between these positions. For to provide a new frame is at the same time to re-enframe the entire field within which things are isolated and placed in meaningful relations with other things. Any single pattern is not stable; what is stable is the human capacity to frame and re-enframe.[4] And this capacity demands that we consider concealment as fundamental to meaningful articulation and communication. Roy Wagner thus gives the following interpretation of the Usen Barok of New Ireland, Papua New Guinea:

> The Usen Barok understand their lives to be grounded in 'power' *a lolos* . . ., that which enables human capability and tests its limits, but also stands outside of it. If power over something is the ability to negate or destroy it, then social power – that which commands society – cannot be merely a function of the social order itself. It cannot . . . amount to society's representation of itself. It may only be elicited or contained (Wagner 1986b: xiv).[5]

In the remaining chapters, I will show what the implications of this critique are and what advantage they might give us in the face of one of contemporary anthropology's most dramatic new forms of representation, film.

## Notes

1. This perhaps is what Nietzsche meant when he identified 'Untruth as a condition of life'.
2. See Lévi-Strauss 1963; Schrempp 1992.
3. Jünger's image of the steel-encased warm body, the organic fusion of man and machine, reminds us that we cannot appeal to em-bodying as a function of the human body *as such*. For the image of that body is itself historical and takes its shape against the background of a body of meanings. And in this realization we find the most potent argument against art as Platonic *mimesis*. The fusion of steel and flesh should also convince us that organicism is not limited to the living body and its functions. In Jünger's view, the machine is just as much an organic entity, and organicism is a way of viewing the constitutive relations of life (which is why Harroway urges us to consider the cyborg, as a way of avoiding an organicism of the machine).

4. This is paralleled by a point made by Bergson and Nietzsche and commented upon by Deleuze.
5. '... the severing is still a binding and a connecting' (Heidegger, 'Logik: Heraklits Lehre vom Logik', in *Heraklit*, 'Gesamtausgabe', Bd. 55 (Frankfurt am Main: Vittorio Klostermann, 1979), p. 337. (Cited by Levin 1988: 197)

# 8

# Prelude: Light and Language

Among both the Kaluli and the Foi of the southern fringe highlands of Papua New Guinea and elsewhere in Papua New Guinea the realm of the acoustic, and consequently, the role of the acoustemic and the acoustemological (Gell 1979, 1995; Feld 1986, 1996; J. Weiner 1991, 1995a) have been well documented. Living in primary rainforest environments, the dense texture of environed sound constitutes a rich field for the mimetic elaboration of social and cultural contrasts and equivalences, typically between the birds of the forests and their characteristic cries, and the language of people, in particular, men. Both Feld and I have spent much time documenting the vocabulary and practices with which the Foi and the Kaluli locate within this soundscape the normative and aesthetic lineaments of their social world.

If our intent was only to document the mechanics of sound as a field of cultural elaboration, or as a cultural system, however, there would hardly be much of interest for us, either anthropologically or phenomenologically. For it still remains that language and visual display, both of which in an important sense oppose and limit the mimetic product of these local forest acoustemologies, also play important and salient roles in the daily life of these Papua New Guinea communities. For the Foi and Kaluli, the major venue in which this forest mimesis of bird and man is made public consists of communal ceremonies where men decorate themselves with oil, cosmetics, feathers and leaves, producing a prominent visual effect. The community assembles in the interior of the communal longhouse, carefully lit by firebrands and torches so as to produce the desired illumination of these men's bodies and decorations. Decorated in this way, both Kaluli and Foi men perform the sung memorial chants in which prosaically as well as mimetically, the equations between birds, men, forest voices and territory are articulated and that become such a central spatial and temporal nexus of Kaluli and Foi sociality.

Let us focus then on the longhouse as a site for both viewing and talking in Foi society. During the day, or at night on non-ceremonial occasions, the men's longhouse is a dark, windowless interior, illuminated only by the two doorways at either end and the shafts of light that manage to penetrate through the gaps in the wall slats or through holes in the sago-leaf roof. On the many occasions I have witnessed men's gatherings for the purpose of public conversation, hearing, dispute, debate and so forth, men do not feel the need to clot together while they converse. They sit at their own fireplaces along the 270-foot length of the longhouse, along with those visitors from other villages that have friends or relatives at such fireplaces. When they speak, men do not feel the need to look at each other and see the face of the speaker or their individual interlocutors. This tendency *not* to bring the body into correlative positioning with voice is even more marked at night. At this time, the invisibility of people is more pronounced. Only the flickering fires or the occasional kerosene hurricane lamp provide illumination. From the sides of the longhouse come the voices of women, who are sitting in the separate women's houses that line the two sides of the men's longhouse. The illusion of the disembodiment of the voice is very tangible at these times, prompting one to consider the longhouse as a space of voices without haptic or visually deictic anchoring.[1]

Perhaps this refusal to allow the anchoring power of illumination and of the visual into the Foi domain of voice during ordinary, quotidian public discourse is what sets the stage for the heightened focus on the visual during ceremonial performances of the memorial songs, the *sorohabora* (see J. Weiner 1991). During these dances, the decorated dancers range themselves along the central corridor of the longhouse. The spectators sit between the fireplaces along the sides, holding torches and flares and kerosene lamps. At this time, all eyes are focused on the bodies of the male singers. The singers themselves perform their songs simultaneously, each group – and there may be twelve or more such groups on such a night – singing their songs in a drawn-out round. The possibility of hearing any one song, unless one is standing right next to the performers (as I have myself when recording these songs) is remote. Here the voices of men serve as a background for their own visual and kinaesthetic embodiment.

The longhouse on these occasions can be considered as one collective moment of public, embodied seeing – perhaps we can call it a distributive panoptic, a spatial configuration that allows a communal but *uncentred* viewing of that which visually marks the potency, temporality and sociality of Foi males. When I say it is embodied, I mean this in at least two senses, neither of which is less literal than the other. First, of course, the act of viewing and gazing is focused on the male human body, specifically the body engaged in one of its most culturally salient vocalacoustemic activities. Secondly, the longhouse itself is a body, the body of the mythical hunter Yibumena, and enhouses the act of seeing within its own human form (see J. Weiner 1991).

We might then consider that the condition of seeing in Foi is always conditional upon a prior embodiment, an already-figured condition of containment that makes socially apprehensible the embodied nature of subjectivity itself in Foi. This would bring an examination of Foi viewing very much into line with what Lacan called the Imaginary:

> A description of the Imaginary will therefore on the one hand require us to come to terms with a uniquely determinate configuration of space – one not yet organized around the individuation of my own personal body, or differentiated hierarchically according to the perspectives of my own central point of view – yet which nonetheless swarms with bodies and forms intuited in a different way, whose fundamental property is, it would seem, to be visible without their visibility being the result of any particular observer, to be, as it were, already-seen, to carry their specularity upon themselves like a color they wear or the texture of their surface. (Jameson 1977: 354–5).

We would also be close to the distinction that Foucault claims between seeing and the condition of visibility:

> . . . the conditions pertaining to visibility are not the way in which a subject sees: the subject who sees is himself a place within visibility, a function derived from visibility . . . (Deleuze 1988: 57).

What then is the relationship between sound, language and vision, and what theoretical resources beyond the phenomenological must we bring to bear to articulate this relationship? Feld observes that there is an overaching Kaluli aesthetic that makes itself apparent across all sensory modalities:

> When [the drum] is 'talking,' *tolan*, it is saying *dowo*, 'father,' and the sound is 'hard' in both the linguistic and aesthetic senses of that metaphor. Similarly, aesthetic evaluation concentrates on the 'hardness' of the drum sound as it 'carries,' *ebelan*. This verb is usually used to describe water motion that is visually evident at one place but then flows out of sight. This carrying property extends to indicate continual auditory sensation and feeling beyond the production of sound (1986: 94).

> The auditory sensation [of the Kaluli drum] is a shifting figure and ground, with strong sense images of the octaves at C and c, and their inner fifth at G (1986: 83) . . . Concretely, it is the moment when the throbbing drum voice is

no longer heard as a bird voice calling *tibo tibo*, but is now heard, on the 'inside' reflection, as a dead child calling *dowo dowo*, 'father, father.' This is the moment when Kaluli listeners are completely absorbed by the sound, reflecting on its inner meaning rather than its outer form . . . The sensation of hearing the voice of a bird 'inside' the sound of the drum, and then hearing a further reflection, the voice of the spirit child coming through the voice of the bird to call 'father,' relates powerfully to the octave and fifth shift (1986: 94).

Goldman also makes an argument for a confederation of sensory modalities in his compelling discussion of Huli expressive strategies:

> The systematic ordering and classification of phenomena accords with the spatially and conceptually defined spheres of *anda* ('house, inside, private'): *hama* ('cleared ground, public'). This environmental categorization is central to the organization and production of most activities in Huli and Duna . . . *Anda* and *hama* are . . . inextricably bound to the sexual distinction. *Anda* signifies the private world of domestic activities and arrangements, the unseen, unrecorded, and 'covert' . . . *Hama* represents the epideictic arena, a forum for the presentation of self and display . . . The Huli conceive an identity between display modes of decoration, exchange of pigs, and oratory, all of which demand the use of 'high-valued' items. These three spheres provide a unitary source of metaphor and figurative allusion in which one's talk is equated with one's decoration, or pigs are symbolically identified with wigs . . . Pigs, paint and parlance are all substances used when 'coming outside' to present oneself through display (Goldman 1983: 101, 102).

In all these examples, we find an acceptance of the transposability of sight and sound, and particularly, of seeing and speaking. It is this transposability that lies at the heart of the phenomenological approach, whether we find it in linguistics, psychoanalysis, or anthropology:

> Seeing, for both [psychoanalysis and existential, semiotic phenomenology], leads to speaking, although each discipline relates seeing and speaking differently, making of Lacanian psychoanalysis (grounded in language) a *phenomenological semiotics* and of Merleau-Ponty's existential philosophy (grounded in embodiment) a *semiotic phenomenology* (Sobchack 1992: 99).

As Marcus and Fischer note, at the end of *Sound and Sentiment* Feld resorts to visual representation, photographs, to capture a sense of the key image of Kaluli life, that of a bird turning into a man, which he had up to that point described chiefly in its acoustic and musical dimensions. They conclude, 'there is, then, no absolute comprehending of other

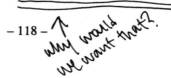
why would we want that?.

*— set yourself up for failure*

cultural experience, only degrees (1986: 64). But might we now want to make the same argument *within* a culture: Can we not argue by the same appeal to the limits of perception and interpretational strategies that our sight cannot convey what our words tell us, and our language cannot put into words what our sight encompasses? *— words can't speak on their own*

Here is where Merleau-Ponty, Heidegger and Foucault converge, for it is a relationship to which all three turned their attention: what is the relationship between seeing and speaking? How are things made visible: through language, or through vision or through some dialectical relationship between the two? Or is there an unbreachable scission between seeing and speaking, such that we can never see what we speak about and will always deny what we see? What then are the conditions of possibility of sight and of communicative praxis? And more broadly, in any given context, what is the site of revelation and what is the counterposed and correlative site of concealment? Does sight reveal what language hides, or vice versa . . . or could it be both at once? Are sight and speech then the limiting form of each other? Finally, how does the articulation of these sensory limits create the spaces wherein perspective, meaning, space and time emerge as phenomenal aspects of any particular mode of being in the world?

Here is where Heidegger's concern with the processes of 'sheltering' and 'concealing' is especially useful. The notion of a 'clearing', or *lichtung*, literally, a 'lighting', was very important in *Being and Time*, and there it was nothing less than ecstatic temporality itself: the being-outside-of-oneself that allowed the possibility of temporality, perspective and the interpretational mode of questioning. We can certainly, in our conventional anthropological manner, see the space and time of such communal ceremonial as the Kaluli *gisalo*, and the Foi *sorohabora*, as ec-static, 'outside time', in that sense: that although they are always within 'practical' time, they serve to create a focusing and enhancement of the expressivist potential of voice and body image; a space of reflection and interpretation on the mundane and the taken-for-granted that practical life cannot and does not.

Heidegger, in his meditations on Being, wanted us to consider that 'illuminating' something like Being was made possible by the act of *bergen*: a prior *sheltering* from the light (Heidegger, 'Logos', in *Early Greek Thinking*; see Krell 1986: 92). In *Being and Time*, Heidegger says '*Dasein is its disclosedness*' (*BT* 1962: 133). And being disclosed (*erschlossenheit*) is something more than being merely visible: it is for something to be preserved in such a way that its own modes of lighting and concealing are made possible. Deleuze says:

Visibilities are not to be confused with elements that are visible or more generally perceptible, such as qualities, things, objects, compounds of objects. In this respect Foucault constructs a function that is no less original than that of the statement. We must break things open. Visibilities are not forms of objects, nor even forms that would show up under light, but rather forms of luminosity which are created by the light itself and allow a thing or object to exist only as a flash, a sparkle or shimmer (Deleuze 1988: 52).

This is why we must also pay attention to the act of enclosure, enhousement, of embodiment in societies such as that of the Foi and Kaluli, as the creation of an 'inside' of vision and viewing contrasted with the exterior space of sound and movement. To see in this special sense of seeing to the heart of something means penetrating to its inside, to see below the surface. Vision for the Foi is not a thing of surfaces but of revealed interiors. We might then consider all Foi acts and artefacts of containment or enhousement as possessing the potential for a visible revealing of interiors of this sort (see J. Weiner 1995a; M. Strathern 1991).

Morphy speaks of the 'Light of the *Wangarr*', the Yolngu creator beings (1991: 193). He refers to the Yolngu aesthetic of 'shimmering' or *bir'yun*: '*bir'yun* is the flash of light – the sensation of light that one gets and carries away in one's mind's eye, from a glance at the *likanbuy miny'tji*' (1991: 194). This shimmering or lightning effect is what gives a Yolngu painting ancestral power. Again, the manifest effect of this lightning is also linked to its protection from unrestricted gaze: women and children must not see paintings that exhibit *bir'yun*. Thus, Yolngu brilliance is made possible by a sheltering or enclosing of its effects, socially and spatially.[2]

We must consider extroversion as a process of the revelation of social knowledge, and in this respect, Papua New Guineans evince as much of a preoccupation with bringing the inside to the exterior as Foucault demonstrates a preoccupation with how the outside folds in upon itself to produce an interior, how the Self is, as it were, an invaginated form of the Other. This is most vividly exemplified in the Abelam initiation ceremony. According to Losche, the Abelam term *wut* refers to womb, a woman's netbag, and the bark paintings that cover the walls of the men's ceremonial longhouse.

> The term signifies the ability of particular forms to intrinsically give forth from a hidden interior. During initiations the haus tambaran is conceived of as a container into which initiates crawl. Once inside, this interior is itself divided into a series of rooms or niches created by painted or plaited walls which are also called by the generic term *wut*. During construction the builders

emphasize the fact that the walls have two sides, one of which is spectacular, bright, revelatory and seductive but whose power and very existence depends on the other, the dark and invisible interior. The structure of initiations over time is also conceived as a set of layered sequences which builds up a cyclical, potentially infinite series of revealed and secret components based on the notion of the simultaneity of covering and uncovering, visibility and invisibility (Losche 1995: 55).[3]

The creation of invisibility, of limits to the social consequences of sight, are just as important as the conscious attempts to channel and control visibilities. With this in mind, I conclude with anthropology's most concerted recent attempt to inscribe subjectivity as the central question of anthropology.

## Notes

1. Helliwell reports the same phenomenon among the Gerai Dayaks of Borneo within their communal longhouse:

   'It can be seen that the partitions separating one *lawang* from another include within their very structure the possibility of the merging of household and community spaces. The permeability of these partitions may be seen as symbolising the nature of human interactions taking place across them; but at the same time they generate and reinforce those interactions by allowing an almost unimpeded flow of light and sound' (Helliwell 1989: 11).

2. Heidegger 1975: 'Seeing is determined, not by the eye, but by the lighting of Being. Presence within the lighting articulates all the human sense' ('The Animaxander Fragment', in *Early Greek Thinking*, p. 36).

3. Hirsch also makes a case for containment as a necessary condition for Fuyuge temporality:

   'Each home then is a realisation of *gab* that have occurred, or are occuring, or are anticipated. The accumulation and concentration of what we see as wealth is the outcome of coercive strategies whereby persons and collectivities of persons reveal and compare their capacities. It is the way in which capacities are hidden and revealed that is the key aesthetic issue for the

Fuyuge. It is an aesthetic issue because the process of revelation is evaluated to see if the hidden capacities appear in an appropriate manner. The manner in which the foregrounded experiences of place and the background horizon of space come to form a single potentiality in the *gab* (that is, to anticipate one another) is achieved through specific processes: of people making visible their capacities in one context to debate or in another context to assemble pigs and dancers, money, pearl shells, etc. These are not necessarily two forms of wealth but two different realisations of the way in which units come into existence' (Hirsch 1995: 68).

# 9

# On Televisualist Anthropology:
# Representation, Aesthetics, Politics

The effacement of memory is more the achievement of an all-too-wakeful consciousness than it is the result of its weakness in the face of the superiority of unconscious processes. In this forgetting of what is scarcely past, one senses the fury of the one who has to talk himself out of what everyone else knows, before he can talk them out of it.

— T. Adorno (1991)

In a paper entitled 'Culture and Media: A Mild Polemic' presented in England and Australia in 1994, Faye Ginsburg argued for anthropological interest in the videos that indigenous and minority people are currently producing themselves. On the face of it, one could not possibly dispute the anthropological importance of such an interest. I share with Professor Ginsburg an interest in exploring the ways in which media technology is altering the terms of cultural articulation in general in the world today. But for me there was a single problem that condenses everything that disenchants me not only about this whole phenomenon but also about what I perceive as the inability to bring to it a critical perspective: the examples of indigenous video and film she showed us seemed inept, trivial, superficial; they were bad to the point of embarrassment, in whatever way one wants to define that – as art, as ethnography, as documentary, as technique, or as composition.

Now in making this judgement of taste I realize I am violating a still powerful unwritten rule of social analysis; that we suspend such judgements in favour of something more like evaluation, in Jameson's terms[1]: trying 'to keep alive (or reinvent) assessments of a sociopolitical kind that interrogate the quality of social life itself by way of the text or individual work of art . . .' (1991: 298), and moreover, to wed this kind of evaluation to analysis, which he describes as a rigorous investigation of the historical and cultural conditions of possibility of specific forms such as these (ibid.). It seems that an earlier anthropology did not have to confront this issue of taste, since we automatically dignified the products of cultural production of our hosts as a result of their very alienness and inscrutability. I don't seem to recall that we anthropologists ever had the same confrontation with what I cannot resist terming 'culture schlock' when we were studying things like rituals and ceremonies. Perhaps the terms of their constitution, display and performance were so different from our own that we did not know enough about them to judge them in that way, though we were always able to elicit much from the people themselves about whether such performances were effective or not as social events.[2]

But we all know quite a bit about video, and we are infinitely more familiar with the kinds of effects it has on us, on our socialized perceptual and imaginistic faculties, and we are all adept these days at turning issues of social and political discrimination into aesthetic judgements and vice versa (the popular form of historical analysis has become the comparison between, for example, the 1950s image of American family life we get from *Leave it to Beaver* and the 1980s version we get from *Murphy Brown*). After all, even bad art has its place in the current interpretative, cultural scheme of things, everything from *Dallas* to McDonalds is grist for the cultural-critical mill, and, Bourdieu notwithstanding, perhaps we should all be grateful for the reaction we have to bad art, bad film and bad literature, lest we forget why we search for its opposite. On the other hand, if there is something about the televisual medium that lends itself to the proliferation of products, ethnic, ethnographic, documentary, experimental or otherwise, too unbearably bad or embarrassingly crude to watch, then perhaps there is more to this medium than meets the eye!

I wish I could show the readers of this chapter the clips that Ginsburg showed the audience in both live versions of the paper; but as is this is not possible, I will have to make do with a textual recreation of them (keeping in mind, however, that at the end of this exercise, we might find reason to prefer a written account over the visual). One of the clips, which was from the film entitled *Qaggiq*, produced by the Inuit man Zacharias Kunuk, seemed to be a dramatization of a marriage negotiation between a young man and his fiancée's recalcitrant father. I hope I was not the only one who found the 'acting' in this clip so incredibly stiff and self-conscious that there was a point where I thought the poor Inuit actors were going to faint, and what was worse, I found myself praying for such an end to the clip, so excruciating did I find the act of viewing it. Now if this is the reaction we have to these films, then to what extent is it effectively telling us about or portraying something critical about Inuit social relations, and further, in what way is the presence of the camera responsible for their portrayal in the form that we saw? Is the camera passively recording these relationships, or more actively creating them through its particular mediatory capacities? Is there something I need to know about the tenor and shape of Inuit social engagement that would allow me to see this portrayed interaction differently or perhaps from my point of view more effectively? And how would that be conveyed to me, apart from an explanatory passage beforehand?

That explanatory passage I refer to is no more nor less than the critical ethnographic background to the film, and in such a case we would desire that the anthropologist perform the same role that we expect of the successful film critic: we want him/her to tell us something about the film that we cannot see for ourselves. We confront at the outset the phenomenological/critical understanding: that film, like all our other artworks, never stands alone – it is always constituted in a relation to the verbal, the narrative and the textual, which gives it its hermeneutical contours and which in dialectical fashion provides the limits of its interpretational ambience. In short, our textual or critical constitution of the film is not something external to the film itself. For as Pinney reminds us in a Heideggerian vein, 'To raise the possibility of the "picture" is to presuppose a frame' (1992a: 45); and the frame in this case is the 'ethnography', generally speaking.

To position ethnography in this way is already to situate it as a theoretical enterprise – our textual account of the film is not a mere rendering of it in verbal terms, but is a far more critical, dynamic counter-point, given that it seeks to account for the film's effects in an entirely different *medium*. But Ginsburg asserts to the contrary that 'The variety and particularity revealed by [ethnographic] research is a necessary corrective to grand theorising that loses touch with the specific, embedded and diverse ways that people use media to make sense of their worlds and, most importantly, to construct new ones' (1994: 14).

This world that indigenous and Third World people are trying to make sense of has been well described by Homi Bhabha. No longer are social and cultural differences guaranteed by an appeal to an authentic cultural tradition; instead, such differences 'are the signs of the emergence of *community envisaged as a project – at once a vision and a construction* – that takes you "beyond" yourself in order to return, in a spirit of revision and reconstruction, to the political *conditions* of the present' (1994: 3, emphasis added).

In Bhabha's formulation I find a curious appeal to history in the very act of denying it any purchase on one's theorizing. I therefore do not find it coincidental that one of the many contentious comments Fredric

Jameson has made about video is that it 'blocks its own theorisation becoming a theory in its own right' (1991: 71):

> . . . in a situation of total flow, the contents of the screen streaming before us all day long without interruption . . . what used to be called 'critical distance' seems to have become obsolete. Turning the television off has little in common either with the intermission of a play or an opera or with the grand finale of a feature film, when the lights slowly come back on and memory begins its mysterious work. Indeed, if anything like critical distance is still possible in film, it is surely bound up with memory itself. But memory seems to play no role in television . . . (1991: 70).

Perhaps memory itself is a function of juxtaposing two different forms of language, two different interpretative modalities, two different forms of mediation itself – at least this is what psychoanalysis has always maintained, confronted with its task of memoriation.[3] But it would seem that Ginsburg is here appealing to 'ethnography' as a means of diverting our attention from the historicity of her particular mode of questioning. We should point out that the issue of the relation between aesthetics and politics has a long pedigree, that it has already been played out within German Marxism through the debates between Adorno, Lukács, Bloch, Benjamin and Brecht earlier this century (Adorno, Bloch, *et al.* 1977). I might find it helpful to refer to certain claims that were made about art, representation and polity in the course of these debates, if only to point out how similar claims have been appealed to by the proponents of indigenous video.

Perhaps theory, then, is the label we give to the effect of this historical positioning, given that it simultaneously reframes the mode of interpretation as well as the thing being interpreted, and does so in a way that preserves the temporality and historical situatedness of our mode of questioning. It could be that the constructionist underpinning of Ginsburg's and Terry Turner's approach to indigenous representation is left unquestioned by virtue of the resistance of film and video to theory. And so, at the risk of losing touch with Ginsburg's world, I am going to defer to what she would label 'grand theory' in order to establish contact with the world of non-Western camera-users. For I totally reject the notion that ethnographic research stands outside theory. Every social science methodology has a theory inscribed within it, and it is the peculiar nature of social science's reflexive effect that it must constantly make this theory visible. In fact, it is this realization that is the theme of this chapter: that if, as Ginsburg asserts, we cannot consider the formal properties of a film apart from the social relations that constituted its formation, no less can we consider visual representation apart from (a) the theory embedded in the textual narrative that accompanies and explains the film; and (b) the particular metaphysic that is reposited in our image-producing technology, a metaphysic that is just as much a part of our culture and the social relations through which we live it and just as accurately descriptive of it as the *djukurba*, or 'Law' or 'Dreaming' is a theory of Walbiri culture. A recognition of the theoretical lineaments of one's mode of questioning is what allows a social analysis to be properly dialectical, and hence provides the possibility of some real social and historical insight.

As Ginsburg herself notes, the camera does not provide merely a '"window" on reality, a simple expansion of our powers of observation', but 'a creative tool in the service of a new signifying practice' (1991: 93). But although, as technology, it is 'present to us only as the phenomenal form of a relation with other people' (Cubitt 1991: 15) – and here we might again point to the necessity of dialectical thinking right at the outset – we as Westerners mask or repress this relational constitution of such technology. And if this is true, the same goes for our other artforms as well. By this reasoning we must then conclude that film is no more – nor less – genuine, and hence *stylized*, a depiction of 'real social relations' than the combination of secco recitative and da capo aria was of emotions and their relational constitution in the Cartesian world of George Friedrich Handel.

From this vantage point, I want to speculate on the effects of media such as film or video on cultures that, in ways reminiscent of our own medieval forebears, have a very different relation to the whole question of representation than ours does. If it is insisted that we see new identities – interstitial, hybrid, subaltern, embedded – as emerging from a deliberate effort at construction, signing and visioning, then it is still anthropology's task to remind us of those traditions for which such processes are not a matter of human action and intention but are immanent in the world itself and not under direct human control. I am therefore interested at first in the transition from the medieval to the modern, if only because it has been commented on so extensively by Martin Heidegger, in whose existential phenomenology I locate a serious exploration of the Western foundations of representation, visualism and subjectivity. I argue that these foundations are integral to the filmic media themselves, as we must agree they are if we are to accept that they are cultural products through and through, and that these foundations could be opposed to and even subversive of non-Western modes of knowledge and its acquisition, revelation and articulation.

The issue is not, however, just one of representation as such. Anthropologically, it concerns the status of social relationality and the manner in which it is represented; whether the representation of relationality belongs to it properly speaking, or stands outside it, as an external commentary on it; whether the representations are constitutive of the relations they depict, or, if not, whether an external perspective on social relations is nevertheless necessary to them at some other level.

I would like to explore these questions by examining the role of film media in anthropology, both as a tool of our own ethnographic craft, and as an object of our ethnographic inspection. With respect to the latter, I am especially interested in indigenously-produced films and videos and also more broadly in what is termed Third Cinema or Third World cinema. I consider a nexus of politics, culture and self-identity within which, so it is maintained by anthropologists such as Faye Ginsburg, the medium of film and video play an integral role. I argue that special issues pertaining to representation and self-representation emerge in the consideration of the role of film in cultural articulation and in our anthropological constitution of it. I want also to raise questions concerning the relationship between different modes of representation and the objects created by representational practices and technologies. And finally, I want to raise once again the question Eric Michaels asked with respect to the non-Western world of Australian Aborigines: 'What is the cost of failing to describe the signifying practices of our cultural subjects in explicit comparison to our own signifying practices?' (1994: 133).[4]

## The Work of Revelation and Elicitation

A woodcut made by Michael Ostendorfer around 1520 shows a crowd of religious pilgrims surrounding the statue of the Madonna, the *Schöne Maria of Regensburg*, which had been set up to commemorate a miracle said to have occurred on the site. The fervour surrounding the popular veneration of this statue aroused the negative reaction among some of Strasburg's citizens:

> It also troubles us, since no scriptures say it is right, that there is that evil idol in the choir of the cathedral, which is not only a blasphemous offence to many of our people in the city, but to all people in the whole region. For every day one sees people kneeling before it, and praying to it, while these same people obstinately refuse to pay attention to God's Word as it is preached to them (in Chrisman 1967: 148).

The good burghers of Strasburg, the founding fathers of our current ambivalently iconoclastic late-twentieth-century Western culture, thus displayed their exasperation at the unenlightened masses who refused to see the statue as a *work of art*, a medium with a message, and insisted on seeing it in medieval terms, as an *epiphany*, a manifestation of divine power. For the supplicants, the statue made visible some aspect of an unseen world; as a statue, as a *mediating artefact*, it took a particular form and shaped the nature of communication with that world through that form. It was not a work of art as much as it was an embodied *poiesis*. More importantly, we cannot, from this evidence, conclude that the statue had the same representational function for the (medieval) supplicants as it did for the emerging moderns, the Reformist burghers of Strasbourg and elsewhere in sixteenth-century Europe.

Walter Benjamin, in his seminal article 'The Work of Art in the Age of Mechanical Reproduction' (1968), argues that the ritual 'use-value' of art works was their most important feature before the advent of techniques of mass reproduction. 'By the absolute emphasis on its cult value', he wrote, the work of art 'was first and foremost an instrument of magic' (1968: 225). He goes on:

> One may assume that what mattered was their existence, not their being on view. The elk portrayed by the man of the Stone Age on the walls of his cave was an instrument of magic. He did expose it to his fellow men, but in the main it was meant for the spirits. Today the cult value would seem to demand that the work of art remain hidden. Certain statues of gods are accessible only to the priest in the cella; certain Madonnas remain covered nearly all year round; certain sculptures on medieval cathedrals are invisible to the spectator on ground level (ibid.).

Turning now to the non-Western world, in many parts of Papua New Guinea the strategy of public discourse is precisely *not* to reveal things – secret or non-public names, magic spells, origin myths, etc. This is found in a most highly developed form among the Manambu of the East Sepik River region, and has been described by Simon Harrison in his book *Stealing People's Names* (1990). The Avatip engage in formal debates where the object is for a subclan to demonstrate that it possesses the secret names of a disputed ancestor. 'By doing so it proves, by implication, that it alone is capable of performing the associated magic' (1990: 153). But since to reveal the names is the very act of demonstrating that one possesses the knowledge and its power, the debate is conducted in a series of whispers between the most senior men of the two disputing groups.

This phenomenon of making something secret in the midst of the most public, communal instances of discourse, is very common in Papua New Guinea. The Foi and other interior New Guinea people make use of metaphorical, allusive language, which is known by men of high status and renown, but not known by other men. Through knowing what the allusions are, through knowing the restricted code, these men of status can converse amongst themselves in public without other men's knowing what they are talking about.

The Avatip thus seek *not* to reveal names and knowledge. Their reasoning seems to be that if people know what you know, the precise identification of ownership could become the opportunity for raids, thefts and the pre-emption of knowledge itself, all of which could be used tactically against others. Discursive strategies then become to force others to reveal these names or other items of restricted knowledge. Such an approach to talk and to the act of 'saying' or revealing does not then support any simple constructivist or mediational approach to knowledge, or one in which public representation and mediation is one of its central constitutive mechanisms. It is my contention that it is precisely this non-constructionist approach to saying, revealing and knowing that is the hardest thing to convey to Westerners who are dazzled by the realism, im-mediacy and power of filmic representation.

In Chapter 2 I described the Foi word *mitina-*, which means 'to show' and which I literally translate as 'to cause to be released'. Not only is the act of seeing tantamount to possession in Papua New Guinea,[5] but the act of showing someone an item of property – a piece of land, a shell valuable, a pig, for example – is also tantamount to relinquishment. A Foi man who wishes passers-by to know that a garden is his property will leave a piece of leaf, usually from his totemic tree species, prominently displayed for all to see. This is not simply a communicative act, or if it is one, it does not function in a simple way. A Foi person coming across such a mark deduces the presence of certain beings and certain activities and intentions from it.

These approaches to revelation underscore the enormous importance attached to the very act of making something visible, whether visually or discursively, and the social restrictions that exist surrounding such practices of making visible. But we late-twentieth-century Westerners inhabit a thoroughly specularized as well as spectacularized society, a world in which the 'tendency *to make one see* the world by means of various specialized mediations . . . naturally finds vision to be the privileged human sense . . .' (Debord 1983: §18). In such a world, we are very much unaware of restrictions placed on seeing itself (see Jay 1992).

– 130 –

In general, when I think about what is embodied in certain features of the landscape in Aboriginal and New Guinea society and the relationship to this act of territorial embodiment and the discursive practice of myth that constitutes it, I feel that we confront something more akin to the medieval phenomenon of *epiphany* – the making visible of a manifestation of divine power, or in general, the unseen, the invisible, the unrepresentable. Van Baal said of the Marind-anim of south New Guinea that their myths are the form that the *dema*, that is, their ancestral creator beings, take in human language. Strategies for epiphanic manifestation – strategies to make such power reveal itself in certain ways – are what social life and ritual are about in these settings, and again, such strategies are not easily glossed by our conventional social constructionist idioms. The whole act of *signing* and of encountering signs must be seen not so much in strict communicative terms as the result of social *strategies of elicitation*.

When I speak of elicitation, I refer not just to a specific, non-representational approach to communication. I also appeal to the more general question of the way form is revealed in any given world of communicative convention. How would we describe the constitution of the effects of filmic communication in such terms? I now turn to the main subject of this chapter.

## The Medium and the Message

In examining the films produced by indigenous, non-Western film-makers about themselves, one of Faye Ginsburg's main points is that there is a relation between the social conditions of production of these filmic texts and their subject-matter:

> If we recognise the cinematic or video text as a mediating object – as we might look at a ritual or a commodity – then its formal qualities cannot be considered apart from the complex contexts of production and interpretation that shape its construction. Films embody in their own internal structure and meaning the forms and values of the social relations they *mediate*, making texts and context interdependent (1994: 6; emphasis added).

In response to this, I offer the following comments: First, the video text and the ritual are composed of and take place in completely different 'times'. Although it could be said in some cases that a ritual invokes and tries to make visible certain dimensions of 'mythic' time, in its practical constitution it is coterminous with the temporal life of the community whose members engage in it. The scenes in a video or cinematic text, on the other hand, are 'never coterminous with the length of such moments in real life' (Jameson 1991: 74). Nor can we solve the problem by comparing the practices of *viewing* or *producing* the video text with the ritual, because it is precisely the gap between video/cinematic text, production, and viewing that we do not find in ritual: the production and viewing of the ritual *are* the ritual. (Inasmuch as, in the case of many rituals, everyone in a community participates in some form or another, its status as mediating 'object' cannot be accepted *prima facie*).[6]

The recognition of this gap leads to the second problem. There is a most crucial ambiguity in Ginsburg's assertion. To which social relations is Ginsburg referring? Those at large in a social system, which are now mediated by film? Or are they specifically the relations between producer and viewer, or consumer, that is, the social relations of production of the film? It is a foundation of anthropology's approach to the issue of social representation that a ritual models, or stands in some relation to, the social world in which it is embedded. If we are to employ this analogy in its strict sense, then the social relations the films portray, even if not of these productive relations themselves, must of necessity be imaged in their terms.

I think it is important to point out that Ginsburg employs an essentially Marxist framework to describe these productive relations, for it indicates where this debate is anchored within the current characterization of postmodernity and anthropology's place in and relation to it. What differentiates social constructionism from a dialectical analysis is precisely the manner in which totality is appealed to. Georg Lukács in his critical treatment of early twentieth-century Expressionism remarked that:

> The underlying unity, the totality, all of whose parts are objectively interrelated, manifests itself most strikingly in the fact of crisis. Marx gives the following analysis of the process in which the constituent elements necessarily achieve independence: 'Since they do in fact belong together, the process by means of which the complementary parts become independent must inevitably appear violent and destructive . . .'.[7]
>
> . . . In periods when capitalism functions in a so-called normal manner, and its various processes appear autonomous, people living within capitalist society think and experience it as unitary, whereas in periods of crisis, when the autonomous elements are drawn together into unity, they experience it as disintegration (Adorno *et al.* 1977: 32).

If we wish to characterize what have been called dialectical societies,[8] such as the Gê and Bororo, or the East Sepik River groups of Papua New Guinea, such as the Avatip, Chambri and Iatmul, we would have to consider a world in which it was not the totality of a culture or society that was the form of social objectification but rather the relations between its unarticulated components. From Lukács's point of view, the conventional articulation of such a social totality would resemble what he describes above as the unity through disintegration that characterizes capitalist society in its non-conventional periods of crisis. We would then have to say that constructionist and dialectical views of social process draw forth totality through opposed means. Therefore, behind the Marxist metonymy by which Ginsburg sees the relations of film production standing for the entirety of a social world[9] lies that particular constructionist appeal to totality that is not inscribed in dialectical analysis: the lure of the self-evident wholeness of the experiential and the phenomenal and the superior powers of film to capture this wholeness. The anthropological film-maker David MacDougall likewise says:

> The film image impresses us with its completeness . . . It is possible that the sense of completeness created by a film also lies in the richness of ambiguity of the photographic image . . . unlike words or even pictographs, [photographic images] share in the physical identity of the objects . . . (1992: 117).

But the whole of social life also includes the concealments, the gaps in knowledge, and the turnings-away that make nescience a positive component of social knowledge.[10] And how are these gaps to be recorded or reproduced by our representational media? Iris Jean-Klein, in her account of social life in the occupied West Bank, described the dilemma of an American photographer who arrived with a group of visiting Western students whom she accompanied to the town of Ramallah. He could find nothing to photograph, nothing that visibly or graphically represented a community in the midst of political struggle, or an indigenous people in the process of cultural and political self-assertion. He and other members of the group did not know what they were being shown. What the photographer was commenting on, Jean-Klein says, was the *absences* that had become salient and noticeable to outside observers. She puts it thus:

> . . . we were presented with glimpses of 'routine' and yet, concurrently (and more paradoxically) we were shown glimpses of 'routine suspended'. These qualities were contrived in part by reference to 'gaps' and absences of various qualities . . . (1993: 124).

Hence, when Collier makes a similar pronouncement: '. . . *only* film or video can record the realism of time and motion or the psychological

of interpersonal relations' (1986: 144), apart from the
...lity of film and video recording 'real time', I submit that
...ment can only be made on the assumption that the act of
...not at the same time an act of transfiguration, and the more
... medium, the more total the depicted object is transfigured –
...is precisely the property of video that in bringing-forth the
co... ...ions of its own production as subject-matter, it conceals this very
transfiguring effect (something I will return to at the end of this chapter).
I would at this point endorse Adorno's early observation that 'there is
even reason to believe that the more closely pictures and words are coordinated, the more emphatically their intrinsic contradiction and the
actual mutedness of those who seem to be speaking are felt by the
spectators'.[11] More to the point, there is no reason why an appeal to
realism *as film technique*, which is all that Collier could be laying claim
to, should be privileged as representational strategy over, say, montage.[12]
As the German film producer Alexander Kluge put it:

> If I conceive of realism as the knowledge of relationships, then *I must provide
> a trope for what cannot be shown in the film, for what the camera cannot
> record*. This trope consists in the contrast between two shots, which is only
> another way of saying montage. At issue here are the concrete relations
> between two images. Because of the relationship which develops between
> two shots, and to the degree that movement (the so-called cinematic) is
> generated between such shots, information is hidden in the cut which would
> not be contained in the shot itself. This means that montage has its object
> something qualitatively quite different from raw material (Kluge 1981–2: 218–
> 19, emphasis added).

I thus take issue with Ginsburg's and Collier's assertions: If film con-
veys to us 'the real', how literally are we to take that, if we must admit
that 'the real' as such is inaccessible to us? And if in our everyday life,
the real is inaccessible, then in what realm does convention, which we
do 'know', reside? Would it not be more accurate to say that film, like
other works of art, like rituals and myths, and most of all like opera, does
not convey 'the real' but rather something like 'the truth' of convention,
which is to say, the revelation of its caricatured form?[13] And can we not
then affirm Adorno's words: 'Art is the social antithesis of society'?

## Visualism and Subjectivity

The main issue that arises now is the problematic status of both representation and subjectivity in the context of non-Western traditions. Given social

science's current concern with these issues with respect to characterizing its position within the phenomenon labelled postmodernity, I consider the problems raised by Ginsburg to be important. I speak as someone who has taken seriously the programme of Marcus and Fischer that they label cultural critique (1986). As does James Faris (1992), I do not think we can consider the issue of indigenous film-making without simultaneously situating it alongside a critique of the filmic medium itself. Film is put forth as a guarantor of both the subjectivity and the autonomy of the film-maker and as a useful and powerful medium of representation and self-representation for non-Western people. I think it is fair, however, to question: (a) whether the people of such traditions were interested in articulating the subject or the subjective; and (b) whether their modes of relational articulation could themselves be labeled representational. In short, I wonder whether our anthropological informants and hosts come from traditions much more like that of our medieval forebears than our current modern one.

Martin Heidegger first raised these issues in powerful form earlier this century. He took note of what we could call in Foucault's terms an epistemic shift between the medieval and the modern periods. It was with the dawn of the modern age that European society arrived at the notion that the world in its entirety could be pictured or represented. For Parmenides, but also for our medieval forebears, 'man is the one who is looked upon by that which is' (Heidegger 1977a: 131), whereas in the modern age, 'that which is . . . come[s] into being . . . through the fact that man first looks upon it, in the sense of a representing that has the character of a subjective perception' (ibid.). Hence, Heidegger remarks that 'the world picture does not change from an earlier medieval one into a modern one, but rather the fact that the world becomes picture at all is what distinguishes the essence of the modern age' (Heidegger 1977b: 130). Guy Debord, characterizing the 'society of the spectacle', notes in similar terms that:

> The spectacle cannot be understood as an abuse of the world of vision, as a product of the techniques of mass dissemination of images. It is, rather, a *Weltanschauung* which has become actual, materially translated. It is a world vision which has become objectified (1983: §5).

Heidegger accurately identified this shift to totalizing picturing as underwriting the emergence of subjectivity itself: '. . . to represent means to bring what is present at hand before oneself as something standing over against, to relate it to oneself, to the one representing it, and to force it back into this relationship to oneself as the normative realm' (1977b: 131).[14] Thus, as Foucault notes, what is made possible by this is not just a relation of subject to perceived objective world; this *external* dualism also finds its *internal* form as *the subject's relation to him/herself* (Foucault 1973).

How would we address this transition in an anthropological context, and specifically with respect to the role of film? Eric Michaels has I feel correctly identified the crux of the matter:

> . . . there is no necessary translation from orality to electronics; we are seeing instead an experimental phase involving the insertion of the camera into the social organisation of events. *The point is the necessity of locating such a position for the camera* (1986: 65, emphasis added).

What Ginsburg and others fail to do is distinguish between *the representation of relations* and *a relation to representative praxis*. This is brought out most vividly when Ginsburg refers to the statement of the Kayapo video maker Mokuka (quoted from Eaton 1992):

> Just because I hold a white man's camera, that doesn't mean I am not a Kayapo . . . if you were to hold one of our head-dresses, would that make you an Indian? (Ginsburg 1994: 9)

Mokuka might sympathize with Jameson's remark that 'no one seems to have asked the Ayatollah whether the use of audio-cassettes marked a corrupt surrender to Western technology and values' (1992: 117), although, unlike the Kayapo, modern day Iranian society is in a more completed stage of modernization. But besides, the observation that Mokuka has made a category mistake here – properly phrased, his question should be reversibly posed back to him in this way: 'If you were to hold one of our cameras, would that make you a *film-maker*?' – I wish to make two other points with respect to Mokuka's pronouncement: (1) Is it not an assertion that the *essence* of culture is not affected by the medium through which it is made visible? And does it not therefore controvert what Ginsburg is trying to say about the intertextuality of indigenous media and their reflexive, relational constitution? Does it not then argue *against* the transformative power of film, or at least against its superior powers *vis-à-vis* other representational media, saying that no matter how radical a transformative effect through its technique and embodied representational praxis we attribute to film and its technology, the constitutive mechanisms and relational practices of non-Western society will nevertheless remain unaffected by it? (2) The difference between myself and Mokuka is that when I hold a Kayapo head-dress, I do not use it to constitute my self-identity, nor to negotiate that identity or construct an image of it for others. It is exactly this *differential social/existential relation to the camera and its technology* that spells the difference between myself and Mokuka.[15]

In her Australian version of this paper, Ginsburg distinguished what these indigenous video-makers are doing – that is, depicting their authentic social relations – from what any ordinary bourgeois Western video owner does when he or she (mostly he's, I would say, judging from my most casual inspection of weekend crowds in various parts of the Western world) makes footage of home, holiday and other events and occasions of his/her social life. Westerners, she seemed to be saying, through their video-making practices are not focusing on creating images of their cultural or social life, at least not for political purposes. But in what sense could Ginsburg possibly maintain that the video camera is not intimately involved in constituting and representing such bourgeois relationality? And who is to say that they don't do it as well or even better than the Kayapo or Inuit?[16] Bourdieu comments on the intimate relationship between such picturing and Western bourgeois relationality:

> The conventionality of attitudes towards photography appears to refer to the style of social relations favoured by a society which is both stratified and static and in which family and 'home' are more real than particular individuals, who are primarily defined by their family connections; in which the social rules of behaviour and the moral code are more apparent than the feelings, desires or thoughts of individual subjects; in which social exchanges, strictly regulated by consecrated conventions, are carried out under the constant fear of the judgement of others, under the watchful eye of opinion, ready to condemn in the name of norms which are unquestionable and unquestioned, and always dominated by the need to give the best image of oneself, the image most in keeping with the ideal of dignity and honour. How, under these conditions, could the representation of society be anything other than the representation of a *represented* society? (Bourdieu 1990a: 83–4).

But while this may be perfectly accurate as a description of the sacred role of the photograph in the European context that Bourdieu focuses on, I wonder whether the American bourgeois relationship to it is as solemn. In fact, as I watched the Inuit in their igloos struggling to appear spontaneous and natural (whatever that might mean for them) in front of the camera, I thought of the ease with which middle-class Westerners stand before the camera. First of all, Westerners can hardly walk into a bank, large department store or shopping mall without entering into the field of view of the now ubiquitous security camera. We are usually unaware of this discreet panoptical visual recording device and, if we were, we would hardly consider that what it records is anything resembling what we consciously and deliberately construct with the camera. But with regularity, we from time to time catch a glimpse of ourselves on a video monitor. What we see is ourselves with faces turned away (since the camera and the monitor are usually not facing in the same direction) even though we are looking at the monitor face on. We see ourselves looking at the monitor, not at our ourselves, or at the camera.

Not only do we picture this viewing relationship to ourselves in our public space; we are brought up from the day of our birth to pose in front of its eye, from the series of photographic prints that constitute the visual record of our development to the meters of video tape that capture our happy and festive occasions with family and friends. We do not just use this footage to mediate encounters with each other; we demonstrate an awareness of filmic sensibility in all these encounters with others.

We look through the viewfinder and the implement itself disappears from the frame that it creates. Technology keeps making it smaller and smaller, not to make it more portable as such but to make it more like a literal extension of the eye and hand. The camera seems to record without being visible for the most part. In this sense, the camera is *zuhanden*, in Heidegger's terms, 'ready-to-hand' or 'available'. We use it without attending to it as such, and our relationship to it cannot then be considered mediatory. We are in an unmediated relationship with a tool that nevertheless exercises a mediational function.[17]

But Western home video footage inevitably includes, if it can, the obligatory several seconds of the video holder being videoed by another video holder. And, inevitably, we the viewers oblige by laughing at this. The videomaker's *relationship to the camera* becomes an item of representation; the videomaker's *standing outside the very relationships s/he is caught in* is captured for a few seconds in this obligatorily funny interlude. In this way we know that what the camera produces is not a documentary record, nor is it constitutive *in the strict realist sense to which Collier defers* of the social relationships it is portraying.[18]

We make it deliberately parodic and exaggerated, for we learn to display that slightly self-mocking defensive clowning in front of the camera, the posing that says that what is captured is not the occasion, or the social relations that constitute it as event, but our own not-taking-it-seriously attitude towards them. Is this what we were seeing the Inuit engaged in? How would we recognize it if it were the case?

Perhaps it is this non-seriousness, this wilful refusal to make of the home video a serious political or cultural text, that causes Ginsburg to dismiss them, though again we can point to a judgement of taste unbalanced by a true evaluation. The home video-maker isn't making images *on behalf* of anyone in the marked political/cultural sense in which Ginsburg is interested. But then who exactly do the indigenous film-makers represent? On whose behalf do they speak?[19] Who authorizes them to produce these important texts of cultural identity? Are they merely some indigenous mirror version of ourselves, which is to say dilettantes, aesthetes and *auteurs-manqués* with the time and resources to worry about culture? Are they in the same position to their society as we imagine 'ritual experts' to be in such places as New Guinea and Africa? Or must we now revise our understanding of the traditional ritual expert, as something of a dilettante him- or herself? There is much to recommend such a revision. And I think that such authors as Ginsburg, Worth and Adair, Eric Michaels and Terry Turner are cognizant of the need to situate the project of contemporary visual and filmic image-making within a communal assessment and evaluatory praxis, and to make such situating part of the subject-matter.

Nevertheless, to compare the role of the camera in this bourgeois world with its role in the Inuit world strikes me as the central task at hand, and it is this task that receives no treatment from Ginsburg. In this unhesitating juxtaposition of images, image-making and framing we find the most convincing demonstration of the postmodern status of Ginsburg's project, a project that is less impressed by one of anthropology's more conventional modernist goals – to see within art an alienating doubling of the world – and more convinced of the self-signifying and equivalizing powers of the visual image in and of itself (see Jameson 1992: 96).[20] Is it unreasonable to speculate on the depth of understanding of Inuit society that is being sacrificed to make these filmic events stand forth?

These questions expose another critical ellipsis in Ginsburg's programme: nowhere in her description of this new space of film practice, its new social-cultural-political positioning, and its producers is there mention of aesthetics – and in fact, Eliot Weinberger (1994) in his mordant commentary identified art and aesthetics as the acknowledged bane of ethnographic film realism. It could be that in the face of the overwhelming ineffectiveness of many of these efforts, we must suspend aesthetic judgement on these films because they are made by people inexperienced both with the technology and its technique. In this case, we must, as Eric Michaels has done (1994: 114–15), explain why it is that Westerners might fail to see what is or is not being framed by non-Western video and film-makers. We could then instead see this failure not as adventitious to the medium but as inherent in the dissonance between a non-Western representational praxis and the one inscribed within the Western filmic. Nor do I necessarily refer to the kind of suspension of judgement that Bourdieu refers to with respect to Western family photographs:

> The taking and contemplation of the family photograph presuppose the suspension of all aesthetic judgement, because the sacred character of the object and the sacralizing relationship between the photographer and the picture are enough unconditionally to justify the existence of a picture which only really seeks to express the glorification of its object, and which realises its perfection in the perfect fulfilment of that function (Bourdieu 1990a: 90).

As Michaels further notes, both a 'failure to value and a banal overvaluation' are bad anthropological approaches to this phenomenon, and I think both postures are evident in current evaluations of indigenous film and video. By invoking the aesthetic I do not mean that we should *only* judge these to be good or bad *as films*; they are an instantiation of an aesthetic in so far as Ginsburg claims that they are now *the form in which social relations themselves are brought forth and made visible* (see J. Weiner 1993a, b; M. Strathern 1988). If exploring the interpretative dimensions of a social world is itself the manner of adducing the proper *form*, then it is an omission to not consider the aesthetic properties of these indigenous videos. Let us now do so.

Ginsburg recognizes that there is an incommensurability between the possibilities of representation enabled by film technology and those extant in non-Western societies. But where we differ is precisely on the *locus* of this incommensurability. Ginsburg says that '. . . the very *form* of Western narratives may undermine traditional modes' (1991: 97). From this point of view, we would have to agree with Cubitt's observation:

> Photocopying, video cameras and edit suites, computing and computer imaging are available for community use already. But those who try to appropriate each newly available technology for new purposes seem constrained to reproduce the patterns of textual production which the medium seems to demand . . .[21] Something of the 'technological' relation is deeply embedded, not simply as peer pressure, but as something far more deeply entrenched (1991: 19).

Ginsburg, along with other anthropologists, prefers, however, to make transparent the structural implications of the technological relationship themselves. For them, it is a matter of the different *styles* afforded by the medium. Ginsburg cites MacDougall (1987), who reports:

The dominant conflict structure of Western fictional narratives, and the didacticism of much of Western documentary, may be at odds with traditional modes of discourse . . . Differences may arise in the conventions of narrative and imagery. At a film conference in 1978, Wiyendji, an Aboriginal man from Roper River, argued against the Western preoccupation with close-ups and fast cutting, saying that Aborigines preferred to see whole bodies and whole events . . . Such objections obviously cry out for more Aboriginal filmmaking (1987: 54)

In a similar manner, Terry Turner has identified the stylistic difference between Western and non-Western film-making (1992):

We have tried to limit editing assistance and advice to *elementary technical procedures* of insertion and assembly, compatibility of adjacent cuts, use of cutaways and inserts, and avoiding abrupt camera movements or zooms. We have made no attempt to teach Western notions or styles of framing, montage, fast cutting, flashback or other narrative or anti-narrative modes of sequencing, nor have we sought to impose length constraints or other features that might render a video more accessible, or acceptable to a Western audience (1992: 7, emphasis added).

But surely this is tantamount to saying something like: 'We have taught them English grammar, syntax and semantics but have made no attempt to teach them the iambic pentameter, the sonnet, or the couplet.'

By its ability to shape our interest in information, television editing conventions and formats encourage a value system that emphasises fragmentation over continuity, repetition over diversity, and familiar messages over unfamiliar ones, all of it in 30-second bits instead of more sustained attentional patterns. It is this video legacy that has shaped modern American politics and business and religion and culture, not through the messages presented on television, but *through specific utilisations of the form and structure of the medium itself* (Hobbs 1991: 44, emphasis added).

I am suggesting, in other words, that the difference between Aboriginal and Western preferences for forms of filmic representation is situated one epistemological step too late. For it presupposes the rôle and function of the picture as self-representation and as a document of subjectivity, and it is this relational *eidos* of Western visualist culture that, as Raymond Williams pointed out long ago, itself *impelled* as well as was enabled by, the development of visual image technology.[22]

Moreover, in theatre or ritual one can always assume a vantage point from which the ritual or play can be seen as a contrivance (see Benjamin

1968: 233). But the camera eliminates this possibility for the viewer of film. To cry out for more indigenous film-making under such circumstances as MacDougall does in the Australian context would then be to cover over even more concertedly the Aboriginal mode of making-things-appear.

To return to an earlier point, we thus need constantly to attend to *theory*, the theory of representation, in order to determine whether modes of cinematic creation are serving to *erase* the pre-cinematic relation to the visual of indigenous and non-Western people. If the use of media technology offers a 'new opportunity for influence and self-expression' (Ginsburg 1991: 97), then surely we are justified in questioning whether *self-expression* was a component of the relational strategies of such people. Terry Turner argues that 'Kayapo culture possesses a well developed set of notions of mimesis and representation that antedate Western cultural influences, but which have also exerted their influence on Kayapo work in video and Kayapo representations of themselves in social and political interaction with the West' (1992: 9). While I feel this would make the Kayapo quite unique among Amazonian societies, judging from what, among others, Hugh-Jones and Reichel-Dolmatoff have written about the pre-contact Amazonian lifeworld,[23] I think what Turner is really trying to convey is more along the lines followed by Fry and Willis, who assert that film creates:

> a cultural space in which innovation is possible; it has a future. This is a new symbol of power in a culture dominated by the media. It doesn't override the effects of the damaged culture in which it functions, but creates a fissure in which a new set of perceptions can seep in (1989: 163).

Against this undeniably vital and useful perspective (though the idea of a *damaged culture* needs some careful thought here) must be balanced what is surely our *practical* understanding of the effect of film, that in the cinema, 'visual pleasure always triumphs over critical resolve' (Kaes 1989: 7).[24] I would like to pose two polemically oriented questions of my own here: (1) If cultural difference can now only take place within the arena of electronically generated visual and audio images, how much scope is there for the uncovering or revelation of such difference? How will we measure what kind of or how much cultural difference we find between, say, American and Soviet society on the one hand, and American and Soviet film on the other? Must not the techniques and material lineaments of film and video technology necessarily limit the range of expressive and social relational modalities available for the articulation

– 142 –

of such difference? (2) More importantly, and again I point to the necessity of dialectical thinking in the characterization of this phenomenon, what new forms of concealment does this new medium also bring with it, given that every form of expression takes shape against a mode of repression which is its background? In considering the power of any medium to represent or picture everyday life, we must not ignore what is repressed or hidden or misrecognized in everyday life, and how these everyday concealments are made inevitable through the conduct of social life itself. How then do we reconcile the power of making visible, or the representational impact of film, with the need to acknowledge the concealing properties of convention?[25] I cannot dissuade myself that we must ultimately judge the social, political and aesthetic value of film in the same way that Brecht suggested we evaluate drama: in terms of what he called the 'alienation-effect':

> A representation that alienates is one which allows us to recognize its subject, but at the same time makes it seem unfamiliar. The classical and medieval theatre alienated its characters by making them wear human or animal masks ... Here is the outlook, disconcerting but fruitful, which the theatre must provoke with its representations of social life (1964: 192).[26]

Only within this experience of self-alienation can we adjudge the complexity of the dramatic and filmic effect, and it is to the issue of complexity that I now turn.

## Complexity

We would all agree that Mephistopheles emerges as one of the most complex characters in our literature in Goethe's *Faust*. But how much of our insight into that character is sacrificed when that role is sung and acted in Gounod's opera? Would we have to say that the opera is a less complex form than literature? Or are we dealing with two different kinds of complexity, two different strategies for the production of form, which are not totally transposable into each other? This is what Peter Kivy (1989: 271) calls the 'fallacy of misplaced depth' – here it refers to the attempt to make commensurate two incommensurate types of complexity, the musical and the literary. And it applies all the more forcefully to film, I suspect – for much of Ginsburg's argument rests on her appeal to the *complex* and to the *complexity* of filmic representations.

I turn to the following statement by Ginsburg: 'My argument is that looking at media made by people occupying a range of cultural positions, from insider to outsider . . . [offers] us a fuller sense of the *complexity* of perspectives on what we have come to call culture . . .' (1994: 6, emphasis added).

What is meant by *complexity* here? Certainly the Inuit actors' dialogue did not appear *complex* – if it is, in Inuit terms, again, we need that explained to us, and such an explanation would probably have to tell us about what precisely was being *not said*, or what was being said in a deliberately banal way. (I must point out that I am responding only to Professor Ginsburg's edited use of certain clips from the various films and videos and her comments on them, and in no way is this meant to be a comprehensive critical assessment of the films and videos.) The footage made by Jean Rouch in his film *Petit à Petit* of an African man taking cranial measurements of Parisians is amusing, but *by itself* how complex is it? The Native American Miguel sisters mimicking Jeannette MacDonald and Nelson Eddy's *Indian Love Song* might provide us with a giggle, but again, where is the complexity in this all-too-predictable (to us) parody? On the other hand, the footage of *Sylvania Waters*, made to look like exactly what it was parodying – home video footage – *was* an extraordinarily complex commentary on and savage mockery of contemporary middle-class Australian family relations. If it is complexity one wants to see, I suggest one look no further than Robert Altman's mordant commentaries on southern Californian social relations in *The Player* or *Short Cuts*. Perhaps it is this *self*-mockery, the portrayal of a seemingly unintended taking-the-micky-out-of-the-film-maker-him/herself (especially in *The Player*), that was missing in the clips that Professor Ginsburg showed us in her presentations. My overwhelming reaction to these clips is that they did not work for me, and I desired more specific information on the manner in which they did or did not work for the producers and viewers themselves.[27]

If they do not work for us, then surely the mere viewing of these videos by us the anthropologists will not suffice. It is not enough for Professor Ginsburg to show us these clips and say, 'Here are the Miguel sisters being hilariously parodic', or 'Here is an Inuit film-maker making a film about himself talking about film-making'. We can judge this for ourselves. Ginsburg's comments do not, any more than do mine now, constitute an analysis of this phenomenon, either critical or otherwise, in any sense. Nor, because of the representational goal towards which they are deployed, can we see them as Sibelius saw his piano music – when asked what a piece of his meant, he merely played it over. Film is not as resolutely pragmatic an art form as music, because it calls forth and makes-visible its own representational, picturing function. I want Professor Ginsburg to tell me what I can't know about the film just by inspecting it, and here I reiterate that a full-blooded anthropological treatment of this phenomenon cannot neglect the critical dimension. We need, in other words, further mediation.

Because these films are *not* the same as a ritual or an artefact. The latter are incomplete without a consideration of the co-presence of an audience from whom a certain social response is elicited in a specific context. They have a specific, usually quite practical goal. This was what, among other things, Sol Worth and John Adair found out in their experiment with Navaho film-making (1974): the Navaho man Sam Yazzie was not interested in film once they found that it had, for him, only a representational and not a practico-transformative effect. Ginsburg, however, does not conclude from this that filmic media might be irrelevant or inutile for the Navaho; instead, she criticizes Worth and Adair for 'focusing almost exclusively on the film text as the site for the production of cultural meaning' (1994: 10). But perhaps the real problem is that, when Worth and Adair were among the Navaho, the production of cultural texts had never been and had not yet become an issue.

Something like a ritual that has such a practico-transformative effect might be considered mediatory in such terms. But film and video can be characterized as what Baudrillard calls 'speech without response' (1988: 207). Far from being a mediating object, as Ginsburg believes them to be, 'What characterises the mass media is that they are opposed to mediation . . .' (ibid.).[28] In this respect, perhaps the comments of the Scottish TV and stage dramatist John McGrath writing in 1985 are worth repeating, since they echo the sentiments of Adorno, Jameson and Brecht to which I have deferred in this discussion:

> Drama has lost the quintessential quality of television – that of being an event brought to us as a nation simultaneously. Ten years ago, I think television drama was still primarily created as an event specially tailored for the one-off moment of transmission . . . This was the quality that made it different from film, and linked it to the heroic unrepeatability of the experience of theatre (McGrath 1985: 52–3).[29]

Eric Michaels has gone further than anyone else in elucidating this performative capacity of film-making, in describing the effects of auto-documentary film on the Walbiri people of Yuendumu (Michaels 1987a). It is quite clear from Michaels's account that the documentary evoked strong emotional and social reactions among the people of Yuendumu – but to evoke and to depict are two distinct things. In such a case, it is reasonable to assume that, just as Walbiri rituals and artefacts and myths did not have the representational function that film and photographic depiction must inevitably have, the films they make are being used in non-representational ways and cannot be simply techniques or tools for the fashioning of identity or self-identity.

## The Aesthetics of Culturalism

Earlier I suggested that memory and history might themselves be the product of juxtaposing two incommensurable interpretational modalities, which creates a space of temporality and within it the possibility of making social and historical transformation visible. I continue with this dialectical orientation by citing a passage from Habermas, in which one could just as easily substitute the word 'culture' for 'history', and which addresses the epigraph of Adorno's at the beginning of this chapter:

> Modern consciousness, overburdened with historical knowledge, has lost the 'plastic power of life' that makes human beings able, with their gaze toward the future, to 'interpret the past from the standpoint of the highest strength of the present'. In other words, the history invoked by many current writers all too easily abandons any pretense at hermeneutical perspectivism; it takes on a 'paralysing relativism' rather than a living perspectivism; it blocks 'the capacity to "shatter and dissolve something [past]" from time to time, in order "to enable [us] to live [in the present]"' (Habermas 1987: 85 ).

Jameson echoes this critique of ahistoricism in his identification of the 'media phenomenon of neo-ethnicity . . . Ethnicity is something you are condemned to; neo-ethnicity is something you decide to reaffirm for yourself' (1992: 117). I now turn to the relationship between the representational strategies we have been discussing and what Ginsburg identified as the exigencies of cultural self-assertion. As she remarks, (1994: 5): "Those . . . from indigenous, ethnic, or diaspora groups who are using such media, are more and more conscious of their activities as vehicles for mediating cultural revival, identity formation and political assertion'.[30] I trust I am not reading too much into that statement when I interpret it as meaning that there is something about filmic media themselves that causes this kind of cultural consciousness-raising even as they at the same time anaesthetize us to theorizing it. Indeed, television has done more than anything to facilitate the development of national identity throughout the world. The 1986 Peacock Report on the funding of the BBC concluded, 'British broadcasting in its existing public service mode should and did assert and reflect Britain as a community, society, and culture and that it was the principal forum by which the nation as a whole was able to talk to itself' (p. 78). Identity in this case is not established strictly speaking through the give and take of social interaction but through co-identification with the same screenly images. For modern citizens, national and cultural selfhood 'is realised in the knowledge that we are all watching the same image at the same time' (Murray-Brown 1991: 21), and it is this usually tacit appeal to the 'sociality' of the co-watchers that grounds the constructionist analyses of what TV or film 'means' or 'signifies'.[31]

If such is the case, then what is being revived and asserted through indigenous video making? It could not be the revival of a world in which visual representation was constituted in terms very different from our own, as was certainly the case with Papua New Guinea peoples and many Australian aboriginal people of the Northern Territory. It would have to be a revival founded on the possibilities and limitations of social and self-constitution inscribed in the new media. It would have to include the mirroring relation of self to self that screen media make necessary and inevitable, including the transitive, unarticulated, tacit sociality of the co-viewer, and it is this kind of peculiarly visualist sociality that I find so inappropriate to the characterization of non-Western ritual and perform-ance and other so-called 'mediatory' practices.[32] Hence, to return to a point made earlier, the nature of political and cultural identity created through filmic media would have to have a most radically different relation to social and political practice itself, and it is some sense of concrete lineaments of this relation that is missing from Ginsburg's account, though Michaels ultimately identifies it as the sole locus of analysis in his approach. Since we only have the video clips with which to judge this relation, the cultural-nationalist message we are told it contains becomes '*a message*' – and ultimately a sociality – '*transmitted by the quality of the image, rather than its structural implications*' (Jameson 1992: 208, emphasis added). While we must always be aware of who authors a film or video, we cannot ask who authors a myth or ritual, and hence the filmic and the ritual-mythic must stand in very contrastive relations of revelation with respect to such structural implications.

But then, of what use is the assertion of a new cultural identity, if it does not differ in its *theory, cosmology and mode of being* from our own? Why should we continue to do anthropology if we can only find a sort of ersatz difference in the manufactured sound bites, video clips and promotional videos that will henceforth be everyone's most important cultural product? It remains for us to place indigenous video alongside all of the more 'traditional' appropriations, if I can call them that, of Western representational and expressive forms – where in our repertoire is a sound anthropological analysis of the lives and works of Wole Soyinka, Chinua Achebe, Albert Namatjira or V. S. Naipaul? Why should video and film alone capture our imagination when it comes to cultural identity and assertion? But then such a question I believe in large part supplies its own answer.[33]

Further, how will we be able to distinguish between different forms of cultural assertion if we only have aesthetic grounds by which to differentiate them? How will we be able to distinguish – culturally, politically or in any other way – between these indigenous film-makers' products and those products of the growing underground video cultures, the porn enthusiasts, sports fans, and other 'vidéastes' who now circulate their own images through the market (see Cubitt 1991: 9)? Who will say that the social relations depicted in the latter are any less authentic a cultural product than the Inuits'? Will the answer to such questions do no more than call forth indignant assertions of moralism or the judgement of taste, or the Bourdieuian mixture of both? Could this not be exactly the manner in which anthropological film-makers unwittingly have helped drive the final nail into the coffin of the non-Western world?

We are witness to a devaluation of the strange and the different in this exercise. No, not so much that. It is something more insidious. It is the replacement of genuine historical, linguistic, social and cultural difference with an ersatz difference among electronic images.[34] As Barthes has noted, we are replacing genuine historical and social difference with the connotation of it, 'the purveying of imaginary and stereotypical differences', signaled by the pervasiveness of the nominalizing constructions '-ness' and '-ity' in talking about culture – 'alterity', 'otherness', 'aboriginality', *'Sinité'*. It could be that this will soon be the only difference available to us, and one wonders whether that will spell the death of anthropology, or at least the death of its modernist foundations.

In fact, to be obsessed with the strange and the different in this 'old-fashioned' sense is to be branded as anachronistic, an exoticist. But when strangeness and difference are disallowed as features of our encounter with non-Westerners, we at the same time deny, in the Freudian sense of *verneinung*, the space of the uncanny, the strange, the inexplicable in our own life, the perception of which makes social difference possible (see J. Weiner 1993b). We deny the possibility of the social visibility of what Lacoue-Labarthe calls *désistance*, the inherent instability or 'infirmity' of the subject, 'without which no relation (either to oneself or to others) could be established and there would be neither consciousness nor sociality' (1990: 83). We could also add that there would be no history either, and to return once again to Adorno's epigraph, we would have to admit that

> ... the logic of the simulacrum, with its transformation of older realities into television images, does more than merely replicate the logic of late capitalism: it reinforces and intensifies it. Meanwhile, for political groups which seek actively to intervene in history and to modify its otherwise passive momentum . . . there cannot but be much that is deplorable and reprehensible in a cultural form of image addiction which, by transforming the past into visual mirages, stereotypes, or texts, effectively abolishes any practical sense of the future and of the collective project . . . (Jameson 1991: 46).

To return to Marcus and Fischer, from whom I take my original cue, it must now be pointed out that cultural critique was advocated years ago by Brecht, who looked toward theatre rather than ethnography for this critical Archimedean leverage. Of a new critical review Brecht was introducing in the early 1930s he wrote:

> Amongst other things the review understands the word 'criticism' in its double sense – transforming *dialectically* the totality of subjects into a *permanent crisis* and thus conceiving the epoch as a critical period in both meanings of the term. And this point of view necessarily entails a rehabilitation of *theory* in its own rights.[35]

By admitting the similarity of the agendas of Brecht and Marcus and Fischer, I draw attention to the broader theoretical and historical frame within which I maintain the inspection of indigenous film and video must take place. This frame is defined by the progress of Marxist theory this century as it has confronted the changes in the form of capital formation upon which Western society has focused, and its appropriation of image production as its latest and perhaps final act of colonization: 'As the indispensable decoration of the objects produced today, as the general exposé of the rationality of the system, as the advanced economic sector which directly shapes a growing multitude of image-objects, the spectacle is the *main production* of present-day society', Guy Debord (1983: §15) says. The only space thus left for the perception of totality – productive, cultural or otherwise – is within the image itself, which leads me to my last characterization of indigenous visualism.

## Conclusions: The Total Work of Representation

Consider again the words of John Kasaipwalova, the Trobriand aesthete:

> ... our process of Kabisawali is a total movement involving our politics, our economy, our villages, our families and our persons, we are as a matter of consequence engaged in changing our given historical reality and at the same time attempting to create a cultural environment that is both contemporary of our times and relevant to our present needs (1975: 1)

This was an introduction to a proposal for the creation of a Modern Art School on the Trobriand Island of Kiriwina, to be called the Sopi Arts Centre. Through the encouraging of traditional graphic, plastic and musical arts, the Trobriand Islanders could establish their directions of cultural development, which would more effectively link present-day society with its own traditions while at the same time not closing off avenues for change and growth.

Let us now compare Kasaipwalova's formulation with Wyzewa's description of Richard Wagner, which I cited in Chapter 6: 'With [Wagner], Art is no longer in painting, nor in literature, nor in music, but in the strict union of these genres and in the total life which is born thereof' (Boon 1972: 171). What Kasaipwalova and Richard Wagner seem to share is the Boasian, Benedictian, belief that the process of forming a community, or a cultural tradition, is similar to the production of a work of art (see Zimmerman 1990: 11).

But such a belief is inextricably linked to the expressivist and expressionist tendencies in nineteenth-century social and artistic theory that still inform our view of culture and social identity and which I maintain are implicit in the approach of Terry Turner, Faye Ginsburg and all of visual anthropology. For Richard Wagner, 'music is called upon to do nothing less than retract the historical tendency of language, which is based on signification,[36] and to substitute expressiveness for it' (Adorno 1981: 99). If we substitute 'film' for 'music' in Adorno's statement, we would then see film as twentieth-century anthropology's latest formulation of the total work of art:

> ... Whenever other arts are foregrounded with a film – and, generally visual, these can range from video to cuneiform, or ... from theatre to painting – what is at stake is always some formal proposition as to the superiority of film itself as a medium over these disparate competitors. There would thus be a kind of built in auto-referentiality in the very cinematographic medium,

which, without having read Wagner, instinctively proposes itself as the fulfilment for the ideals of the *Gesamtkunstwerk* . . . (Jameson 1992: 158–9).

In considering these imperialistic qualities of video, we might want to recall Raymond Williams's description of television as 'whole flow' (1990). If Ginsburg appeals to the totalizing medium of video as a privileged site of cultural articulation, she must by that token ask us to consider both social relations and culture as equivalent to a total image or total work – be it of art, or production or the fusion of both.[37] Under what conditions could this equivalence be established? What characteristics do works of art have that societies also have? And how to reconcile such a position with the equally valid intuition that art *opposes* conventional sociality and culture? I acknowledge that my critical view of indigenous film is from what some would label the 'high culture/low culture' dichotomy whose last great theorist this century was Adorno. But I maintain that this contrast is generated by a more general appreciation of the alienating effects of art, without which anthropology's own techniques of making culture visible would be seriously compromised.

Let me repeat what Ginsburg said: 'Films embody in their own *internal* structure and meaning the forms and values of the social relations they mediate, making texts and context interdependent' (1994: 6, emphasis added). But included in this *internal* embodiment of relations must also be the relation between the viewer and the filmic text (see Cubitt 1991: 87–8). It sites representation as a basic feature of relationality itself. It is in this very fusion of aesthetics and politics that Ginsburg situates her subject-matter within a postmodern project, and I maintain that one of the effects of this particular postmodern position is the obliteration of the kind of cultural difference that anthropologists have been used to and by which they have defined their discipline and its replacement with an illusion of difference. In the words of Wolf Lepeneis, 'If you believe in the unity of aesthetics and politics, you are already living in the period of *post-historie*' – and therefore of post-culture.

Now elsewhere I have said that this isomorphy between methodology and subject-matter is one of the defining characteristics of both anthropology and psychoanalysis. To study social relations, anthropologists have to enter into social relations with their hosts; to elicit from a patient the possibility of discourse, the psychoanalyst must inevitably become the focus of those anxieties the patient cannot at first speak about. In both cases, *the appearance of the transference and of the countertransference must at first be concealed from both parties to the analysis.* The reflexive effects of the analytical engagement are only made tangible or palpable by focusing one's attention elsewhere. In anthropological terms, this can be rendered in the following way: By focusing on the anticipated constructionist outcome of an act of representation, we conceal the constructionist origin of the transfiguration that accompanies such a representational act (see Wagner 1981). Drawing these social and psychoanalytical perspectives together, McCabe puts it this way, '. . . the unproblematic taking up of the position of the subject entails the repression of the whole mechanism of the subject's construction' (McCabe 1974: 17).

But to me, this is no more than an affirmation of what has been (up until now perhaps) one of anthropology's central tenets, one that was adumbrated by Victor Turner nearly forty years ago: '. . . the participant is likely to be governed in his actions by a number of interests, purposes, and sentiments, dependent upon his specific position, which impair his understanding of the total situation' (1964 [1957]: 29). Anthropology exists only because it can poise the promise of a description of total system against the perspectivism of its members. This promise cannot be secured by isolating and exalting the subjectivity of any of those members, whether anthropologist or indigenous 'other'. The position of externality, of outsider, is still necessary to anthropology.

The anthropological study of art, and of representation more generally, models this dialectic between inside and outside. We confront again the Brechtian paradox of art – and of ritual, to which Ginsburg originally compared the cinematic or video text: it is something produced within the social relations of life but which, if it is to be recognised as such, must stand apart from it. In his commentary on Adorno, Fredric Jameson thus says:

> . . . every work of art is 'of the world' and . . . everything about it is social – its materials, its creator, its reception, art itself (or culture) as a leisure class activity, and so forth; as a thing in the world it is social, yet the most important thing about it is not 'in' the world at all, in that sense (1990a: 185–6).

In so far as the self in Western society is included within this arena of representable things, then in its practice and conceptualization it is 'always a production rather than [a] ground' (Spivak 1992: 212). It is this productionist self that is inevitably consolidated through televisual media. But to the extent that the self and the body were components of such a ground for (among others) the Walbiri, Foi, Chambri, Manambu, and many native American peoples, the use of film will always work counter to their strategies of self-revelation.

* * *

Gewertz and Errington, in their compelling account of the Chambri (Papua New Guinea) experience of the modern world system argue that as part of representing the Chambri's relationship with the developing Nation-State, one must not neglect to make visible the way the Chambri *resist* representation itself (1991: 168). The promoters of indigenous video insist that such people should have the power to produce their own images of their own society and culture. The implication of course is that this culture and society already exist as knowable entities, and the people themselves have to be assumed to possess the rationalizing and expressive urges so bound up with our own notions of the individual and its autonomy. That the Chambri importantly and decisively speak for others – the ancestors in particular – is clear. But let us not gloss too quickly over the other patent observation that for the Chambri, *not* speaking is both a necessity and a prerogative of the powerful. As the ethnography of this region shows so pronouncedly, for some Melanesian peoples self-objectification is not the final and desired outcome of discursivity but a positive danger looming over all social life and discourse (J. Weiner 1991: 193–4).[38]

The last film clip we were shown by Ginsburg in her Australian lecture was to my mind the most significant: It consisted of the camera fixed on the face of an Inuit director, his own face masked by opaque aviator sunglasses, explaining in – what was for me, I must admit – an expression-less way the manner in which he had utilized this new technology of expression. If this is to be the ultimate product of video production – the mock-discursive elaboration of its own productive conditions of possibility – then all videotexts ultimately have the same subject-matter, and culture as such becomes merely another contrived effect within the confines of the screen. I was finally amazed that such an artificially constructed closed loop of pointless auto-referentiality could ever pass as an interesting, much less an authentic artistic or social event for anyone. I thought about a famously-reported Native American propensity to 'give up on words' – the 'stolidness' we so often think of with respect to Native Americans[39] – and wondered how useful a medium that calls forth acting, overacting, projecting and overprojecting as expressive modalities of the subject would be to people for whom the avoidance of such projection is a virtue.

# Notes

1. See also Gow 1994.
2. Schieffelin, in a seminar given at the University of Manchester in 1992, describes how a Kaluli séance failed as a performance and provides insight into the evaluative criteria employed by the Kaluli themselves in this regard.
3. See Ricoeur 1970; J. Weiner 1995a.
4. Foucault: '. . . it is in vain that we say what we see; what we see never resides in what we say. And it is in vain that we attempt to show, by the use of images, metaphors or similes, what we are saying; the space where they achieve their splendour is not that deployed by our eyes but that defined by the sequential elements or syntax' (1973: 9).
5. See Gillison's (1994) comments on the Gimi of the Eastern Highlands Province for comparison.
6. Eric Michaels's account (1986) of the producing and viewing of *Coniston Story* at Yuendumu, Northern Territory, Australia, is the most successful attempt so far to show how the time of filmic production is coeval with the time of social and community life in a non-Western setting.
7. Marx, *Capital* vol. 1, p. 209.
8. See Wagner 1981; Maybury-Lewis 1979; Bateson 1968.
9. '*It is not just the objective conditions of the process of production that appear as its result. The same thing is true of its specific social character*. The social relations and therefore the social position of the agents of production in relation to each other, i.e. the *relations of production*, are themselves produced: they are also the constantly renewed result of the process' (Marx, *Capital*, vol. 1: 1065).
10. Film is, if anything, a decidedly un-organic depiction of this. We can say, paraphrasing Sartre, that film theory '. . . while rejecting organicism, lacks weapons against it' (Sartre 1963: 77).
11. Adorno (1978). The translator, Robert Hullot-Kentor, goes on to say: 'Although the effort to mimetically achieve organicity ultimately leads to stiltedness, which it is the role of film to obscure, a true organicity can be achieved only by way of a dissonant composition' ('Foreword: Critique of the Organic', in Adorno (1989: xvii)).
12. Both Marcus (1994) and Taussig (1987) advocate the use of montage, both filmic and textual, as a solution to the problem of the transparency of one's representational praxis.
13. The dilemma between realism and representation in ethnographic film is addressed by several contributors to the volume *Visualizing*

*Theory*, edited by L. Taylor. The terms of this dilemma are articulated so effectively by Jameson that it is worthwhile quoting him at length:

> 'Realism' is, however, a peculiarly unstable concept owing to its simultaneous, yet incompatible, aesthetic and epistemological claims, as the two terms of the slogan, "representation of reality," suggest. These two claims then seem contradictory: the emphasis on this or that type of truth content will clearly be undermined by any intensified awareness of the technical means or representational artifice of the work itself. Meanwhile, the attempt to reinforce and to shore up the epistemological vocation of the work generally involves the suppression of the formal properties of the realistic "text" and promotes an increasingly naive and unmediated or unreflective conception of aesthetic construction and reception. Thus, where the epistemological claim succeeds, it fails; and if realism validates its claim to being a correct or true representation of the world, it thereby ceases to be an *aesthetic* mode of representation and falls out of art altogether. If, on the other hand, the artistic devices and technological equipment whereby it captures that truth of the world are explored and stressed and foregrounded, "realism" will stand unmasked as a mere reality- or realism-*effect*, the reality it purported to deconceal falling at once into the sheerest representation and illusion. Yet no viable conception of realism is possible unless both these demands or claims are honored simultaneously, prolonging and preserving – rather than "resolving" – this constitutive tension and incommensurability' (Jameson 1990b: 158).

14. These statements of Heidegger's are also forcefully discussed in an anthropological context by Chris Pinney (1992a).
15. As Bourdieu notes: 'An art of illustration and imagery, photography can be reduced to the project of showing what the photographer chose to show, . . . with which it becomes, one might say, morally complicit, since it approves of and bears witness to what it shows' (1990a: 86)
16. 'Our familial and social relations are very much in play in the uses to which we bend media technologies, as are the vagaries through which they become elements of psychic life' (Cubitt 1991: 16).
17. '*Tele*vision delivers near to sight that which almost always appears remote. Television is dealt with at arms length (now usually via "the *remote*"), it seemingly bridges distance without making material connection' (Fry 1993: 14).
18. 'For the film, what matters primarily is that the actor represents himself to the public before the camera, rather than representing someone else' (Benjamin 1968: 229).
19. These points have also been cogently raised by James Faris (1992).

20. Barthes identifies a photograph which does not contain a 'point of rupture' as *unary*. In this form 'it emphatically transforms "reality" without doubling it, without making it vacillate . . .: no duality, no indirection, no disturbance' (1981: 40).

21. See Ang 1987.

22. 'The enlargement of a snapshot does not simply render more precise what in any case was visible, though unclear; it reveals entirely new structural formations of the subject. So, too, slow motion not only presents familiar qualities of movement but reveals in them entirely unknown ones . . . Evidently a different nature opens itself to the camera than opens to the naked eye – if only because an unconsciously penetrated space is substituted for a space consciously explored by man. Even if one has a general knowledge of the way people walk, one knows nothing of a person's posture during the fractional second of a stride. The act of reaching for a lighter or a spoon is familiar routine, yet we hardly know what really goes on between hand and metal, not to mention how this fluctuates with our moods. Here the camera intervenes with the resources of its lowerings and liftings, its interruptions and isolations, its extensions and accelerations, its enlargements and reductions. *The camera introduces us to unconscious optics as does psychoanalysis to unconscious impulses*' (Benjamin 1968: 236–7, emphasis added).

23. Of the Desana, Reichel-Dolmatoff says: 'Generally, the dances imitate animals and the songs that accompany them refer to the movements and colors of the animals they represent. "But underneath goes the invocation," says the informant, and by "underneath" he is referring to the symbolic language of the songs (*vaí hayári*/ fish song) in which all the references to the river, the traps, and the catch are, in reality, allusions to sexual intercourse' (pp. 163–4). Stephen Hugh-Jones appeals to epiphanic processes among the Barasana when he relates that the Yurupary trumpets are the form that the bird spirits (*He* or *minia*) take in human ritual (1979: 140–1). He goes on: 'The *He* state is known indirectly through myths or bukura keti, the stories of the ancients, but it also experienced directly' (1979: 247), neither of which appeals to representation or mimetic imitation as such. Finally, with respect to the Navaho, it might be valuable to recall Gary Witherspoon's observation: 'In the Navajo view of the world, language is not a mirror of reality; reality is a mirror of language . . . Ritual language does not describe how things are; it determines how they will be' (1977: 34).

24. See Barthes 1981.

25. 'The unstable dialectic of the real and the apparent, the present and the absent, the visible and the invisible, is the condition under which TV enters into the social' (Cubitt 1991: 33).

26. '. . . the photographic 'shock' . . . consists less is traumatizing than in revealing what was so well hidden that the actor himself was unaware or unconscious of it' (Barthes 1981: 32).

27. In this respect I am taking a position analogous to that of James Faris, but for precisely opposite reasons: Faris too questioned the role of Western filmic technology in traditions that had very different relations to visuality and representation. But whereas he saw Western consumption of indigenous videos as their driving force, I desire to know more about the conflict engendered by the production of videos, which should be producing such an effect on the Western world but can only do so within the world of the video makers themselves.

28. We should recall the words of Benjamin (1968):

> 'The performance of the movie actor is transmitted to the public by means of an array of technical instruments, with a twofold consequence. The camera that presents the performance of the film actor to the public need not respect the performance as an integral whole. Guided by the camera-man, the camera continually changes its position with respect to the performance. The sequence of positional views which the editor composes from the material supplied him constitutes the completed film . . . Hence the performance of the actor is subjected to a series of optical tests. This is the first consequence of the fact that the actor's performance is presented by means of the camera. Also, the film actor lacks the opportunity of the stage actor to adjust to the audience during the performance, since he does not present his performance to the audience in person. This permits the audience to take the position of the critic, without experiencing any personal contact with the actor. The audience's identification with the actor is really an identification with the camera. Consequently, the audience takes the position of the camera; its approach is that of testing.'

29. What emerged as the discursive constitution of American sociality through the relationship of co-viewing provided by the televised trial of O. J. Simpson seems to me a critical ethnographic opportunity for anthropology at this juncture.

30. Thorp utters a similar pronouncement: 'Given a concentration of technical equipment and the energetic potentials it represents, video may become the condensor or catalyst of concrete attitudes and behaviours, a certain way of looking at things that stems from genuine historical and cultural concerns' (1991: 103).

31. In this respect, commentators on the role of mass media in constituting present day Western sociality are confirming the observation that de Tocqueville made over 150 years ago. In early nineteenth-century American society, where the dispersal of population meant weak social ties, and where there was little centralization of political authority, newspapers flourished. The political character of Americans' association was disclosed in the profusion of newspapers, "which bring to them every day... some intelligence of the state of their public weal." A newspaper survived, he understood, by "publishing sentiments of principles common to a large number of men," and hence "it always represents an association which is composed of its habitual readers" ... who through it were able "to converse every day without seeing one another, and to take steps in common without having met" [A. de Tocqueville, 1954, *Democracy in America*, New York: Vintage, pp. 121–2, 119–20]', quoted in Zynda 1984: 253.

32. As Zynda (1984) points out, such appeals to the community of viewers, or of readers, 'rest on a comparison of mediated communication to the directness of face-to-face communication. This comparison ignores the alienation of the receivers of mass-mediated messages from their senders, not to mention the content of what is printed or televised' (1984: 251).

33. Even so, where is a specifically anthropological interest in Third Cinema, for example, the work of the Filipino producer/director Kidlat Tahimik?

34. '... In the new dimensionality of postmodern cultural space, ideas of the older conceptual type have lost their autonomy and become something like by-products and after-images flung up on the screen of the mind and of social production by the culturalization of daily life' (Jameson 1992: 24–5).

35. From Brecht's *Sur le Realisme*. This passage is translated by Colin McCabe and is quoted in McCabe 1974: 7.

36. Although Heidegger shared this notion of the congruity between polity and art work, he nevertheless distrusted the Dionysian sentiments of Richard Wagner (as he makes explicit in *Nietzsche*, Vol. 1) and he rejected the Platonic theory of art as mimesis – as the mirror of the world, just as he rejected the Romantic view of art as the expression of the subjective perception of the artists (both of these notions are well-entrenched in anthropological analyses of art and ritual). (But see Taylor in Dreyfus and Hall 1992a for an expressionist view of Heidegger's theory of art).

37. Adorno, who otherwise was an implacable opponent of Heidegger and his philosophy, nevertheless reached the same conclusion concerning the role of film in achieving this totalization of representational subjects and subject-matter.
38. Pinney (1992a: 48): '... modern Western selves ... consolidated themselves through an accumulating externality, an ineluctable accretion of possessions – presences – which effaced (through a displacement) the absence of the very self they purported to reflect'.
39. '"The Bororo call civilized people *kidoe kidoe*, 'parakeet, parakeet,' because, like these birds, they talk too much" ... The white man thus has his place in the native bestiary ... In return, white observers have often mentioned oral retention, "a fierce reluctance to speak except when absolutely necessary," as a behaviour typical of American Indians ...' (Lévi-Strauss 1988: 164–5).

# 10

# The Scale of Human Life

Rameses means nothing to us . . . *We* know better than to use our science for the *reparation* of the mummy, that is, to restore a *visible* order, whereas embalming was a mythical labor aimed at immortalizing a *hidden* dimension (Baudrillard 1983: 19).

There was a time in anthropology when, if one were presenting the analysis of a ritual in a seminar, one had to make sure that one provided the audience with all the information about the ritual one needed in order to sustain the analysis. One couldn't count on everyone's being able to travel to Tikopia or Ghana or New Guinea to see the ritual for themselves, nor would one have been able to substitute for one's analysis a full-length film version of the ritual. Ginsburg and many other anthropological film-makers continue to speak as if the analysis of the films and their productive matrix is somehow immanent in the very act of showing them, and it is their faith in the transparency of what the films do and mean that impelled me to this exercise in the first place.

Let me continue by returning to the question of ritual, which Ginsburg originally invoked as a model for what she perceived was at work in indigenous film and video production. There are two points I wish to make. First, in considering mythico-ritual performances in Australia and Papua New Guinea, one must recall the sheer scale and size of the performance, and its associated objects, relative to that of the human community. Throughout Australia, ceremonial grounds had to be large enough to accommodate a number of dancers and viewers, who through the form of their dance inscribed an iconic version of a mytho-geographic track of certain Creator Beings, a track that was very large in size (see for example Keen 1994: 199). Among the Marind-anim of south New Guinea, certain artefacts such as the bull-roarer were considered to be the voice and other parts of the giant creator being Sosom. We witness here the attempt to fashion some gigantic version of human action and life, wherein the actions of beings had cosmological and geomorphic consequences of a permanent and vast nature, and to thus precipitate human community and sociality as some smaller version, component or effect of it. But in filmic representation, only the technological relations of production supporting the global cinematography and video industry are 'vast' (though because they are invisible in Ginsburg's accounts, they acquire what Gell and Bourdieu would call enchanted qualities), whereas the products are themselves a small effect on a small screen. The effect created, in other words, is that humans and their technology are big and all-powerful in relation to their 'ritual' productions, which have become small. When a stroke of a politician's or bureaucrat's pen in Canberra can eliminate the elaborate channels of funding that keep some of the central Australian Aboriginal media projects going, whose power and autonomy are more surely and definitely being made visible? On the other hand, there may be some comfort in knowing that a few Aborigines plodding along a ritual dance track, unfilmed and untelevised, may retain their own sense of the gigantic in their lives by escaping the government's and developer's miniaturizing attention.

The second point about ritual concerns anthropology's conventional approach to it. From Malinowski through to Rappaport, anthropologists were convinced that large-scale, important ritual activity had to have effects and consequences beyond the overt performative and symbolic properties of the ritual itself, however central these properties were to our analysis of them. Paradoxically (though only so by today's perspective it seems) it was this tacit acceptance of what lay beyond the representational that gave our symbolic analysis that much more depth. But if such productions are only seen to have symbolic properties as such, when we take too literally what 'symbolic' means in Bourdieu's term 'symbolic economy', then our symbolic analysis itself becomes a small thing.[1] There is no reason why such ecological, economic and sociological dimensions must drop out of our anthropological analysis of contemporary 'ritual', whatever its form, cinematographic or otherwise, for it is only by anchoring our symbolic analysis in them that such analysis does more than replicate its own terms.

Let me digress momentarily in order to comment on the place of an ecological field of relations within a broader symbolic anthropology.

## Revealing the Grounds of Human Life in Papua New Guinea

The rhetoric of constructionism cancels or obviates the dualism of nature and culture that characterized an earlier structuralist anthropology. Constructionism's language of negotiation and voluntarism also serves by implication to erode dualism in general. But the theme of this book is not that all dualisms deserve to be sublated – it is rather that *without an understanding of the work of opposition, the task of concealment and sublation is itself masked.*

In the place of an earlier dualism of nature and culture, I propose a contrast that meets the language of constructionism half-way, as it were: Roy Wagner's contrast between the domain of human action, intention and transformation, and that which lies outside this domain, or in other words, that which is acted upon. This contrast accounts for one of its specific forms, the opposition between culture and nature, but is not exhausted by it. In *The Invention of Culture* (1981), Roy Wagner suggests that what is perceived as innate, natural or external to human life cannot be dissociated from the symbolic acts by which humans implement and recognize their own domain of intention and meaning – their constructioning activity, if you will. But because of their intersubjective, communal origin, the effects of symbolization always outstrip any particular subjective, intentional appropriation of or relation to them (see J. Weiner 1997). What an actor perceives as happening counter to or in opposition to his/her constructioning activity is placed outside the register of human will and consciousness, but it is just as symbolically mediated as the acts and entities upon which the actor is focused. Their human origin is concealed from the actor as a result of the focusedness of his/her intention.

In broader terms, this is a phenomenon that Marx, Freud, and Heidegger (among others) have all tried to put at the centre of their portraits of the limits of the human world: that it is the various dimensions of our interest in and engagement with the world that actually shape the extent and contours of what is concealed from us. For Heidegger, Freud and Marx it was respectively our Being, our desire and our productive relations, realms that we Westerners have been prone to label 'natural' at one time or another. For Heidegger in particular, what was concealed was the Earth, 'the non-historical, spontaneous, self-generating aspects of things' (Zimmerman 1990: 122) as the ground of human existence, against which the humanly-made World stood as figure, but which it did not precede ontologically.

The value of this framework is that it admits that the way in which these non-human realms emerge in human consciousness is not simply a matter of symbolic construction. Instead, these theories of concealment, as we can call them, recognize a place for the non-constructed in human action and symbolization, and therefore avoid some of the obvious analytic limitations of the idea that nature is a social construction.

I partially explore these limitations by posing a second question: What is gigantic in human life? If we consider nature itself as only a social construction, we lose the sense of a domain that lies beyond the power and limits of the human and that is therefore large in comparison to it. We then might want to ask, what confronts human life with something that exceeds it? What lies beyond human life but nevertheless exerts an influence on it? This is the question of ecology as a study of relations that exceed the system's ability to cognize them, and again, it is this sort of question that is stricken off the agenda by an overly strong constructionist approach to these issues.

Let me continue by talking about trees.

In the Foi myth, 'The Origin of Leeches' (see Weiner 1988a), a man hides inside a *cyrtostachoid* palm and moves around the forest, spying on and publicly revealing men and women meeting in the woods for adulterous liaisons. The sustained analogy between trees and humans barely needs extended acknowledging here, since Papua New Guineans comment on and elaborate this analogy to a great extent (for example, the Foi, Umeda [Gell 1975], Muyuw, and Kamea). In Foi, a man and his sons, and his sons' sons are called an *ira*, a 'tree', a line of realized procreative destiny and territorial coherence within a broader local patrilineally composed territorial unit, the *amenadoba*, literally, 'man-line'. What I'd like to point out is that we might think, contrary to what the Foi myth says, that the difference is that the trees are rooted and people are not – but Maschio (1994), Bamford (1998) and Wagner (1988), as well as others like myself (J. Weiner 1991) have demonstrated that anthropogenically, trees move around in response to human movements and cannot be said to be rooted in any more literal a sense than a 'base man' is the 'root' or cause or grounds of his coalesced 'tree', faction or clan. The transgenerational continuity of trees like coconuts, sago, breadfruit or areca is still shallow by tree standards, but long enough for human reproductive and productive purposes, and other fruit- and edible leaf-bearing trees like pandanus and *Gnetum gnemon* need human attention if they are to be maintained.

The forest hides things. The Foi term for metaphor is 'tree leaf talk' – words that conceal their base or grounds, as tree leaves hide from sight what goes on behind them. What human activity does in the bush is to unconceal what occurs there (Kirsch says that the Yonggom of the Western Province speak of magic spells as causing game animals to reveal themselves from the forest).[2] We might see this as the Foi's or the Yonggom's version of ecological analysis. Let me expand on this metaphor.

## The Ground of Human Life

To do this, I would like first to return to another Heideggerian discussion I introduced in Chapter 5, that of Leibniz's notion of grounds (see Heidegger 1996) – What are the grounds of human life? – and I would like to play upon the double meaning here, of ground as reason, cause, principle, and as literally the earth upon which humans live and move and create a trace of their existence. Those of us who have lived with forest-dwelling peoples of Papua New Guinea have usually spent time observing how our interlocutors' bodies create a 'plenum', as Merleau-Ponty once put it, of human space by means of the very kinetic and kinesthetic acts of walking, stopping, turning, grasping, reaching, searching, etc. This appreciation of how physically and actively the moving hunter or gatherer dynamically orients him/herself in space is surely the first step to the most empirically rigorous account of a human relation to land we can provide in any context. But it is also no less primordially a verbally-mediated reaching out to the world, as witness the continual acts of pointing, gesturing and naming that accompany movement through terrain in Papua New Guinea: 'there is where my father gathered bush-fowl eggs; here is where X set his cassowary snares; this is where they killed and ate a man after a raid', and so on. The land speaks, as it is often said in the similar Australian Aboriginal context, but only through the human voice and hand in their appropriative manipulability, from which we are unable to dissociate the contribution that poetry and myth make with regard to their own historical and deictic functionality.

We know much about the importance of the revelation of ownership of land and resources, of trees and named places (among, for example, the Rauto [Maschio 1994], the Kamea, the Foi [J. Weiner 1991], and the Sepik River groups [see Harrison 1990; Wassmann 1991). Although publicly, in their confrontation with other like units, tracts of land are associated with specific local clans, historically it is individual men and their sons who carve out specific paths and contours across the clan terrain, which they then personalize as a result of this historical productive activity. The manner in which these particular territorial life-lines are revealed is furtive, allusive and poetical, rather than ostensive and didactic. In Foi, this revelation is the making visible of the grounds (in both senses) of human life and sociality. Hence, Leibniz's famous dictum, translated by Heidegger in one version as 'nothing is without grounds', which translates fairly well into New Guinea *tok pisin*: 'olgeta samting i gat as'. *As* in *tok pisin* is, among other things, the base of a tree, and the reason or explanation for some state of affairs. It is also used to refer to human causation, as in the founder of a line, or the instigator of a fight or an exchange.

Leibniz said 'nothing is without a reason' or a grounding. As Bamford (1998) and Maschio (1994) have indicated, in Papua New Guinea human sociality cannot be detached from its 'ground', which is literally the earth, but also its historical grounding, as a spatial record of human life-span, a track consisting of a linked series of inhabited places. As I have said, and as Maschio (1994), Feld (1982), and others have discovered, normally this ground is concealed, or at least, people's relationship and connection to it is not unlimitedly public knowledge. We might then confirm Heidegger's and Wagner's observation that it is always the nature of human Being to conceal its own grounding – again, this is the existential point that is elided in the strong constructionist account of culture, knowledge and meaning. In another context, Ivy (1995) observes that 'social categories become visible at the moment they cease to operate'. We can interpret this as what Heidegger referred to as the 'breakdown of equipment' (Heidegger 1962: 105), which nevertheless produces relationality. Human life under such conditions, including the conditions of possibility of knowledge itself, rests often in Papua New Guinea on techniques for unconcealing, for revealing connections that are hidden by convention.

Ecological analysis of the sort that played an important role in anthropological theorizing about total systems always insisted that the regulatory functions of adaptive behavior took a concealing, disguising form – as ritual, for example – although in this case we might say that the grounds of ritual were phrased in terms external to it (as adaptive behaviour with respect to land, pigs and other resources). For Papua New Guinea people like the Foi, what are external to humans yet able to exert power over them are spirits of the dead, something that seems far less 'natural', far more personalized and hence provocative in terms of our understanding of what we intuit to be external to the domain of human construction.

Papua New Guineans also set up their own domain of externality in terms of exchange, the ground of human relationality, though these grounds take a decidedly spatial form – most often they are described as the roads or paths that are the historical preconditions of ritual and exchange and that reveal the spatial and territorial configuring of human life as much as anything. But these spatial groundings made visible through ritual and exchange were by the same token thought to be very different from the regulatory mechanisms originally thought to come before them, like warfare and horticulture, which it was felt in some sense accounted for them.

Ecological analysis posited a logic and a compunction of a system that was 'bigger' than the human world, because it included the human domain as a component or effect of it. You could say that the ecosystem and its homeostatic qualities were 'large' in comparison to the system of human persons, whose logic and effects were 'small' and particular in relation to it, even though in the last analysis, it was not nature that was determinative of human action but another form of human action. To use a phrase that has been mentioned in relation to Melanesian public discourse (A. Weiner 1983), this was *our* 'hard talk'. We see some of this in Robbins's notion of the Urapmin's 'big bush', which seems to overwhelm human attempts to appropriate it.[3]

What happens then when human being is detached from its grounding, as a result of, for example, large-scale mineral extraction, deforestation, migration, or more recently, drought? Papua New Guinea ethnographers such as Maschio, Robbins, Kirsch, Rodman and Jorgensen[4] preview a Papua New Guinean world in which this proportionality is reversed, through contact with the Western technological mode of being. Certainly it was Heidegger at the end of his famous article 'The Question Concerning Technology' (1977c) who suggested that 'gigantism' was the peculiar effect of the technological mode of being. What we can say in anthropological terms is that through the human enhancement and magnification that technology enables, everything human becomes 'big' in relation to that which is non-human. In the paper he gave at the original conference, Joel Robbins remarked that the Urapmin of the Mountain Ok area are overwhelmed by the size of Western towns, which seem forest-like in size but are nevertheless human artefacts.

What is 'big' in New Guinea life – or in the model of ecological regulation – however, does not seem to be the result of human action in the same way, or even at all, in the case of the Kaluli, for whom 'vastness' is a quality of the ambient soundscape (Feld 1996) that provides an aural plenitude to their sensual lived world. We also hear from our Papua New Guinea interlocutors that certain creator beings such as Souw or Sosom or Afek or Umoim are gigantic in size, and their actions have or have had gigantic consequences for the landscape and for the condition of human social life, against which the realm of human action and production seems tiny in comparison.

Human beings replicate, or attempt to replicate or mimetically instaurate these productive originary acts, through their own human-sized acts of naming, marking, chanting, clearing and so forth, so that what we would call the 'everyday' and the 'practical' is suffused with the mythopoetical, a point I hardly need elaborate upon to those familiar with the manner in which myth and person are intertwined in Melanesian life.[5] In so doing, they reproduce internally the same contrast between the 'big' acts of incisive creation, and their 'small' effects of precipitated human action and sociality – so that the Paeila working body may be 'large' or 'small',[6] a man's name can be 'big' or 'small' (cf. e.g. A. Strathern 1971; Wagner 1972); Daribi settlements may house veritable 'swarms' of men, which, like Foi longhouses, yet produce the small fragments of refugees, exiles and remnants from which originary founding acts of migration and adoption can occur. And anthropologists who have worked in Papua New Guinea such as Biersack (1990) and Battaglia (1995) also show us what happens when that 'small'-scale network becomes too mediated, too spread out over a 'vast' landscape of air-linked urban centres: the elicitory, confrontational scale of public encounters has become detached to a marked extent from what Arendt once described as 'the space of appearance [which] comes into being wherever men are together in the manner of speech and action' (Arendt 1958: 199):[7] the tenor and rhetorical values that inflect this public space in Papua New Guinea are brought to the arenas of national and international dialogue without noticeable alteration in either scale or anticipated perlocutionary effects. There is a nation of landowners without there yet being a 'homeland' upon which to construe the body of a nation.

Anthropologists of contemporary Papua New Guinea such as Gewertz and Errington (1991) and Foster (1995) have recently given us the image with which I can conclude, the image with which we can now comment on the currently popular contrast in scale between the global and the local. For however many coke bottles, video cassettes and pop songs fall out of the sky into Papua New Guinea villages, the body from which they purportedly have been shed still remains unarticulated, its vastness hidden from the forest appropriators. And this invisibility is what has, from the first moments of 'cargo cult', always secured its own mythopoietical dimensions. We can recall the moment of unconcealment for Yali, the leader of the Madang area cargo movement (see Lawrence 1956), who performed his own ecological-ritual analysis of Western production when he was confronted with the museums and factories of Australia, turning his confrontation with the industrialized moral economy of the West into an insight into the moral and soteriological implications of such a productive system. Papua New Guineans, as in the Telefolmin and Kaliai (Lattas 1992) cases for example, and like ourselves, can only fashion a visible global totality out of their own mythopoetical fragments, an act that posits an external, concealed ground and sees human acts as a consequence of its own hidden, embodying processes.

## Nugurunderi's Landscape

This brings me back finally to those who would dismiss this still resolutely non-Western world as no longer of interest to contemporary anthropology. Annette Hamilton firmly tells us that 'the brute fact' (a phrase also invoked by Appadurai [1991] in a similar context) is that our erstwhile radically non-Western interlocutors are 'already "viewers," with all the disruption to indigenous subjectivity which this implies', though 'indigenous subjectivity' was the very thing the existence of which I am trying to render problematic. Behind this rueful acknowledgment of brute fact I suspect lies the barely concealed relief that anthropology will now be spared the irksome task of learning difficult languages and the distasteful business of living in boring, out-of-the-way places. But if anyone really thinks that anthropology can now safely ignore these so-called colonial backwaters, I invite them to join me on one of my visits to the Foi of Lake Kutubu, Papua New Guinea to watch the Chevron Oil Company in full operation at one of its most important petroleum reservoirs. And I would be truly discouraged if I had to spell out to my colleagues how and why the work I have done over the past twenty years on Foi language, myth, social structure, geography, ritual and poetry was necessary so that I could arrive at the stage where I could contemplate an anthropologically informed *Foi* account of what they have experienced since the Chevron Company arrived.

If we neglect this task, then we only have one version of representation, one version of subjectivity, one version of power, and that is our own. This is what I tried to draw attention to, and what was demonstrated to terrifying effect by Turner's erasure of the social reality of the non-representational in non-Western societies: for Turner and Ginsburg, 'the real is not only what can be reproduced, but *that which is always already reproduced*' (Baudrillard 1983: 146), and the evidence for this is that they don't think seriously about why I should see no difference between their position and that of Collier.

What Hamilton, Turner and Ginsburg hope to salvage from this brute fact is the possibility of the reassertion of the autonomy of our interlocutors. We would perhaps see the exchange of their non-Western, amodern culture for a new autonomy and subjectivity as a fair bargain under today's conditions. But the autonomy and the subjectivity secured is as much an illusion as our own. Allow me, then, to turn on my own virtual projector and give you a screening:

In June 1995, the state of South Australia began a Royal Commission into whether certain Aboriginal women of the Ngarrindjeri nation, the traditional residents of the Lower Murray River region of this part of Australia, had recently and deliberately fabricated a claim of secret women's religious knowledge associated with Hindmarsh Island (in the Murray mouth) and its surrounding channels for the purposes of blocking the construction of a proposed bridge that was to link the island with the town of Goolwa on the mainland. The year before, these women had successfully applied under the terms of the Commonwealth Aboriginal and Torres Strait Islander Heritage Protection Act of 1984 for this site to be judged one of particular significance to Ngarrindjeri tradition. The then Federal Minister for Aboriginal Affairs responded to the application by imposing a 25-year ban on the construction of the bridge. The Royal Commission was instigated subsequently by the South Australian State government shortly after the Adelaide media prominently reported the views of a group of 'dissident' Ngarrindjeri women, as they came to be called, who publicly denied that the women's restricted business was part of their tradition.

In July of 1995, in the early days of the Royal Commission, representatives of the women who had made the original application asked for a private audience with the presiding Commissioner, Iris Stevens. Away from the courtroom, consisting of media reporters, the developers, various anthropologists, historians and archeologists and their legal counsel, the women revealed to the Commissioner two secret objects associated with the mythological foundation of the restricted women's knowledge. Like Ginsburg, these women must have had faith in what they surely felt were the immanent meanings visible in the objects themselves, but which, to their dismay, ultimately failed to be perceived by the Commissioner. Shortly after this, through their own counsel, an Anglo-Australian Queen's Councillor, the 'proponent' Ngarrindjeri women, as they would come to be called, withdrew in protest from what they proclaimed was a racist inquiry into the religious beliefs of Aboriginal people. The Royal Commission henceforth heard testimony, with one exception, only from Ngarrindjeri women who had publicly disputed the existence of this women's ritual knowledge on Hindmarsh Island.

A key witness for the Royal Commission was a young cultural geographer from the South Australian Museum, Philip Clarke, who had recently finished his doctoral dissertation at the University of Adelaide on the cultural history of the Lower Murray region, and who had extensive knowledge of Ngarrindjeri history and culture. Philip Clarke was to spend many hours documenting the lack of evidence for gender-based restrictions on ritual knowledge among the Ngarrindjeri, such as were being put forth by the applicant women, in what came to be revealed as a considerable body of literature, ethnographic and quasi-ethnographic.

His testimony at one point was illustrated by reference to a central Ngarrindjeri creation myth, the story of the male ancestral creator Ngurunduri, who traveled along the length of the Murray estuary and the south Australian coastline creating various features of the landscape as he journeyed. Ngurunduri, so the myth goes, was chasing after his two wives who had run away from him. In the course of various adventures during which he creates all the fresh- and salt-water fish of the Murray estuary, and various features of the landscape and heavens, he catches up with his wives, whom he kills in revenge for their action. This myth was accorded centrality in a compendious summary of pre-Contact Ngarrindjeri culture recorded during the 1940s by Ronald and Catherine Berndt,[8] two young anthropologists working with three aged Ngarrindjeri informants, two men and one woman, who gave accounts of these practices and stories, which at that point had been all but obliterated from Ngarrindjeri communal consciousness.

A dramatization of this myth, featuring people who were members of a prominent Ngarrindjeri family as the actors, had been produced in 1987 as a highly successful and effective video, made with the help of the South Australian Film Corporation, and another young South Australian Museum scholar, Steven Hemming, a historian who was also to appear before the Royal Commission in support of the claim of the proponent women. In fact, the man who played Ngurunduri in the video, Henry Rankine, was one of the most important supporters of the proponent women and a former member of the Lower Murray Heritage Committee, a Ngarrindjeri committee that negotiated local cultural heritage issues with various government and business development interests.

At one point, when his testimony was being led by the Counsel assisting the Commissioner, Philip Clarke screened the video (entitled 'Ngurunduri: A Ngarrindjeri Dreaming'). The courtroom was not cleared for this screening. Indeed, the video is a most public artefact in Adelaide. It is screened continuously without stop at the South Australian Museum during its public opening hours, as part of its permanent display of Ngarrindjeri material culture and photographs.

I am only capable at this point of saying a few things about this incredible appropriation, presentation, representation and interpretation of images surrounding the very public issue of cultural difference in Australia.[9] I could say that nowhere did any of the participants in this inquiry show any interest in the *myth of Ngurunduri*, and the implied obliteration of women's lives and activity within the context of inscriptive activity along the Murray estuarine coast, nor was it conceded that the myth was now being used by Euro-Australian 'social scientists' (I am glad to say that none of those persons deferring to it in this way were anthropologists) to undermine a political claim that the Aboriginal actors in the film were themselves supporting. I could say that what was at stake were two versions of the gigantic, the personalized version of Ngurunduri the Creator, and the Anglo-Australian version of a man-made nature, where, under the accords made by the Australian states of Victoria, South Australia and New South Wales earlier this century, the large-scale use of the Murray–Darling River system for agricultural irrigation permanently altered the estuarine geography of the south Australian coast, and gave to the farmers' water pipes the same place-making power that Ngurunduri's club, canoe and spear had once had (this evidence, recounted by an official of the South Australian Water Commission, of the recent, 'anthropogenic' alteration of the coastline was adduced by the Royal Commission as a counterweight to the 'mythic' rationale for its contours and its sacredness given by the Ngarrindjeri proponents). How are we to juxtapose these accounts except as explanatory, theoretical totalities? We can reverse Lévi-Strauss's famous description of mythopoeia: it is the mythographic that is determined in our theories of knowledge, as much as the other way around, and this includes visual interpretation as well as all the 'hydraulic' theories appealed to, Aboriginal and Western, in the course of the Hindmarsh Island Bridge Royal Commission.

The local and national media, particularly television, played a prominent role throughout this affair, first in bringing to public attention the 'dissenting' opinion of the eleven women who disputed the claim of the proponent or applicant women, and subsequently in covering the Royal Commission itself. They turned the courtroom proceedings into local melodrama, turning the restricted nature of the Ngarrindjeri's mode of knowledge revelation into another item of evidence adduced towards the inauthenticity of Ngarrindjeri culture, fostering the view that dispute can only indicate a deficient knowledge rather than a relationally constituted one and that mythic knowledge must be revealed as defective in relation to its scientific counterpart. Having originated within the vast, productive nexus of Western images, which we all concede has its own mythic dimensions, the myth of Ngurunduri in its filmed form, and the Ngarrindjeri people who appeared in it, returned themselves and their life to the symbolic economy of image production that reproduced them as a Western form of seeing. Pinney is therefore correct: the effects of film will not be predictable, especially when filmic relations of production are themselves embedded in a matrix of global economic formations far removed from the intentions and concerns of film-makers.

Ngurunduri means *nothing* to us, any more than the tri-State Murray–Darling Authority means anything to Ngurunduri. They can only come to reflect each other in the anthropologist's account of a contemporary South Australian society in which they find themselves staring incredulously at each other, as if astounded at the turn of events that should bring them face to face in such a manner. Neither for the Ngarrindjeri nor for Euro-Australians can Ngurunduri's creation any longer assume the gigantic scale it once literally did. Henry Rankine, whether as Ngurunduri the film character, or as the member of various Ngarrindjeri committees who must travel back and forth between Ngarrindjeri communities and the board rooms and council chambers of different governmental and business organizations in South Australia, traces the path along which will sprout new marinas, highways, and ecological caravan parks and convention centers, as well as Aboriginal 'culture centres', and the sites of productivity in this contemporary Ngarrindjeri mythographic inscription will be created as a result of conflicts over land and power between the Ngarrindjeri and the non-Aboriginal people and government of South Australia. It is left to the anthropologist to continue as he or she has always done, to return the sense of the gigantic, that is the global, to myth, both Western and non-Western, in cases like this, and to reinsert these images into an ethnographic analysis, out of which the creative incommensurability of cultural difference can once more emerge as our irreducible subject-matter and ultimate goal.

# Notes

1. As Wagner notes:

   '. . . if the action of the ritual is considered as wholly symbolic in its effect, then it will be of the same "scale," or phenomenal order, as its translation . . . But if the ritual communication is freighted with sociological or ecological implications as well, then as mere translation, however sensitive it may be, it cannot possibly bring across all of its implications and effects' (1984: 144).

2. In the paper 'Time, Space and Loss on the Ok Tedi', presented at the session 'Environment and Sociality in Melanesia', American Anthropological Association Annual Meetings, 1996.

3. In the paper 'Welcome to Big-Bush Urapmin: Environment, Development and the Construction of Poverty in A Papua New Guinea Society', presented at the session, 'Environment and Sociality in Melanesia', American Anthropological Association Annual Meetings, 1996.
4. In papers given at the session 'Environment and Sociality in Melanesia', American Anthropological Association Annual Meetings, 1996.
5. See for example, Leenhardt 1979; Clifford 1982; J. Weiner 1995b; Wagner 1978; Ballard and Goldman 1997.
6. See Biersack, 'The Human Condition and its Transformations: Nature and Society in the Paiela World', presented at the session, 'Environment and Sociality in Melanesia', American Anthropological Association Annual Meetings, 1996.
7. This passage was cited by Biersack in her conference paper cited above. I wish to acknowledge the appropriateness of her invocation of Arendt in this context.
8. Berndt, R. and C. Berndt, 1993. *A World that Was*. Melbourne: University of Melbourne Press.
9. See J. Weiner 1997, 1995c, 1999 and 'Anthropologists, Historians and the Secret of Social Knowledge'. *Anthropology Today* 11(5): 3–7.

# References

Acker, W. (1952). *T'ao the Hermit: Sixty Poems by T'ao Chi'en*. London: Thames & Hudson.

Adorno, T. (1981). *In Search of Wagner*. London: Verso.

—— (1978). 'Vers une musique informelle', *Gesammelte Schriften*, vol. 16, ed. Rolf Tiedemann, trans. Robert Hullot-Kentor. Frankfurt: Suhrkamp Verlag.

—— (1989). *Kierkegaard: Construction of the Aesthetic*, trans. Robert Hullot-Kentor. Minneapolis: University of Minnesota Press.

—— (1991). *The Culture Industry: Selected Essays on Mass Culture*, ed. J. M Bernstein. London: Routledge.

Adorno, T., Bloch, E., *et. al.* (1977). *Aesthetics and Politics*. London: Verso.

Ang, I. (1987). 'The Vicissitudes of "Progressive Television"'. *New Formations* 2 (Summer).

Appadurai, A. (1991). 'Global Ethnoscapes: Notes and Queries for a Transnational Anthropology', in R. Fox (ed.), *Recapturing Anthropology*. Santa Fe: School of American Research Press.

Arendt, H. (1958). *The Human Condition*. Chicago: University of Chicago Press.

Augé, Marc. (1995). *Non-Places: An Introduction to an Anthropology of Supermodernity*. London: Verso Books.

Ballard, C. and Goldman, L. (eds) (1997). *Fluid Ontologies: Myth, Ritual and Philosophy in the Highlands of Papua New Guinea*. Westport, CT: Greenwood Publishing.

Bamford, S. (1998). 'Humanized Landscapes, Embodied Worlds: Land and the Construction of Intergenerational Continuity among the Kamea of Papua New Guinea'. *Social Analysis* 42(3): 28–54.

Barthes, R. (1989). *Camera Lucida*, trans. Richard Howard. New York: Polity Press.

Basso, K. (1984). '"Stalking with Stories": Names, Places and Moral Narratives among the Western Apache', in Edward Brunner (ed.), *Text, Play and Story*. Washington, DC: American Ethnological Society Publications.

—— (1988). '"Speaking with Names": Language and Landscape among the Western Apache.' *Cultural Anthropology* 3(2): 99–130.

Bateson, G. (1968). *Naven*. Stanford: Stanford University Press.

Battaglia, D. (1990). *On the Bones of the Serpent*. Chicago: University of Chicago Press.

—— (1995). "On Practical Nostalgia: Self-Prospecting among Urban Trobrianders", in D. Battaglia (ed.), *Rhetorics of Self-Making*. Berkeley, CA: University of California Press.

Baudrillard, J. (1983). *Simulations*. New York: Semiotext(e).

—— (1988). *Selected Writings*, ed. Mark Poster. Cambridge: Polity Press.

Benjamin, W. (1968). 'The Work of Art in the Age of Mechanical Reproduction', in *Illuminations*, trans. H. Zohn. New York: Schocken Books.

Berndt, R. and C. Berndt. (1993). *A World that Was*. Melbourne: University of Melbourne Press.

Bhabha, H. (1994). *The Location of Culture*. London: Routledge.

Biersack, A. (1990) 'Histories in the Making: Paiela and Historical Anthropology'. *History and Anthropology* 5: 63–85.

Boon, J. (1972). *From Symbolism to Structuralism: Lévi-Strauss in a Literary Tradition*. Oxford: Basil Blackwell.

Boorse, C. (1975). 'The Origins of the Indeterminacy Thesis'. *Journal of Philosophy* 72: 369–87.

Bourdieu, P. (1977). *Outline of a Theory of Practice*. Cambridge: Cambridge University Press.

—— (1984). *Distinction: A Social Critique of the Judgement of Taste*. London: Routledge and Kegan Paul.

—— (1989). 'The Historical Genesis of a Pure Aesthetic', in *Analytic Aesthetics*, ed. R. Shusterman. Oxford: Basil Blackwell.

—— (1990a). *Photography: A Middle-Brow Art*, trans. by Shaun Whiteside. Cambridge: Polity Press.

—— (1991). *The Political Ontology of Martin Heidegger*. London: Polity.

Brecht, B. (1964). 'A Short Organum for the Theatre', in *Brecht on Theatre: The Development of an Aesthetic*, trans. John Willett. London: Methuen.

Brown, P., R. Keesing, M. Jolly, and M. Strathern (1992). 'Book Review Forum: M. Strathern *The Gender of the Gift*'. *Pacific Studies* 15(1): 123–59.

Casey, E. (1996). 'How to Get from Space to Place in a Fairly Short Stretch of Time: Phenomenological Prologemena', in *Senses of Place*, ed. K. Basso and S. Feld. Santa Fe: School of American Research Press.

Chrisman, M. (1967). *Strasbourg and the Reform*. New Haven, CT and London: Yale University Press.

Clifford, J. (1982). *Person and Myth: Maurice Leenhardt in the Melanesian World*. Berkeley, CA: University of California Press.

—— (1988). *The Predicament of Culture*. Cambridge, MA: Harvard University Press.

Collier, J. (1986). *Visual Anthropology* (revised edition). Albuquerque, NM: University of New Mexico Press.

Cubitt, S. (1991). *Timeshift: On Video Culture*. London: Routledge.

Debord, G. (1983). *Society of the Spectacle*. Detroit: Black and Red.

Deleuze, G. (1983). *Nietzsche and Philosophy*. London: Athlone.

—— (1988). *Foucault*, trans. Seán Hand. London: The Athlone Press.

Dreyfus, H. (1991) *Being-in-the-World: A Commentary on Heidegger's Being and Time, Division I*. Cambridge, MA: MIT Press.

Dreyfus, H. and H. Hall (eds) (1992a) *Heidegger: A Critical Reader*. Oxford: Blackwell.

Dreyfus, H. and H. Hall (1992b). 'Introduction', in *Heidegger: A Critical Reader*. Oxford: Blackwell.

Eaton, M. (1992). 'Amazonian Videos'. *Sight and Sound*, 17 November.

Faris, J. (1992). 'Anthropological Transparency: Film, Representation and Politics', in P. Crawford and D. Turton (eds) *Film as Ethnography*. Manchester: Manchester University Press.

Feld, S. (1982). *Sound and Sentiment*. Philadelphia: University of Pennsylvania Press.

—— (1986). 'Sound as a Symbolic System: The Kaluli Drum', in D. Howes (ed.), *The Varieties of Sensory Experience: A Sourcebook in the Anthropology of the Senses*, Detroit Monographs in Musicology, 9. Detroit: Information Coordinators.

—— (1996). 'Waterfalls of Sound: An Acoustemology of Place Resounding', in S. Feld and K. Basso (eds), *Senses of Place*. Santa Fe: School of American Research Press.

Fell, J. (1979) *Heidegger and Sartre: An Essay in Being and Place*. New York: Columbia University Press.

Foster, R. (ed.) (1995). *Nation Making: Emergent Identities in Postcolonial Melanesia*. Ann Arbor, MI University of Michigan Press.

Foucault, M. (1973). *The Order of Things*. New York: Vintage.

Freud, S. (1919). 'The Uncanny'. *Standard Edition* 17: 219–54. London: Hogarth Press.

Fry, T. (1993). 'Introduction', in T. Fry (ed.), *RUA/TV?: Heidegger and the Televisual*. Sydney: Power Arts Institute.

Fry, T. and A.-M. Willis (1989). 'Aboriginal Art: Symptom or Success?'. *Art in America* 77(7): 108–11, 160, 163.

Geertz, C. (1973). *The Interpretation of Cultures*. New York: Basic Books.

—— (2001). 'Life among the Anthros'. *New York Review* 48(2): 18–22.

Gell, A. (1975). *Metamorphosis of the Cassowaries*. London: Athlone.

—— (1979). 'The Umeda Language Poem.' *Canberra Anthropology* 2(1): 44–62.

—— (1992a). 'The Technology of Enchantment and the Enchantment of Technology', in J. Coote and A. Shelton (eds), *Anthropology, Art and Aesthetics*. Oxford: Oxford University Press.

—— (1992b). 'Under the Sign of the Cassowary', in B. Juillerat (ed.), *Shooting the Sun: Ritual in West Sepik*. Washington, DC: Smithsonian Institution Press.

—— (1995). 'The Language of the Forest: Landscape and Phonological Iconism in Umeda', in E. Hirsch and M. O'Hanlon (eds), *The Anthropology of Landscape*. Oxford University Press.

Gelven, M. (1989). *A Commentary on Heidegger's* Being and Time. DeKalb, IL: Northern Illinois University Press.

Gewertz, D. and F. Errington (1991). *Twisted Histories, Altered Contexts: The Chambri in the World System*. Cambridge University Press.

Gillison, G. (1993). *Between Culture and Fantasy: A New Guinea Highlands Mythology*. Chicago: University of Chicago Press.

Ginsburg, F. (1991). 'Indigenous Media: Faustian Contract or Global Village?'. *Cultural Anthropology* 6(1): 92–112.

—— (1994). 'Culture/Media: A Mild Polemic'. *Anthropology Today* 10(2): 5–15.

Goldman, L. (1983). *Talk Never Dies: The Language of Huli Disputes*. London: Tavistock.

Gow, P. (1994). 'Against the Motion (II): Aesthetics is a Cross-Cultural Category'. *Group for Debate in Anthropological Theory* No. 6, ed. J. Weiner. Manchester: Department of Social Anthropology, University of Manchester.

Habermas, J. (1987). *The Philosophical Discourse of Modernity*, trans. F. Lawrence. Cambridge: Polity.

Harrison, S. (1990). *Stealing People's Names: History and Politics in a Sepik River Cosmology*. Cambridge: Cambridge University Press.

—— (1993). *The Mask of War*. Manchester: University of Manchester Press.

Haugeland, J. (1992). 'Dasein's Disclosedness', in H. Dreyfus and H. Hall (eds), *Heidegger: A Critical Reader*. Oxford: Blackwell.

Heidegger, M. (1962). *Being and Time*, trans. J. Macquarrie and E. Robinson. Oxford: Basil Blackwell.

—— (1969). *Zur Sache des Denkens*. Tubingen: Max Niemeyer.

—— (1971a). 'The Origin of the Work of Art', in *Poetry Language Thought*, trans. A. Hofstadter. New York: Harper and Row.

—— (1971b). *On the Way to Language*. New York: Harper and Row.

—— (1971c). *Poetry, Language, Thought*, trans. A. Hofstadter. New York: Harper and Row.

—— (1975). *Early Greek Thinking*, trans. David F. Krell and F. Capuzzi. New York: Harper and Row.

—— (1977a). *Basic Writings*, ed. David F. Krell. New York: Harper and Row.

—— (1977b). 'The Age of the World Picture', in *The Question Concerning Technology and Other Essays*, trans. W. Lovitt. New York: Harper and Row.

—— (1977c). *The Question Concerning Technology*, trans. W. Lovitt. New York: Harper and Row.

—— (1979). *Nietzsche*, Vol. 1: *The Will to Power as Art*, trans. D. F. Krell. New York: Harper and Row.

—— (1982b). *The Basic Problems of Phenomenology*, trans. and ed. by A. Hofstadter. Bloomington, IN: Indiana University Press.

—— (1984). *Nietzsche*, Vol. 2: *The Eternal Recurrence of the Same*, trans. David F. Krell. New York: Harper and Row.

—— (1986). *Nietzsche*, Vol. 1: *The Will to Power as Art*, trans. David F. Krell. New York: HarperCollins.

—— (1987). *Nietzsche*, Vol. 3: *The Will to Power as Knowledge and Metaphysics*, trans. J. Stambaugh, D. Krell and F. Capuzzi. New York: Harper and Row.

—— (1996). *The Principle of Reason*, trans. Reginald Lilly. Bloomington, IN: Indiana University Press.

Helliwell, C. (1989). 'Good Walls Make Bad Neighbours: The Dayak Longhouse as a Community of Sound', Seminar Presentation, Department of Prehistory and Anthropology,' Australian National University, Canberra.

Herf, J. (1984). *Reactionary Modernism: Technology, Culture and Politics in Weimar and the Third Reich*. New York: Cambridge University Press.

Hirsch, E. (1995). 'The Coercive Strategy of Aesthetics: Reflections on Wealth, Ritual and Landscape in Melanesia', in J. Weiner (ed.), *'Too Many Meanings': A Critique of the Anthropology of Aesthetics. Social Analysis* special issue 38: 61–71.

Hobbs, R. (1991). 'Television and the Shaping of Cognitive Skills', in *Video Icons and Value*, ed. A. Olson, C. Parr and D. Parr. Albany, NY: State University of New York Press.

Hugh-Jones, S. (1979). *The Palm and the Pleiades*. Cambridge: Cambridge University Press.

Ingold, T. (ed.) (1996). *Key Debates in Anthropology*. London: Routledge.

Ivy, M. (1995). *Discourses of the Vanishing: Modernity, Phantasm, Japan*. Chicago: University of Chicago Press.

Jameson, F. (1977). 'Imaginary and Symbolic in Lacan: Marxism, Psychoanalytic Criticism and the Problem of the Subject'. *Yale French Studies* 55/56: 338–95.

—— (1990a). *Late Marxism: Adorno, or the Persistence of the Dialectic*. London: Verso.

—— (1990b). *Signatures of the Visible*. New York and London: Routledge.

—— (1991). *Postmodernism: Or, the Cultural Logic of Late Capitalism*. London: Verso.

—— (1992). *The Geopolitical Aesthetic: Cinema and Space in the World System*. Bloomington, IN: Indiana University Press.

Jay, M. (1992). 'Scopic Regimes of Modernity', in *Modernity and Identity*, ed. S. Lash and J. Friedman. Oxford: Blackwell.

Jean-Klein, I. (1993). 'The Animation of "Community": An Anthropological View from a Town in the Israeli-Occupied West Bank Territories of "Palestine"', Ph.D. thesis, Department of Social Anthropology, University of Manchester.

Kaelin, E. F. (1967). 'Notes Towards an Understanding of Heidegger's Aesthetics', in E. Lee and M. Maudelbaum (eds), *Phenomenology and Existentialism*, pp. 59–92. Baltimore, MD: Johns Hopkins University Press.

Kaes, A. (1989). *From* Hitler *to* Heimat: *The Return of History as Film*. Cambridge, MA: Harvard University Press.

Kasapwailova, J. (1975). *Sopi: The Adaptation of a Traditional Aesthetic Concept for the Creation of a Modern Art School on Kiriwina*. Port Moresby: Institute of Papua New Guinea Studies.

Keen, I. (1994). *Knowledge and Secrecy in an Aboriginal Religion*. Oxford: Clarendon Press.

Kivy, P. (1989). *Osmin's Rage: Philosophical Reflections on Opera, Music and Text*. Princeton: Princeton, NJ: University Press.

Klee, P. (1970). 'Creative Credo', in V. Miesel (ed.), *Voices of German Expressionism*. Englewood Cliffs, NJ: Prentice-Hall.

Kluge, A. (1981–2). 'On Film and the Public Sphere'. *New German Critique* 24/25.

Kockelmans, J. (1972). *On Heidegger and Language*. Evanston, IL: Northwestern University Press.

Kolb, D. (1986). *The Critique of Pure Modernity: Hegel, Heidegger and After*. Chicago: University of Chicago Press.

Krell, D. (1986). *Intimations of Mortality: Time, Truth and Finitude in Heidegger's Thinking of Being*. University Park, PA: The Pennsylvania State University Press.

—— (1993). *Daimon Life: Heidegger and Life Philosophy*. Bloomington, NJ: Indiana University Press.

Lacoue-Labarthe, P. (1990). *Heidegger, Art and Politics: The Fiction of the Political*. Oxford: Blackwell.

Langlas, C. and J. Weiner (1988). 'Big-Men, Population Growth and Longhouse Fission among the Foi, 1965–1979', in J. Weiner (ed.), *Mountain Papuans*. Ann Arbor, MI: University of Michigan Press.

Lattas, A. (1992). 'Skin, Personhood and Redemption: The Doubled Self in West New Britain Cargo Cults'. *Oceania* 63(1): 27–54.

Lawrence, P. (1956). *Road Belong Cargo*. Manchester: Manchester University Press.

Leenhardt, M. (1979). *Do Kamo: Person and Myth in the Melanesian World*, trans. Basia Miller Gulati. Chicago: University of Chicago Press.

Lefebvre, H. (1968). *The Sociology of Marx*. Harmondsworth: Penguin.

Lévi-Strauss, C. (1963). *Totemism*, trans. Rodney Needham. Boston: Beacon Press.

—— (1966). *The Savage Mind*. Chicago: University of Chicago Press.

—— (1988). *The Jealous Potter*, trans. B. Chorier. Chicago: University of Chicago Press.

Levin, D. (1988). *The Opening of Vision: Nihilism and the Postmodern Situation*. London and New York: Routledge and Kegan Paul.

Losche, D. (1995). 'The Sepik Gaze: Iconographic Interpretation of Abelam Form', in *Too Many Meanings: A Critique of the Anthropology of Aesthetics*, ed. J. Weiner. *Social Analysis* special issue 38: 48–63.

MacCabe, C. (1974). 'Realism and the Cinema: Notes on some Brechtian Theses.' *Screen* 15(2): 7–27.

MacDougall, D. (1987). 'Media Friend or Media Foe'. *Visual Anthropology* 1(1): 54–8.

—— (1992). 'Beyond Observational Cinema', in P. Crawford and D. Turton (eds), *Film as Ethnography*. Manchester: Manchester University Press.

McGrath, J. (1985). 'Strike at the Fiction Factories'. *Edinburgh International Television Festival Magazine* no. 10.

Marcus, G. (1994). 'The Modernist Sensibility in Recent Ethnographic Writing and the Cinematic Metaphor of Montage', in L. Taylor (ed.), *Visualizing Theory*. New York: Routledge.

Marcus, G. and M. Fischer (1986). *Anthropology as Cultural Critique*. Chicago: University of Chicago Press.

Maschio, T. (1994). *To Remember the Faces of the Dead*. Madison, WI: University of Wisconsin Press.

Maybury-Lewis, D. (ed.) (1979). *Dialectical Societies: The Gê and Bororo of Central Brazil*. Cambridge, MA: Harvard University Press.

Merleau-Ponty, M. (1962). *Phenomenology of Perception*. London: Routledge and Kegan Paul.

Meyer, Nicholas. (1974). *The Seven Per Cent Solution*. New York: Ballantine Books.

Michaels, E. (1986). *The Aboriginal Invention of Television in Central Australia, 1982–86*. Canberra: The Australian Institute of Aboriginal Studies.

—— (1987a). 'Aboriginal Content: Who's Got it – Who Needs it'. *Art and Text* 23/4: 58–79.

—— (1994). *Bad Aboriginal Art: Tradition, Media, and Technological Horizons*. Sydney: Allen and Unwin.

Mimica, J. (1993). 'The Foi and Heidegger'. *The Australian Journal of Anthropology* 4(2): 79–95.

Morphy, H. (1991). *Ancestral Connections*. Chicago: University of Chicago Press.

Murray-Brown, J. (1991). 'Video Ergo Sum', in *Video Icons and Values*, ed. A. Olson, C. Parr and D. Parr. Albany, NY: State University of New York Press.

Okrent, M. (1992). 'The Truth of Being and the History of Philosophy', in H. Dreyfus and H. Hall (eds), *Heidegger: A Critical Reader*. Oxford: Blackwell.

Pandya, V. (1990). 'Movement and Space: Andamanese Cartography'. *American Ethnologist* 17(4): 775–97.

Pinney, C. (1992a). 'Future Travel: Anthropology and Cultural Distance in an Age of Virtual Reality; or, a Past Seen from a Possible Future'. *Visual Anthropology Review* 8(1): 38–55.

Rabinow, P. (ed.) (1984). *The Foucault Reader*. Harmondsworth: Penguin.

Reichel-Dolmatoff, G. (1971). *Amazonian Cosmos: The Sexual and Religious Symbolism of the Tukano Indians*. Chicago: University of Chicago Press.

Relph, E. (1976). *Place and Placelessness*. London: Pion Limited.

Ricoeur, P. (1970). *Freud and Philosophy*. New Haven, CT: Yale University Press.

Rorty, R. (1979). *Philosophy and the Mirror of Nature*. Princeton, NJ: Princeton University Press.

—— (1989). *Contingency, Irony, and Solidarity*. Cambridge: Cambridge University Press.

—— (1991). 'Heidegger, Contingency and Pragmatism', in *Essays on Heidegger and Others*. Cambridge University Press [Reprinted in Dreyfus and Hall (1992a).

Sapir, E. (1992). 'Language and Environment'. *American Anthropologist* 14: 226–42.

Sartre, J.-P. (1963). *Search for a Method*. New York: Alfred Knopf.

Schieffelin, E. (1976). *The Sorrow of the Lonely and the Burning of the Dancers*. New York: St Martin's Press.

Schrempp, G. (1992). *Magical Arrows: The Greeks, the Maori and the Folklore of the Universe*. Madison, WI: University of Wisconsin Press.

Sobchack, V. (1992). *The Address of the Eye: A Phenomenology of Film Experience*. Princeton: Princeton, NJ: University Press.

Spinosa, C. (1992). 'Derrida and Heidegger: Iterability and *Ereignis*', in H. Dreyfus and H. Hall (eds), *Heidegger: A Critical Reader*. Oxford: Blackwell.

Spivak, G. (1992). 'Subaltern Studies: Deconstructing Historiography', in G. Spivak, *In Other Worlds: Essays in Cultural Politics*. London: Methuen.

Steinberg, L. (1983). *The Sexuality of Christ in Renaissance Art and in Modern Oblivion*. London: Faber and Faber.

Steiner, G. (1978). *Heidegger*. London: Fontana.

Strathern, A. (1971). *The Rope of Moka*. Cambridge: Cambridge University Press.

—— (1975). 'Veiled Speech in Mt. Hagen', in M. Bloch (ed.), *Political Language and Oratory in Traditional Society*. New York: Academic Press.

Strathern, M. (1988). *The Gender of the Gift*. Berkeley, CA: University of California Press.

—— (1990a). 'The Concept of Society is Theoretically Obsolete: For the Motion (I)'. Group for Debate in Anthropological Theory No. 2, ed. by Tim Ingold. Manchester: Department of Social Anthropology, University of Manchester.

—— (1991). *Partial Connections*. Savage, MD: Rowman and Littlefield Publishers.

# References

────── (1992). *After Nature: English Kinship in the Late Twentieth Century*. Cambridge: Cambridge University Press.

Taussig, M. (1987). *Shamanism, Colonialism and the Wild Man: A Study in Terror and Healing*. Chicago: University of Chicago Press.

Thorp, E.D. (1991). 'In Video Veritas: The Mythic Structure of Video Dynamics', in *Video Icons and Values*, ed. A. Olson, C. Parr and D. Parr. Albany, NY: State University of New York Press.

Turner, T. (1992). 'Defiant Images: The Kayapo Appropriation of Video'. *Anthropology Today* 8(6): 5–16.

Vycinas, V. (1961). *Earth and Gods: An Introduction to the Philosophy of Martin Heidegger*. Amsterdam: Nijhoff.

Wagner, R. (1967). *The Curse of Souw*. Chicago: University of Chicago Press.

────── (1972). *Habu*. Chicago: University of Chicago Press.

────── (1975). *The Invention of Culture*. Englewood Cliffs, NJ: Prentice-Hall.

────── (1977). 'Analogic Kinship: A Daribi Example'. *American Ethnologist* 4: 623–42.

────── (1978). *Lethal Speech*. Ithaca, NY: Cornell University Press.

────── (1981). *The Invention of Culture*. Chicago: University of Chicago Press.

────── (1984). 'Ritual as Communication: Order, Meaning, and Secrecy in Melanesian Initiation Rites'. *Annual Review of Anthropology* 13: 143–55.

────── (1986a). *Symbols that Stand for Themselves*. Chicago: University of Chicago Press.

────── (1986b). *Asiwinarong*. Princeton, NJ: Princeton University Press.

────── (1987). 'Daribi and Barok Images of Public Man: A Comparison', in L. Langness and R. Hays (eds), *Anthropology in the High Valleys*. Novato, CA: Chandler and Sharp Publishers.

────── (1988). 'Visible Sociality: The Daribi Community', in J. Weiner (ed.), *Mountain Papuans*. Ann Arbor, MI: University of Michigan Press.

────── (1991). 'The Fractal Person', in M. Godelier and M. Strathern (eds), *Big Men and Great Men*. Cambridge: Cambridge University Press.

Wassman, J. (1991). *The Song to the Flying Fox*. Boroko, Papua New Guinea: National Research Institute.

Weinberger, E. (1994). 'The Camera People', in L. Taylor (ed.), *Visualizing Theory*. New York: Routledge.

Weiner, A. (1976). *Women of Value, Men of Renown*. Austin, TX: University of Texas Press.

## References

—— (1983). 'From Words in Objects to Magic: Hard Words and the Boundaries of Social Interaction'. *Man* 18: 690–709.

Weiner, J. (1985). 'Sunset and Flowers: The Sexual Dimension of Foi Spatial Orientation'. *Journal of Anthropological Research* 40(4): 577–88.

—— (1986). 'Men, Ghosts and Dreams among the Foi: Literal and Figurative Modes of Interpretation'. *Oceania* 57(2): 114–27.

—— (1987). 'Diseases of the Soul: Illness, Agency and the Men's Cult among the Foi of Papua New Guinea', in M. Strathern (ed.), *Dealing with Inequality: Analyzing Gender Relations in Melanesia and Beyond*, pp. 255–77. Cambridge: Cambridge University Press.

—— (1988a). *The Heart of the Pearl Shell*. Berkeley, CA: University of California Press.

—— (1988b). 'Durkheim and the Papuan Male Cult: Whitehead's Views on Social Structure and Ritual in New Guinea.' *American Ethnologist* 15(3): 567–73.

—— (1991). *The Empty Place*. Bloomington, IN: Indiana University Press.

—— (1992a). 'Anthropology *contra* Heidegger Part I: Anthropology's Nihilism'. *Critique of Anthropology* 12(1): 75–90.

—— (1992b). 'Language is the Essence of Culture: Against the Motion (II).' Groups for Debate in Anthropological Theory No. 4, ed. Tim Ingold. Manchester: Department of Social Anthropology, University of Manchester.

—— (1993a). 'Anthropology *contra* Heidegger Part II: The Limit of Relationship.' *Critique of Anthropology* 13(3): 285–301.

—— (1993b). 'To be at Home with Others in an Empty Place: A Reply to Mimica'. *The Australian Journal of Anthropology* 4(3): 233–44.

—— (1995a). *The Lost Drum: The Myth of Sexuality in Papua New Guinea and Beyond*. Madison, WI: University of Wisconsin Press.

—— (1995b). 'Technology and *Techne* in Trobriand and Yolngu Art', in J. Weiner (ed.), *'Too Many Meanings': A Critique of the Anthropology of Aesthetics. Social Analysis* special issue 38: 32–46.

—— (1995c). 'The Secret of the Ngarrindjeri: The Fabrication of Social Knowledge'. *Arena Journal* 5: 17–32.

—— (1997). 'Must Our Informants Mean What They Say?' *Canberra Anthropology* 20(1–2): 82–95.

—— (1999). 'Culture in a Sealed Envelope: The Concealment of Australian Aboriginal Heritage and Tradition in the Hindmarsh Island Bridge Affair'. *Journal of the Royal Anthropological Society* 5 5(2): 193–210.

# References

White, D. (1978). *Heidegger and the Language of Poetry.* Lincoln, NB: University of Nebraska Press.

Williams, R. (1990). *Television: Technology and Cultural Form*, 2nd edn. London: Routledge.

Witherspoon, G. (1977). *Language and Art in the Navajo Universe.* Ann Arbor, MI: University of Michigan Press.

Worth, S. and J. Adair (1974). *Through Navajo Eyes: An Exploration in Film Communication and Anthropology.* Bloomington, IN: Indiana University Press.

Zimmerman, M. (1990). *Heidegger's Confrontation with Modernity: Technology, Art, Politics.* Bloomington, IN: Indiana University Press.

Zynda, T. (1984). 'Fantasy America: Television and the Ideal of Community', in *Interpreting Television: Current Research Perspectives. Sage Annual Reviews of Communication Research* v. 12, pp. 250–65. London: Sage Publications.

# Index

ritual 161, 162
Robbins, J. 167, 174n.3
Rodman, M. 167
romanticism 95
Rorty, R. 11, 72, 82n.2

Sapir, E. 20
Sartre, J.-P. 154n.10
Schieffelin, E. 154n.2
science 72
Sepik River 165
social constructionism 10, 52, 111, 133,
    162, 163, 166 (*see* constructionism)
social relations 132
sound 115
South Australia 169
Spinosa, C. 113
Spivak, G. 152
Steinberg, L. 63, 64, 65
Steiner, G. 34, 35
Strathern, A. 168
Strathern, M. 52, 70, 71, 73, 76, 77, 86,
    87, 93, 105, 107, 109, 120, 130
    and aethetics 87
    and mediation 82n.8
subjectivity 80
symbolic anthropology 58, 89, 93, 162

Taussig, M. 154n.12
Taylor, L. 154–155n.13
Technology 3, 85
television 155n.17, 157n.25
temporality 34, 35, 44
    and language 45
*The Empty Place* 55, 57, 60
the fourfold 57
*The Gender of the Gift* 74, 80, 86, 105
*The Heart of the Pearl Shell* 62, 69
*The Invention of Culture* 88, 89, 93, 163
*The Magic Flute* 63
the soul 79
the uncanny 53
Thorpe, E. 157n.30
Trobriand Islands 33, 46, 90, 95, 150
    Trobriand art 96

Trobriand gender 33, 46, 47 47
Trobriand magic 85
Turner, T. Chapter 9 *passim*, 152, 169

Umeda 90, 91, 164
unconcealing 72
Usen Barok 113

Van Baal, J. 131
video 131, 137–138, 147–148, 153
vigilance 59
vision 120
visuality 116
Vycinas, V. 28

Wagner, R. 29, 52, 56, 59, 62, 73, 75–76,
    77, 79, 88, 93, 95, 107, 108, 110,
    113, 152, 163, 164, 166, 168,
    173n.1
    and metaphor 58
    and obviation 73
Wagner, Richard 93, 150
Walbiri 127, 145–146
Wassmann, J. 165
Weinberger, E. 139
Weiner, A. 33, 46, 167
Western Apache 23, 30
White, D. 16, 27
Will to Power 76
Williams, R. 141, 151
Witherspoon, G. 156n.23
Wittgenstein, L. 12
women and death 32
women and temporality 44
work of art 28, 94, 95
Worth and Adair 145

Yagwoia 55
Yolngu 91, 96–97, 99
    painting 120
Yonggom 164

Zimmerman, M. 100n.3, 110, 111, 150,
    163
Zynda, T. 158n.32

CPSIA information can be obtained at www.ICGtesting.com
Printed in the USA
LVOW06s2129251215

467875LV00010B/224/P